THE THEORY OF CU
AND SOCIAL SELE

CW00430041

In *The Theory of Cultural and Social Selection*, W. G. Runciman presents an original and wide-ranging account of the fundamental process by which human cultures and societies come to be of the different kinds that they are. Drawing on and extending recent advances in neo-Darwinian evolutionary theory, Runciman argues that collective human behaviour should be analyzed as the acting-out of information transmitted at the three separate but interacting levels of heritable variation and competitive selection – the biological, the cultural, and the social. The implications which this carries for a reformulation of the traditional agenda of comparative and historical sociology are explored with the help of selected examples, and located within the context of current debates about sociological theory and practice. *The Theory of Cultural and Social Selection* is a succinct and highly imaginative contribution to one of the great intellectual debates of our times, from one of the world's leading social theorists.

W. G. RUNCIMAN has been a Fellow of Trinity College, Cambridge, since 1971 and of the British Academy, as whose President he served from 2001 to 2004, since 1975. He holds honorary degrees from the Universities of Edinburgh, London, Oxford and York. He is an Honorary Fellow of Nuffield College, Oxford, and a Foreign Honorary Member of the American Academy of Arts and Sciences.

THE THEORY OF
CULTURAL AND SOCIAL
SELECTION

W. G. RUNCIMAN

Trinity College,
Cambridge

CAMBRIDGE
UNIVERSITY PRESS

CAMBRIDGE UNIVERSITY PRESS

Cambridge, New York, Melbourne, Madrid, Cape Town, Singapore, São Paulo, Delhi

Cambridge University Press
The Edinburgh Building, Cambridge CB2 8RU, UK

Published in the United States of America by Cambridge University Press, New York

www.cambridge.org
Information on this title: www.cambridge.org/9780521136143

First published 2009

Printed in the United Kingdom at the University Press, Cambridge

A catalogue record for this publication is available from the British Library

Library of Congress Cataloguing in Publication data
Runciman, W. G. (Walter Garrison), 1934–
The theory of cultural and social selection / W. G. Runciman.
p.   cm.
ISBN 978-0-521-19951-3 (hardback)
1. Social evolution.   2. Sociology.   3. Natural selection.
4. Darwin, Charles, 1809–1882   I. Title.
HM626.R86 2009
303.4–dc22   2009029185

ISBN 978-0-521-19951-3 Hardback
ISBN 978-0-521-13614-3 Paperback

Contents

Preface

The aim of this book is to bring the concepts and methods of current evolutionary theory to bear on the agenda of comparative sociology – that is, on the study of the underlying process by which the human cultures and societies documented in the historical, ethnographic, and archaeological record come to be of the different kinds that they are. Its principal contention is that collective human behaviour-patterns should be analysed as the outwardly observable expression of information affecting phenotype transmitted at three separate but interacting levels of heritable variation and competitive selection – biological, cultural, and social. A neo-Darwinian approach of this kind is by now commonplace in many areas of the more specialized behavioural sciences. But its potential contribution to sociology has hardly begun to be realized.

Since a preliminary formulation of a recognizably selectionist sociology already underlay the trilogy on social theory which I published between 1983 and 1997, this volume might be thought to be no more than a postscript to views which I have already put into print. But my *Treatise on Social Theory* was, as I now recognize, little more than an introductory exposition of its theme. Since it was published, I have not only become increasingly aware of its deficiencies and increasingly indebted to the many other authors on whose contributions to selectionist theory it is now possible to draw, but increasingly conscious of how much still remains to be done before sociology can be said to have moved decisively beyond the agenda set for it by Herbert Spencer, Karl Marx, Max Weber, and Emile Durkheim. What has not changed as much as it might is the hostility still provoked not only among sociologists but among anthropologists and historians by the extension of the concepts and methods which have proved so successful in the explanation of the evolution of species to the explanation of the evolution of human cultures and societies which is directly continuous with it. Much of this hostility is based on misunderstanding, whether wilful or not, and some of it may reflect a deep-seated unwillingness to acknowledge how much of human, as of natural, history is due to chance. But if this book can help to diminish the antagonism which neo-Darwinism still attracts, and thereby encourage sociologists younger and better qualified than myself to carry forward the research programme to which it points the way, its publication will have been fully justified.

My thanks are due to John Davis, who as Warden of All Souls arranged for me to give a series of seminars on these topics at Oxford in the academic year 2002–3; to an anonymous referee for constructive comment on, and criticism of, the penultimate draft; to Ian Hacking for pointing out the weaknesses of an earlier version of the Epilogue; to Richard Fisher of Cambridge University Press for his encouragement and help in seeing the book through to publication; to Zeb Korycinska for compiling the index; and to Hilary Edwards for many years of indispensable secretarial assistance.

Trinity College, W.G.R.
Cambridge
November 2008

The Darwinian legacy

'THE SINGLE BEST IDEA ...'

I

When Karl Marx wrote to Ferdinand Lassalle in January 1861 that *On the Origin of Species* had furnished him with a natural-scientific grounding for the class struggle in history, he could hardly have guessed the extent to which, by the end of the following century, Darwin's theory of natural selection would have been triumphantly vindicated but his own theory of class struggle falsified by subsequent events. It was not as if Darwin succeeded in his lifetime in meeting the objections to the theory of natural selection which his critics levelled against it. Nor could he, since he had no possible way of knowing how biological inheritance actually works. The irony on which many of his biographers and commentators have remarked is that he could have read Mendel's subsequently world-famous paper about cross-pollinated garden peas. But, even if he had, it would not have given him all the answers he needed. Decades later, self-styled Mendelians could still be anti-Darwinians. It was only when the 'new synthesis', as it came to be called, brought together evolutionary theory and population genetics that it became possible to resolve the seeming conundrum that if biological inheritance was blended selection couldn't operate at all (which in fact it can), while if it was particulate it couldn't operate in the way that Darwin supposed (which in fact it does). Still less could Darwin have anticipated the discoveries of molecular biology which made it possible to integrate evolutionary theory with an understanding of how information affecting phenotype through the construction of proteins is transmitted from one organism to another by being encoded in strings of DNA, or the developments in statistics, game theory, and computer science which practising behavioural scientists now take for granted.

It might therefore seem that to comparative sociologists of the twenty-first century seeking to explain the evolution of distinctive patterns of collective human behaviour, Darwin's own writings can be of no more than antiquarian interest. But nobody who has read *The Descent of Man* as well as *On the Origin of Species* can continue to think so. Darwin's prescience is all the more remarkable in the light of what he didn't and couldn't know not only about population genetics and molecular biology but also about primate ethology, palaeoanthropology, archaeology, linguistics, demography, and developmental and cognitive psychology. Sexual selection, which, except for its treatment by R. A. Fisher in one early paper and then his classic *The Genetical Theory of Natural Selection* of 1930, was almost completely ignored for a century after Darwin's death, was to become one of the fastest-growing areas of evolutionary biology (Miller 1998) and to bear directly on issues central to feminist theory (Campbell 1999); Darwin's observations of animals' capacity for deception and manipulation were to be fully borne out in studies of the 'Machiavellian' intelligence which we share with other species (Byrne and Whiten 1988; Whiten and Byrne 1997); his view of linguistic ability as 'an instinctive tendency to acquire an art' directly anticipates the late twentieth-century alliance of traditional linguistics with developmental psychology and neuroscience (Pinker 1994: 20); his discussion of the derivation, as he put it, of the 'so-called moral sense' from the 'social instincts' anticipates the whole modern literature on altruism and the evolution of cooperation between unrelated conspecifics in both animal and human populations; and he was as aware as any present-day theorist of cultural group selection of the possibility that selective pressure can operate not only on competing individuals but also on competing groups.

It has often been remarked that the idea of variation was no more original to Darwin than the idea of selection. But it was by combining them as he did that he took the teleology out of evolutionary theory altogether. It is because what he called 'descent with modification' – hereafter 'heritable variation and competitive selection' – resolves the age-old problem of qualitative change without recourse to either special creation or a predetermined goal that the philosopher Daniel Dennett can call Darwin's 'the single best idea anyone has ever had' (Dennett 1995: 21). The psychologist Donald T. Campbell, who was perhaps the first behavioural scientist to appreciate the implications of natural selection being only one among other special cases of a more general evolutionary theory, aptly credited the Darwinian paradigm with providing what Campbell called 'the universal nonteleological explanation of teleological achievements' (1974: 420). Not only does natural selection explain more about human behaviour than the overwhelming majority of twentieth-century sociologists were willing to concede, but the heritable variation and competitive selection of information which affects behaviour in the phenotype is a process which operates also at both the cultural level, where the information is encoded in *memes* – that is, items or packages of information transmitted from mind to mind by imitation or learning – and the social level, where it is encoded in rule-governed *practices* which define mutually interacting institutional roles. The definition of 'institution' in the literature of sociology has been almost as troublesome as that of 'culture' and 'society' themselves, and some sociologists talk about 'social practices' when they have informal, interpersonally acquired behaviour-patterns as well as, or instead of, formal, institutionally imposed ones in mind. But a categorical distinction has to be drawn between behaviour regulated by formal inducements or sanctions attaching to extra-familial economic, ideological, or political roles designated as such and behaviour regulated by informal habits and conventions. The mechanisms of heritable variation and competitive selection are quite different in biological, cultural, and social evolution. No less important than the recognition that natural selection cannot by itself account for the diversity of collective human behaviour-patterns is the recognition that cultural and social selection, which have too often been assimilated (including by Campbell) under the rubric of 'sociocultural evolution', are, as subsequent chapters will abundantly demonstrate, not at all the same thing.[1] There are not two but three levels at which evolution drives human populations down the open-ended, path-dependent trajectories which continue to generate new patterns of collective behaviour out of old.

2

The purpose of this book is not so much to defend selectionist theory against its critics as to suggest how the agenda of comparative sociology should be reconstructed in its terms. Yet anti-Darwinism is, to this day, as much a part of the Darwinian legacy as neo-Darwinism is. It may no longer be fuelled by the righteous indignation of pious Victorians

[1] As pointed out by Brown (1991: 40), anthropologists have been particularly prone not only to contrast 'cultural' and 'social' jointly with 'biological' but to treat '*a* culture' and '*a* society' as synonymous. This is understandable where, as in much of the ethnographic record, cultural and social boundaries coincide. But sociologists will seldom if ever find an exact fit if they map the distribution of shared memes onto the distribution of interacting practices across a designated institutional catchment area.

determined to remain on the side of the angels when confronted with the distasteful suggestion that we are all descended from apes. But there are still many people, sociologists included, for whom 'neo-Darwinism' implies either the social-Darwinian racism of the late-nineteenth century or the reductionist sociobiology of the late-twentieth. They may agree that the theory of natural selection is no more likely to be discarded in favour of Archdeacon Paley's theology than present-day physical theory to be discarded in favour of Aristotle's. But they are as resistant as any pious Victorian to the application of Darwin's fundamental insight to the behaviour of creatures with minds like ours. They may no longer believe that we are distinguished from our primate ancestors by our possession of immortal souls. But they are not persuaded that the conduct of self-conscious human beings who actively choose between alternative courses of purposive action can be explained within a paradigm which was inspired by, and should be restricted to, the behaviour of creatures guided only by perception and instinct.

To this, there are two related answers. The first is that, as Darwin well knew, purposive decision-making is not unique to humans. The second is that there is nothing about purposive decision-making which removes it, and the behaviour resulting from it, from the possibility of selectionist explanation. Darwin himself was, in his own words, 'very far from wishing to deny that instinctive actions may lose their fixed and untaught character, and be replaced by others performed with the aid of the free will' (1882: 66). Nowhere in this book will it be implied, let alone asserted, that there is no such thing as choice between alternative possible courses of action. It is a truism of sociology that social relationships are created, interpreted, and negotiated by the interacting individuals whose relationships they are. But purposive decision-making, whether by human beings or the members of any other large-brained species, is a natural, not a supernatural, phenomenon. We need to explain without recourse to what Dennett calls 'skyhooks' how the behaviour of organisms with minds and therewith purposes affects the course of cultural and social evolution. Behind all individual decisions there are detectable genetic, cultural, and social influences which have guided them, and there are detectable mechanisms through which they have played their part in the evolution of the collective behaviour-patterns which distinguish one kind of culture or society from another.

The implication for sociology of Darwin's fundamental insight is not that heritable variation in culturally or socially transmitted information affecting phenotype is random in the same sense that genetic drift is random. It is that the causes of variation in information affecting behaviour in the phenotype cannot by themselves provide the explanation of what turn out to be its consequences. To cite a familiar topic to which I shall return in Chapter 3, the causes of variation among different human populations in their shared attitudes to, and beliefs about, what Darwin called 'unseen spiritual agencies' are at the same time readily ascertainable and extremely diverse: the exemplary preacher, the hallucinated visionary, the charismatic prophet, the vengeful moralist, the shamanistic interpreter of dreams, the world-abjuring hermit, the messianic cultleader, and the author or reinterpreter of holy writ may be acting under any number of different influences, giving expression to any number of idiosyncracies of character, and seeking to realize any number of practical as well as spiritual aims. But the success or failure of their teachings depends not on how their own mental states have come to be what they are but on the features of their environment which do or don't favour the reproduction and diffusion of the memes which they transmit to their disciples by imitation or learning and then, if things go well, propagate through institutional roles like those of priest and schoolteacher in which successive incumbents replace one another independently of purely personal relationships.

That is very different from claiming that innovators' aims have no part whatever to play in the explanation of the ongoing course of cultural and social evolution. Innovators often act with deliberation and design with foresight. Suppose, to remain with the same example, that a cynical evangelist has conducted careful market research before formulating a doctrine then spread by well-incentivized acolytes among a gullible population of prospective converts. This may not be the way that visionaries, preachers, and prophets usually proceed. But in such fields of human endeavour as engineering or medicine or architecture – to say nothing of advertising – innovations are launched, tested, and modified (or discarded) as part of a deliberate strategy of competitive selection directed to finding and then exploiting the fittest mutations. In that sense, creative innovation is the antithesis of random variation, even where randomization is itself, as it sometimes is, a deliberate strategy. But Campbell, who in an early paper argued for what he called 'blind variation and selective retention' (Campbell 1960), meant by 'blind' not that engineers, doctors, or architects don't know what they're doing, or that there is no distinction to be drawn between the winnowing of alternative designs by personal choice and their winnowing by external agency, but that would-be innovators cannot anticipate the consequences of their own or other people's discoveries until they have made them. On this point, neo-Darwinians can wholeheartedly agree with a twentieth-century philosopher resolutely hostile to the very idea of social science who quoted with approval the remark of Humphrey Lyttelton that if he knew where jazz was going he'd be playing it already (Winch 1958: 94). The human capacity for active pursuit of innovation doesn't remove the mutations and combinations of information affecting phenotype which result from it into a creationist world beyond the reach of selectionist theory. That, in turn, does not mean that comparative sociologists can answer the questions which concern them by directly applying the models which have served the theory of natural selection so well to the very different, although in some ways analogous, mechanisms by which cultural and social evolution are driven. But it does mean that they can profitably put the idea of heritable variation and competitive selection to use in the service of the 'just what is going on here?' approach which the economist Robert M. Solow sees as distinguishing biological from physical science (1997: 56–7) and recommends to human behavioural scientists in consequence.

3

There is, however, another view of the Darwinian legacy which is perhaps more insidious because it is held with equal conviction by anti-Darwinians on the one side and ultra-Darwinians on the other. It is that to the extent that Darwinian theory can be applied to the evolution of human cultures and societies, it can only be as the theory of natural selection itself. To both anti- and ultra-Darwinians, a Darwinian sociology is either applied biology or it is not Darwinian. To bring the paradigmatic conception of heritable variation and competitive selection and its associated terminology to bear on human cultural and social behaviour as such is, on both their views, a merely metaphorical exercise.

The answer is again twofold. In the first place, much of the vocabulary of science is metaphorical and none the worse for that: ought we to stop talking of electricity as a 'current' because it isn't in fact a liquid? In the second, the objection has force only where demonstrably metaphorical terms are used to disguise the weaknesses of propositions which, when construed literally, can be shown not to be as well validated as the metaphor implies that they are. Thus, to say that cultures evolve through the heritable variation and competitive selection of information affecting phenotype which has been transmitted from mind to mind by imitation or learning would be illegitimately metaphorical either if there were no such information affecting phenotype or if the information transmitted was always reproduced in the receiving mind without any possibility of mutation. But the information is not a metaphor. It is the reality. There is no other thing for which it is standing proxy. Nor does the transmission of information have to mirror the genetic analogy directly. Both 'mutation' and 'combination' can have as precise a meaning to comparative sociologists studying the reproduction and diffusion of memes and practices as to computer scientists splicing codes for programs and crossing them over in order to see what happens next. It is the language in which historians' accounts of cultural and social change are conventionally narrated which is metaphorical: new ideas do not literally 'march forward' or 'take off' or 'surmount barriers', as they do in countless history books, any more than rebellions against the institutional *status quo* are literally 'ignited' or 'defused' or 'undermined' in countless others.[2] 'Fall of the Roman Empire' is as much a metaphor as 'changing climate of opinion', or 'bourgeois ascendancy', or 'industrial revolution', or 'seeds of popular discontent', or 'wave of protest'. The two most famous metaphors in the literature of sociology – Marx's 'base and superstructure' and Weber's 'elective affinities' – have been as misleading as they have been influential. However difficult it may be to explain why some items or complexes of information affecting phenotype are favoured over time by competitive selection where others are not, it is a matter of literal fact that in cultural evolution some mutations or combinations of information transmitted by imitation or learning are more successfully reproduced and diffused in adjacent or successive populations of carriers than others, just as in social evolution are some mutations or combinations of information encoded in practices defining institutional roles.

At this point, the alliance between the anti-Darwinians and the ultra-Darwinians breaks down, since they have wholly incompatible opinions about how it comes about that the collective behaviour-patterns observed

---

[2] When, for example, a historian of Britain tells how in the late seventeenth century 'high culture moved out of the narrow confines of the court into diverse spaces in London. It slipped out of palaces and into coffee houses, reading societies, debating clubs, assembly rooms, galleries and concert halls; ceasing to be the handmaiden of royal politics, it became the partner of commerce' (Brewer 1997: 3), what he is literally narrating is the diffusion of competitively selected memes previously carried within aristocratic status-groups into environments favourable to their probability of further reproduction. And when another (Blanning 2002: 15) says that 'The public sphere was a neutral vessel, carrying a diversity of social groups and ideologies. Depending on the date of its journey, its carrier is usually labelled 'scientific revolution', the 'crisis of European conscience', or the 'Enlightenment'. These, together with plenty of others, do not have to be thrown overboard, but the argument will be advanced here that room needs also to be found for freight with a less modern or progressive appearance', his metaphorical way of putting it cries out – metaphorically speaking – to be cashed in the literal language of selectionist theory.

in different human cultures and societies are what they are observed to be. To the ultra-Darwinians, cultural and social selection must ultimately be reducible to natural selection: mutations in heritable information, however transmitted, are fit and hence selected if and only if they somehow maximize the inclusive reproductive fitness of the organisms carrying them. But to the anti-Darwinians, this presumption is even more unpalatable than the suggestion that cultural and social selection, although not reducible to natural selection, are significantly analogous to it: for them, human cultures and societies can only be explained in their own terms without reference to any theory, model, or analogy drawn from biology. But on any serious reading of the literature of comparative sociology, it is as obvious that not all cultural and social variation can be explained by natural selection as it is that there are many aspects of human cultural and social behaviour which natural selection does explain (however reluctant the anti-Darwinians may be to acknowledge it). Some behavioural ecologists, when confronted with as challenging a counterexample as a creed which enjoins monastic and clerical celibacy, will go to extravagant lengths to find some hypothesis about inclusive reproductive fitness which is consistent with the data, just as some cultural anthropologists, when confronted with as challenging a counterexample as the universally higher probability of young adult males engaging in lethal violence than either older males or coeval females, will go to extravagant lengths to find some hypothesis which will link the data to presumptively autonomous cultural variables. But once Campbell's general point is taken, the question to be addressed is not which mechanism of heritable variation and competitive selection of information affecting phenotype is at work, but how those which are simultaneously at work relate to each other. At the three different levels of natural, cultural, and social selection, there are three different types of behaviour: *evoked* behaviour, where the agent is responding directly and instinctively to some feature of the environment; *acquired* behaviour, where the agent is imitating or has learned from some other agent, whether directly or indirectly; and *imposed* behaviour, where the agent is performing a social role underwritten by institutional inducements and sanctions. To cite another familiar topic – warfare: a comparative sociologist who studies it is at the same time studying the evoked behaviour of young adult males genetically predisposed to initiate or respond to violence under arousal or provocation, the acquired behaviour of members of cultures in which violence on behalf of the in-group is positively valued and successful warriors admired, and the imposed behaviour of recruits into their societies' military roles in which they are subject to formal punishments for disobedience or desertion whatever the memes acquired by imitation or learning which they are carrying inside their heads.

Darwin's legacy to comparative sociology, therefore, carries an injunction to reanalyse the evidence of the archaeological, ethnographic, and historical record in terms of heritable variation and competitive selection of information affecting phenotype in something of the same way that Darwin himself reanalysed evidence reported by 'pre-Darwinian' observers of animal species. His own occasional sociological asides are, admittedly, not very felicitous. No present-day sociologist will gain much from being told that 'The Greeks may have retrograded from a want of coherence between many small states, from the small size of their whole country, from the practice of slavery, or from extreme sensuality' (1882: 141).[3] But the neo-Darwinian sociologist's objective is in principle no different from that of the neo-Darwinian biologist as set out by Francis Crick (1988: 139): 'To produce a really good biological theory one must try to see through the clutter produced by evolution to the basic mechanisms lying beneath them, realizing that they are likely to be overlaid by other, secondary mechanisms.' In comparative sociology, Crick's 'clutter' is 'noise' in its information-theoretic sense: sociologists have somehow to identify and trace from among all the enormous amounts of information affecting behaviour in the phenotype the heritably variable and competitively selected memes and practices without which the distinctive cultures and societies documented in the archaeological, ethnographic, and historical record would not have evolved into being what they are.

'ANY ANIMAL WHATEVER ...'

4

Like Hume, to whom nothing was (in his own words) 'more evident' than that 'beasts' are endowed with thought and reason as human beings are, and Aristotle, who regularly calls animals *phronimoi* (i.e. endowed with practical reasoning), Darwin had no hesitation in attributing to both primates and domestic animals a range of both intellectual and emotional capacities shared with ourselves. Indeed he credits animals with jealousy, gratitude, emulation, vengefulness, shame, curiosity, deliberation, memory, association of ideas, imagination, wonder, and even the rudiments of

---

[3] A very different answer to this longstanding question is put forward in tentatively selectionist terms in Runciman (1990).

a moral and aesthetic sense and a sense of humour. To many of his readers then and since, this has seemed unwarrantably anthropomorphic. But his observations have largely been vindicated by primatologists and ethologists who have been working in the field since the 1960s. Not only did he anticipate their findings about tool-use as well as deception, but unlike many twentieth-century ethologists he was fully aware of the significance of intra-specific variation in attributes and capacities. When, therefore, the primatologist Frans de Waal, in his book *Chimpanzee Politics* of 1982, made the names of 'Luit', 'Nikkie', and 'Yeroen' almost as familiar to a large general readership as those of the characters in the novels of Dickens, his observations would have been less surprising to Darwin than they initially were to de Waal himself.

But although the accumulated long-term field-studies of chimpanzee behaviour have revealed far more extensive cultural variations than previously supposed (Whiten *et al.* 2003; McGrew 2004), rapid and cumulative cultural evolution is unique to humans. Social, as opposed to individual trial-and-error, learning generates traceable cultural traditions in many other species. But ready as Darwin was to assign meaning to the sounds made by dogs and birds as well as monkeys and apes, he willingly conceded human beings' 'almost infinitely larger power of associating together the most diversified sounds and ideas' (1882: 85–6). He never underestimated the difference made by language, and would not have expected other than that even the most carefully trained adult chimpanzee should still lack the linguistic capacity of any normal human three-year-old. He only insisted, as he was right to do, that it is natural selection which explains how we come to have a capacity for language which other primates don't. We are an ape whose distinctive characteristics, including that one, arise out of 'descent with modification', not out of 'special provision'. The anti-Darwinians who like to point out that Darwin conceded to his critics that natural selection might not be able to explain as much as he had appeared to claim have themselves to concede that he would not have needed to do so if he had known what we now know about how natural selection actually works.

Darwin, accordingly, set the agenda for the study of human as well as animal behaviour to a degree that his successors for a long time failed to recognize. In particular, the joint influences of twentieth-century cultural anthropology on the one side and twentieth-century behaviourist psychology on the other can be seen with hindsight to have done as much to retard as to advance our understanding of the relation of the outward and visible uniformities in behaviour which make human cultures and societies what they are to the mental states of their individual members. The cultural anthropologists, for all the undoubted significance of their findings about human communities very different from their own, were too reluctant to accept that there are psychological capacities, dispositions, and susceptibilities which are innate in the human species, while the Behaviourists, for all the undoubted significance of their findings about operant conditioning, were too reluctant to accept that inner mental states are as legitimate a subject of scientific enquiry as their public expression. The questions about behaviour which Darwin posed are questions whose answers require equal attention to be given both to what is going on in individual minds and to its observed phenotypic effects.

It may still be that Darwin was too concerned to emphasize the resemblances between the minds of animals and of humans at the expense of the differences: that to some extent depends on what different readers find more or less important or interesting. But he did see not only that the transition is continuous but that the workings of the human mind and their outcomes in human behaviour can be accounted for within the same paradigm of heritable variation and competitive selection. The neo-Darwinian observer confronted with a consistent and distinctive behaviour-pattern, whether bower-birds decorating their nests, chimpanzees in the Gombe rain-forest conducting a raiding-party, Melanesian big-men dispensing yams to their followers, Roman *haruspices* diagnosing the entrails of their sacrificial victims, wage-workers selling their labour to capitalist factory-owners, or electors in a parliamentary democracy casting their votes, will in each case seek to frame an explanatory hypothesis which will correctly locate the selective advantage attaching to the information, whether genetically, culturally, or socially transmitted, of which the distinctive and consistent behaviour-pattern observed is a more or less extended phenotypic effect.

5

Once, however, it is accepted by comparative sociologists that they both can and should 'get inside the natives' heads', as the saying goes, without compromising their academic credentials in the process, they are confronted with the long-standing question of just how far inside the natives' heads it is necessary or possible to go. The question is no less relevant to the study of behaviour from within the neo-Darwinian paradigm than it is from within any other. If all behaviour is a phenotypic effect of information internalized by its carriers, does or doesn't a sociologist studying a distinctive behaviour-pattern have to be able to say exactly how that information is subjectively understood by 'them'? Darwin was well aware that empathy has its limits: 'who', as he asks, 'can say what cows feel, when they surround or stare intensely at a dying or dead companion?' (1882: 201), thus implicitly anticipating the disdain which Evans-Pritchard was later to express, in the context of anthropological fieldwork, for what he called 'if-I-were-a-horse' arguments. But any systematic and diligent observer of other people's behaviour will be able not only to report what it is they are doing but also to *describe*, at least to some extent, 'how it feels' or 'what it is like' to be one of 'them'.[4] Evans-Pritchard denied that it was possible for an Oxford don to 'work himself into' the mind of a serf of the time of Louis the Pious (1962: 58). But Oxford dons who have mastered the documentary sources for the reign of King Louis do have a better idea than other people of what was going on in the minds of the serfs of that time, just as Evans-Pritchard had a better idea than people who had not lived as he had done in the 1930s among the Azande and Nuer of what was going on in theirs. Sociologists seeking to decode complexes of culturally and socially transmitted information whose phenotypic effects they observe, even if they make no claim to be reliving in their own imaginations the natives' inner mental states, can and do both ascertain and distinguish between the natives' intentions and their motives.

This applies, moreover, no less to chimpanzees who lack the means to put their intentions and motives into words than it does to Oxford dons who debate their own and other people's intentions and motives with a fluency and subtlety which encompass both their intentions in, and their motives for, doing so. Under the right observational conditions, Darwin, if taken to the Arnhem Zoo, could tell readily enough whether Luit has come into violent physical contact with Yeroen with the intention of inflicting physical harm and not merely by accident, and if with the intention of inflicting physical harm, whether from a motive of revenge or of unprovoked aggression. It is true that these terms are notoriously difficult to define precisely. But sociologists have no need to join – although all may, and some do – the philosophical debates which surround the notions of intentionality and agency as such. They need only to recognize that intentions are constitutive of actions (what are the natives doing in making the sounds and gestures observed?), whereas motives are causes of actions (why are the natives performing the actions constituted by

---

[4] 'Describe' is here and throughout used in the sense taken by Runciman (1972) from Toulmin and Baier (1952) and expounded more fully in Runciman (1983: Ch. 4).

these intentions?). It follows that, although the natives know better than anyone else what their intentions are, they can be not merely uncertain but mistaken about their motives. Decoding the information affecting phenotype which is inside their heads still leaves it to be established why *that* is the heritably variable and competitively selected information which causes them to behave as they do; and that involves ascertaining causal relationships of which they may not themselves be aware at all.

The distinction between intentions and motives has added force where the behaviour observed is not what it seems because the agent wishes it to be seen as what it isn't. Darwin was sure not only that monkeys, apes, and domestic animals are dissemblers but that elephants used as decoys 'intentionally practise deceit, and well know what they are about' (1882: 69), thereby raising precisely the issue which a century later came to dominate the agenda of empirical research into the evolved ability to attribute mental states to others and in consequence to behave towards them in a different and sometimes deliberately disingenuous way. For the purposes of comparative sociology, it doesn't matter exactly when and how the ability evolved or exactly when and how young children come to possess what psychologists call an 'intentionality detector'. What does matter is that the psychologically normal, fully grown members of any and all human cultures and societies can both recognize their own intentional states – hence the phenomenon of 'role distance', where people see themselves as if from outside performing the roles that they occupy – and hypothesize about the intentional states of others. The watchful sociologist has not only to be aware that understanding intentions can involve understanding what the agent supposes that other people suppose about what the agent supposes, but also to distinguish 'genuine' behaviour from the behaviour of liars, tricksters, dissemblers, jokers, fraudsters, hypocrites, imposters, and mountebanks.[5] Natural selection, although it has no purposes of its own, has given organisms with minds not only the capacity to formulate purposes but the ability to pursue them by means, among others, of both feigning the intentions constitutive of their actions and concealing the motives which have caused them to do so.

The practical problems which thereby confront observers of human behaviour are thoroughly familiar to anthropologists studying alien cultures in the field. Not only do they have to learn, through the medium of

---

[5] This includes the special cases discussed by the historian Quentin Skinner (2002: Ch. 8), where political actors invoke principles to which they are not genuinely committed, but the principles enter into the causal explanation of their behaviour precisely because their motive is to legitimate their behaviour in the minds of other people.

a language other than their own, how to distinguish the intentions constitutive of the actions they observe, but they have to guard against the
risk that even when they have, the natives may use the language deliberately to mislead them about their motives for doing what they intentionally do. Difficult as it may be for primatologists to tell whether the motive
for an obviously intentional, not accidental, attack on a fellow member
of a group is or isn't revenge for some previous hostile act, at least they
are not required to listen to an elaborate rhetorical performance designed
to persuade them that it isn't when they strongly suspect that it is. But
historians have the same problem as anthropologists do. Suppose that a
historian of the later Roman Empire is contrasting pagan with Christian
behaviour-patterns, and in particular the difference between pagans and
Christians in the giving of money by the rich to the poor. There is first
of all the difficulty of ensuring that the apparent gift is indeed intended
as a gift and not as a loan or a bribe or a reward. But suppose the documentary evidence leaves no room for doubt. The rich – or some of them,
at least – are consciously and deliberately giving money away to the poor.
What is their motive for doing so? The Christians, so the sources tell us,
are doing it because they are persuaded that it is a pious thing to do. But
how can we be sure that the motive is love for fellow beings and not, say,
fear of supernatural sanction? The pagans, on the other hand, do it from
a wish to advertise their superior status.[6] But how can we be sure that
genuine benevolence may not be concealed behind the mask of arrogance
and contempt – or, come to that, that behind the mask of Christian piety
there may not lurk a desire to signal superior status? Or might it be that
the giving of gifts without expectation of return should be explained as
motivated by the pursuit of status as a means of indirectly enhancing
reproductive fitness, whether the gift-giver realizes it or not?

To raise this last possibility is not to imply, even indirectly, that the
search for the selective advantage which attaches to an ostensibly unself-
interested behaviour-pattern will, after all, lead to an explanation in
terms of maximizing the gift-giver's inclusive reproductive fitness. But
the distinction between intentions and motives, and recognition of the
possibility that either or both may be either consciously or unconsciously
concealed by the behaviour constituted by the intention and caused by
the motive, are fundamental to the testing of alternative hypotheses about

---

[6] Ammianus Marcellinus (XXVII.3.6) gives a memorable account of Lampadius, the pagan
urbis moderator of Rome, summoning a few paupers from the Vatican and lavishing money
on them precisely in order to display his contempt (*'ut et liberalem se et multitudinis ostenderet
contemptorem'*).

the evolution of cooperative behaviour-patterns in large human groups. The value, in relation to this all-important topic, of Darwin's assimilation of human to animal behaviour is the reminder that our capacity for dissimulation and manipulation, together with our sexuality, our sociality, and our capacity for reciprocity and collaboration, is part of a genetically transmitted inheritance which goes back long before our ancestors had evolved the capacity to talk about it – or anything else.

6

So just how unselfish are the unselfish almsgivers with their 'so-called moral sense'? Arguments over this longstanding conundrum have remained peculiarly intractable from Darwin's day to this, not least because it has been an additional matter of dispute whether they are for psychologists or philosophers to arbitrate. But sociologists will do well to leave philosophy to the philosophers. Sociology's concern is with the differences of motive between generosity to relatives and friends, unrecognized generosity in which the donor takes pride in remaining anonymous, generosity in pursuit of a reputation for generosity and the resources to be able to afford it (the so-called 'handicap effect'), and generosity inspired by the hope of future favours in return (including reward after death), together with the second-order category of 'strong reciprocators' (Gintis 2000) or 'altruistic punishers' (Boyd *et al.* 2003) who are motivated by a desire to punish those who fail to punish the selfish non-cooperators even at personal cost to themselves. How far such behaviour is to be admired or not is up to you. Darwin, having remarked that 'any animal whatever, endowed with well-marked social instincts ... would inevitably acquire a moral sense of conscience, as soon as its mental power had become as well, or nearly as well developed, as in a man', goes on to pose the 'extreme case' of human beings 'reared under precisely the same conditions as hive-bees': in that event, he says, 'there can hardly be any doubt that our unmarried females would, like the worker-bees, think it a sacred duty to kill their brothers, and mothers would strive to kill their female daughters; and no one would think of interfering' (1882: 98–9). Although this invites the obvious objection that human beings couldn't be reared as hive-bees without having ceased to be human beings, it is an effective rhetorical device for bringing home to readers of the *Descent* the point that the altruistic dispositions on which they may pride themselves are no less than the behaviour of animals, including the insects, a product of the same long process of heritable variation and competitive selection.

The difficulty is rather that Darwin at the same time continues to credit human beings with what he calls a 'higher' standard of morality and to deny to other species 'disinterested love for all living creatures, the noblest attribute of man' (1882: 126). He even at one point, when discussing reciprocal altruism, uses the word 'low' for the motive which leads one person to help another 'in the expectation of receiving aid in return' (1882: 132).[7] To the extent that he is pointing to the importance of the distinction between a strategy of unconditional cooperation and the strategies of 'tit-for-tat', 'generous tit-for-tat', or 'win-stay, lose-shift' in iterated plays of Prisoner's Dilemma, he is anticipating a whole field of subsequent game-theoretic research. But by wording it as he does, he returns to his readers in one hand the conventional moralizing judgements which he had earlier taken away in the other.

Perhaps, in Darwin's case, this was a perlocutionary move to calm his respectable readers' fears about his own respectability.[8] Or perhaps it reflects a descriptive interest in the subjective experience of acting, as it seems to the agent, out of conscience, a sense of duty, and a wish to be good. But he ought, if he was to be consistent, to have held fast to his example of the hive-bees. Selectionist sociology is, and cannot but be, neutral between the different moralities whose content it reports and whose reproductive success (or failure) it seeks to explain. Despite Darwin's references to Kant, his and his neo-Darwinian successors' ideas about the evolution through natural selection of the 'so-called moral sense' stand or fall whatever his own or anybody else's agreement or disagreement with the arguments expounded in Kant's *Fundamental Principles of the Metaphysic of Ethics*.

TWO FALSE TRAILS

7

But if Darwin's idea was such a good one, why did his legacy not sooner and more effectively influence sociology for the better? In the event, its early influence was for the worse – not through any fault of Darwin's own,

---

[7] Which might be bound up, as for example among the virtuous female patrons of the early Jesuits, with 'an evident sense of satisfaction arising from an initiative allocated to them' (Hufton 2001: 331) as well as the hope of reward in the life to come.

[8] As, it has been suggested, he may have sought to make his views about the mental and emotional capacities of animals more palatable to his readers by singling out domestic dogs as models of fidelity and obedience rather than concentrating on monkeys and apes (Kroll 1997).

but because of the way in which the idea of evolution was deployed by the two most influential sociologists of the nineteenth century: Herbert Spencer and Karl Marx.

For all their differences, Spencer and Marx shared a common conception of social evolution as leading, in due course, to a state of the world in which technological advance would ensure universal prosperity and violent conflict would give way to peaceable cooperation. For Spencer, the driving force of social evolution was competition between individuals, whereas for Marx it was conflict between classes. But both believed that the final outcome of the struggle would be benign. This resolute optimism, however groundless, no doubt increased the attraction of both of their respective theories to their respective disciples at the opposite ends of the political spectrum. But both failed equally to draw from Darwin's original insight what would have been the appropriate lesson for both of them. It was not simply that they both retained a teleological notion of evolution as leading to a pre-determined end-state, or even that they both conflated their confident predictions of the future of mankind with their personal values and preferences. They also, albeit for opposite reasons, diverted the study of cultural and social evolution away from analysis of the relation between information affecting phenotype, its carriers, and the environment in the direction of celebration of the winners and dismissal of the losers in the struggle between (for Spencer) more and less vigorous and therefore deserving individuals or (for Marx) economic classes whose triumphs derive from a dialectic of successive antitheses and their subsequent resolution.

This is not to say that their respective influence was wholly retrograde. Much of Spencer's sociology has helped to make the subject what it is quite independently of his value-judgements about social policy, including his analysis of the feedback between structure and function, his perception of the part played in social evolution by the unintended consequences of purposive actions, his emphasis on the influence of military as distinct from administrative leadership, and his recognition of the simultaneity of trends towards both heterogeneity and integration in social institutions. Nor can Spencer himself be charged with all the prejudices of his disciples: he was, as his commentators sometimes forget, a fervent anti-imperialist. Likewise, there is a sense in which even anti-Marxist sociologists are Marxists too: nobody attempting a comparative analysis of human societies and the relations of economic, ideological, and political institutions to one another can neglect what Marx called the social relations of production. But out of Marx's theory of class struggle there developed a whole erroneous school of thought which came to be labelled 'Historical Materialism', and out of Spencer's theory of individual competition there developed a whole erroneous school of thought which came to be labelled 'Social Darwinism'. How could this have happened? How could both these opposite versions of evolutionary theory have so misinterpreted the idea of heritable variation and competitive selection?

8

Since it was Spencer who coined the phrase 'survival of the fittest', and since, for all the differences between Spencer's idea of evolution and Darwin's, Darwin never repudiated it, it is not surprising that Social Darwinism should be derivable from premises both conceptually and empirically consistent with 'descent with modification'. There *are*, after all, genetic differences between members of the same population, and their environment *does* impose a selective pressure on individuals who *do* compete with each other for shares of what *are* limited resources. But to get from there to the doctrines of the late nineteenth-century Social Darwinists requires a series of inferences which are in no way entailed by the theory of natural selection. If, as it seemed to many of Darwin's contemporaries, there was a clear correlation between inherited behavioural aptitudes and observable physical differences, it by no means followed that differential aptitudes are evidence of innate superiority rather than of the effects of different environments on an evolved anatomy and psychology common to the human species as such; and if, at the same time, the competition for scarce resources between rival populations was visibly intensifying, an ethic of 'rugged individualism' and 'strenuous life' was by no means the only adaptive response to it. Darwin himself remarked not once but twice in the *Descent* (1882: 65, 178) how he was struck, on the *Beagle*, by how closely the Fuegians on board 'resembled us in disposition and in most of our mental faculties' and by 'the many, little, traits of character showing how similar their minds were to ours'.

The diffusion and reproduction of Social Darwinism, accordingly, has itself to be given a selectionist explanation. Spencer's doctrines were particularly adaptive in the economic, ideological, and political environment of the United States in the 1880s and '90s – an environment of rapid expansion, unbridled competition, aggressive individualism, and rampant plutocracy. When, later on, Social Darwinism came to be criticized almost as vehemently as it had previously been welcomed, it was equally easy to point to the changes in that environment which had made it an altogether less plausible, as well as less appealing, guide to either the foreign or the domestic policy-makers of a society which had, for the time being at least, lost some of its previous certainty about its 'manifest destiny'. But that was not the end of the story. By 1937, when the American sociologist Talcott Parsons opened his book *The Structure of Social Action* by quoting from the historian Crane Brinton the rhetorical question 'Who now reads Spencer?', it seemed that it was. But Spencer was then rediscovered – with or without acknowledgement – by a new generation of sociologists under the rubrics of 'development' and 'modernization' as the United States increased its economic, ideological, and political power in the aftermath of the Second World War. Teleology of a kind which all nineteenth-century sociologists would have recognized came back into its own.

But this was not, any more than the Social Darwinism of the 1880s and '90s had been, an authentically Darwinian understanding of heritable variation and competitive selection. 'Modernization theory', of which more in Chapter 4, extrapolated from a selective narrative of 'Western' history a projection of the future of the less 'developed' world, and in so doing surreptitiously invoked the very presupposition which Darwin had undermined. No doubt the neo-Spencerians were as entitled to speculate that the other societes in the world would come to resemble the United States as were the neo-Marxists to speculate that the United States, along with the other societies in the world, would in due course evolve into a single-party state and command economy on the model of the Soviet Union. But once teleology is unsustainable, no culture or society is or ever can be historically privileged over the rest.

9

Historical Materialism, like Social Darwinism, starts from premises consistent with Darwin's own. Competition for scarce resources *does* give rise to collective as well as individual conflict, and heritable variation in information affecting forms of social organization *does* generate different modes of production. But to get from there to the doctrines of Marxism-Leninism requires a series of inferences no more entailed by selectionist theory than is Social Darwinism. There is no support in anything that Darwin wrote for the idea of evolution as a cumulative series of antagonisms in which the conflict between successive pairs of exploiting and exploited classes culminates in the revolutionary victory of the proletariat. It was not completely illogical for Engels, in his speech at Marx's graveside, to claim that Marx had 'discovered the law of development of human history' in the same way that Darwin had done for 'organic nature'. But nor was it illogical for Darwin, during his own lifetime, to retain even more reservations about Marx than he did about Spencer.

Marx can no more be held responsible for everything said and done in his name than Spencer can for everything said and done in his. But Marx was categorical in his prediction of the overthrow of capitalism, whether (as he originally foresaw) through the revolution of a fully industrialized proletariat or (as he later came to think possible) by a revolutionary transformation within a still part-agricultural, part-industrial economy. To that extent, he can be read as a group-selectionist who saw economic classes as winners in the competitive struggle where and when their members have subordinated their individual interests to the collective cause. But neither Marx's original theory nor his later conjectures can be reconciled with heritable variation and competitive selection understood in non-teleological Darwinian terms. Marx ignores, or at best grossly underestimates, the range of observable variation both in the form and the content of the information affecting phenotypic behaviour and in the environmental influences which affect its probability of reproduction and diffusion. It is not just that modes of persuasion and coercion can influence the evolution of modes of production as well as the other way round, but that even where similar-looking sequences of social evolution occur they are not the outcomes of a dialectical process of the kind to which he subscribed.

In one respect, moreover, Marx's theory of social evolution could be said to be even more unabashedly teleological than Spencer's, since Marx saw the attainment of the predestined goal as being hastened by the bourgeois converts to Marxism who would help to bring about the proletarian revolution which, as Marxists, they knew to be inevitable. But neither Spencer nor Marx conceived of competitive selection as acting on variations in heritable information which, however they come about, are selected only for their own likelihood of continuing reproduction and further diffusion. It is true that Marx's individual capitalists are not required, any more than Spencer's are, to be aware of the harmonious long-term future to which their short-term self-interested actions will in due course lead. But paradoxically, it was Max Weber who saw competition between both individuals and groups continuing indefinitely into an unknowable future; and he, although explicitly sceptical of the applicability to it of the notions of adaptation (*Angepasstheit*) and selection (*Auslese*), was, as I have argued elsewhere (Runciman 2001), something of a selectionist in spite of himself.

'OUR FORMER SELF-RESPECT'

10

The quotation this time is from Nietzsche, in the *Genealogy of Morals* (III.25), where he says, echoing Kant, that both the natural and what he calls the 'unnatural' – that is, the human, self-referential sciences – 'talk human beings out of their former self-respect'. And so they do. It has often been complained that science has undermined traditional complacencies about what used to be called 'man's place in nature' without offering anything similarly comforting in their stead. But what does it mean to charge Darwin, in particular, with having done so? The distinctive properties of the human mind are no less distinctive for being the outcome of many millennia of heritable variation and competitive selection which cumulatively differentiated the brains of our ancestors from those of their primate cousins. The 'dignity of man', to echo a phrase of Kant's quoted by Darwin himself, is not made less dignified because of the length of time it has taken to become such or the nature of the mechanism which has enabled it to do so. If we see ourselves as the beauty of the world and paragon of animals, noble in reason, infinite in faculty, and godlike in apprehension, does it matter what had to happen to the physiology of our species before Shakespeare could express it in words like these?

One answer is that for some human beings, at least, it is still a seriously disturbing idea that our minds should be nothing more than an unusually complex kind of physical system. Although for T. H. Huxley's grandson Andrew, joint winner of the Nobel Prize for Physiology in 1963, 'the possibilities of a physical system as complicated as the brain are so vast that there is no need for a human being to feel that he is reduced in stature if his thoughts and feelings are governed by physical events in his brain cells' (1983: 15), that is not going to satisfy those who still feel that, as they are likely to put it, mind is more than matter and people more than things. Behind such responses is a long history of suspicion that scientists like the Huxleys are seeking not to explain, but to explain away, our deep and subtle meditations and conjectures about ourselves and our relations to the world and to each other. Even the most intelligent of animals lack, as Darwin conceded, our speculative capacities and our moral and aesthetic sense, and to be told that these are merely events on a par with sensations of pain or pleasure shared with conscious but not *self*-conscious organisms is to be told that they are something other than

what many people will say that they know them from their own subjective experience to be.

But suppose you are standing awestruck in contemplation of the beauty
of what you regard as one of the masterpieces of your cultural tradition. Is
the significance to *you* of your aesthetic experience modified by whatever
explanation you are given of the evolutionary origins of artistic sensibility
as such? Suppose it is indeed the case that sexual selection explains much
more about our taste for what we call 'beauty' than has generally been
supposed, and that our remote female ancestors were disproportionately
attracted to potential mates who had the skills to decorate their bodies
and ornament their dwelling-places in original and striking ways. If so,
it follows that we have something closely in common with the bower-
birds whose reproductive success is, as Darwin remarked in Part II of the
Descent (and subsequent research has fully confirmed), directly linked to
both the quantity and the quality of bower-decoration by males. But that
is not going to make any difference to what you feel when you contem-
plate your chosen masterpiece,[9] any more than if our aesthetic sense has,
after all, no biological function as such but is an incidental by-product of
the ongoing process of natural selection during the Pleistocene.

There is nothing controversial in the idea that our subjective experiences are causally influenced by both history and environment. As J. S.
Mill put it in his essay *On Liberty*, the same causes which have made a
man a 'Churchman' in London would have made him 'a Buddhist or
Confucian in Peking'. But whatever those causes may be, the subjective
mental experiences which result can be given a phenomenological description of what it feels like to have them in exactly the same way. It is true
that for people to be told why they believe what they do can sometimes
lead them to change their beliefs, or at least to realize that they need some
other reason to accept them than unthinking deference to their childhood
mentors. To be educated by Mill (or Marx or Weber or Durkheim or anyone else) in the comparative sociology of religion may cause the London
Churchman to question the Christian doctrines in which he was reared
in a way that he would not otherwise have done. But Darwin undermined
human beings' self-respect only where, for the human beings in question, self-respect depended on retaining a conviction that we are the special creations of God destined to fulfil a pre-ordained purpose; and that

---

[9] The same applies to the 'beauties of nature'. If it is true that our aesthetic responses to land-
scape are to be explained because they made our ancestors more likely to choose habitats which
enhanced their reproductive fitness (Orians and Heerwagen 1992), is that going to diminish your
enjoyment of your favourite view?

conviction has been repudiated both before and since by human beings who have felt no loss of self-respect in consequence. Indeed, it has sometimes been those who reject any idea of an all-knowing Creator whose sense of human self-respect has been the stronger on that very account.

II

The Darwinian legacy, therefore, denies neither the meaning nor the value to you of your awareness of self and the feelings which accompany it. What it may, on the other hand, do – which is a very different thing – is make you more aware than you would otherwise be that your subjective mental experiences are a seriously unreliable guide to the explanation of why you behave as you do. Introspection can, *pace* the Behaviourists, tell us quite a lot about ourselves. But it cannot tell us whether our intuitively persuasive explanations of our own behaviour, and that of the group or community to which we belong, are valid. As to freedom of will, it is undeniable that if any sociologist studying your behaviour is foolish enough to offer you a prediction of how you will vote, what product you will buy, whether you will go to work tomorrow morning, or who you will choose to invite to a meal, you can falsify the prediction from no other motive than to discomfit the predictor. But once you have decided to do what you then proceed to do, your behaviour becomes part of the large-scale collective behaviour-pattern which makes the distinctive culture and society of which you are a member the culture and society that they are, and the sociologists who want to explain that pattern can start to frame and test whatever population-level hypotheses they think will best do so. If a neo-Darwinian hypothesis stands up better than its rivals, it may thereby expose a disconcerting discrepancy between the selectionist answer to the 'just what is going on here?' question and what the natives themselves take the answer to be on the strength of what it feels like to them to be doing what they do. But that no more invalidates the neo-Darwinian explanation than the neo-Darwinian explanation disauthenticates the phenomenological description in terms of the natives' subjective mental states.

The resulting disjunctions between the underlying process at work and the experience of change (or the lack of it) as described by those who live through it may, accordingly, undermine the self-esteem of those who have persuaded themselves and others that events which they claim to have predicted and worked for came about because and only because they did. But once again, selectionist explanation of the evolution of the culture and society within which they held their beliefs and attitudes and occupied and performed their institutional roles neither underwrites nor undermines their own accounts of how it felt to them to be doing what they did. Darwin's legacy leaves us still inhabiting the conceptual world within which we describe our own and other people's inner mental states – the metaphors and similes, the 'it seemed as ifs' and 'it was as thoughs', the adjectival and adverbial embellishments, the appeals to fiction and poetry, the imaginative depictions of loves and hates and joys and sorrows, and the hermeneutic exploration and discussion of all the thoughts and feelings which between them make up what is conventionally meant when we talk about 'the human condition'.

12

But Darwin did, all the same, have a lasting impact on one hitherto comforting assumption, as Nietzsche did too. It was an unconscious alliance in the sense that Nietzsche's own references to Darwin make it clear that he didn't understand – or, perhaps, chose not to understand – what the theory of natural selection actually says. But between them they mounted a powerful joint assault on the faith in human progress which was shared by so many nineteenth-century Christians and non-Christians alike. Again, it is not a matter of self-respect – or not unless your sense of self-respect depends on a sense of playing a part in a historical drama with a guaranteed happy ending. But *On the Origin of Species* and *The Descent of Man* give as little encouragement as *Beyond Good and Evil* and *The Genealogy of Morals* to those who would like to believe that despite all the mistakes, crimes, and sufferings of the past mankind is bound to come through in the end to a world of universal reason, freedom, and peace. Ironically, it was not that Darwin's contemporaries all saw it that way. Just as Spencer and Marx both managed to reconcile what they took Darwin to be saying with their own triumphalist predictions of the harmonious future which would in due course evolve out of the competitive struggle between individuals (for Spencer) or classes (for Marx), so did many Christians of different denominations, Prime Minister Gladstone included, manage to reconcile an acceptance of what they saw as the unchallengeable conclusions of the theory of natural selection with their belief in the providence of God. The widely different reactions of the Protestant churches, in particular, is a topic on its own. There were probably not many who shared the view of the Congregationalist minister Myron Adams that 'that society is most fit which is most Christlike' and 'the relatively superior, in respect of mildness and reasonableness, has been gradually supplanting the inferior and fiercer' (quoted by Roberts 1988: 182) – a tendency about which Nietzsche wholeheartedly agreed but which he equally wholeheartedly deplored. But once seemingly teleological outcomes have been shown to be explicable in terms of heritable variation and competitive selection, the damage has been done. It is always possible to argue, with Archbishop Temple of Canterbury and others, that natural selection must itself have been designed by the mind of God. But once God has chosen to design a non-teleological world, those who are trying to explain what they observe in the world have to come up with non-teleological explanations of it.

It does not follow that the idea of progress has been deprived of any meaning whatever, or that Darwin's contemporaries and compatriots who saw themselves as living in an 'Age of Improvement' were not entitled to do so. The natives of nineteenth-century Britain could, and did, point to advances in transportation, technology, sanitation, diet, and real income per head which meant that by criteria shared by Darwinians with their opponents the world – or, at any rate, their part of it – was to that extent getting better all the time. But they had then to recognize the force of the argument that there might be nothing immutable about those criteria, and nothing inevitable about the continuation of improvement as defined by them. Evolution is by definition movement away from a previous state of a system towards a new and different one. But that is all. For those who cannot bear to abandon the conviction that competition and conflict will somehow be reconciled in a peaceable and harmonious future for the human species, it may not be enough. But as Darwin himself said in the concluding paragraph of the *Descent* (1882: 619): 'we are not here concerned with hopes or fears, but only with the truth so far as our reason permits us to discern it'.

CHAPTER I

The neo-Darwinian paradigm

CONCEPTS AND PRESUPPOSITIONS

I

For all the influence that neo-Darwinian evolutionary theory has had over the past few decades across the human behavioural sciences all the way from economics to archaeology, sociology is still at the stage likely, in Thomas S. Kuhn's original words about 'paradigm-change', to be characterized by 'deep debates' about 'methods, problems, and standards of solution' which 'serve rather to define schools than produce agreement' (1962: 48). But its agenda too is being changed in ways that the diehards – or 'hold-outs', as Kuhn called them – may continue to deplore but can no longer reverse.

Some of Kuhn's followers claimed – and he himself sometimes seemed to imply – that rival paradigms are radically incommensurable. But commitment to a neo-Darwinian conception of heritable variation and competitive selection of information affecting behaviour in the phenotype doesn't make it impossible for sociologists who are so committed to talk to others about 'just what is going on here' in terms readily comprehensible to, and translatable *salva veritate* between, both sides. Confronted with the same set of uncontested observations of a routine occurrence of a wage negotiation in a capitalist economy, a Selectionist sees an institutional practice which has out-competed its rivals where a Marxist sees exploitation of proletarians by a capitalist class, a Behaviourist sees a history of operant conditioning, and a Rational Choice Theorist sees a bargain being struck between self-interested utility-maximizers. No amount of more detailed reportage of the behaviour observed in the particular case will lead them to discard their respective presuppositions. But they can all understand each other perfectly well. They can all recognize that their different ways of seeing the same thing apply to a wider range of collective behaviour-patterns than the one instance of wage-bargaining and that if their different approaches are used to frame and execute alternative research programmes, some will in due course generate explanations which fit more closely than those of their rivals with evidence which they can all check for themselves. There is no implication that the successes of even the most successful of the rival programmes can be shown to be conclusive beyond the possibility of rejection or modification, or that a single crucial experiment or case-study can decide between them. But the failures of the least successful do have a way of turning out to be terminal. It is no more likely that phrenological explanations of behaviour culturally defined as criminal will reappear in twenty-first-century textbooks of sociology than that twenty-first-century textbooks of biology will come to include exposition of Bergson's concept of *élan vital*.

At the same time, it is not as if the neo-Darwinian paradigm has comprehensively displaced its predecessors, or ever will. Even the most extravagant claims for what it can do for comparative sociology will not require that the previous literature of the subject be consigned to the flames, as will be readily apparent from the topics chosen for discussion in Chapters 3 and 4. Reconciliation is categorically impossible only if, for example, the rival research programme is directed to establishing which of the behaviour-patterns offensive in the eyes of God cause sinners to be punished in this world rather than waiting for the next. This is not because theological explanation of accidents, sicknesses, and misfortunes is without a history of its own which is as intellectually coherent and copiously documented as its rivals. When the Rev. Thomas Jackson, in the first half of the seventeenth century, said that 'Pestilence is above all other diseases catching, and such as have been most observant of its course tell us men of covetous minds or unseasonably greedy of gain are usually soonest caught by it, though exposed to no greater or more apparent visible danger than others are' (quoted by Thomas 1971: 88), he could not be accused of advancing a hypothesis unrelated to empirical evidence. Indeed, he might even be construed as advancing a hypothesis grounded in a theological version of selectionist theory. But the eventual abandonment of this kind of providential epidemiology is a textbook instance of a paradigm-change. Not only was divine punishment theory overtaken by the findings of medical research, but it threw up two anomalies of just the kind that bring the presuppositions underlying a hitherto plausible theory into question: first, the 'greedy of gain' were on balance less, not more, likely to die of pestilence than the poor; and second, those smitten included infant children incapable of behaviour which under any plausible definition could be classified as 'covetous'. Hypotheses like these are perfectly comprehensible to rival theorists who reject them.[1] It is as clear what 'sin' meant to Thomas Jackson as what 'descent with modification' meant to Charles Darwin. But selectionist sociology excludes providential retribution as an explanatory concept as categorically as it does both the dialectical *'Aufhebung'* of Historical Materialism and the 'Manifest Destiny' of Social Darwinism.

2

The neo-Darwinian sociologist's short answer to the 'just what is going on here?' question accordingly is: 'the phenotypic behavioural outcomes at population level of information transfer.' Once the collective behaviour-patterns of the members of any culture or society chosen for study are traced back to the items or packages of information which are being acted out in them, the agenda is to ascertain what that information is, where it is encoded, how (and how accurately) it has been reproduced, and why it and not another item or package has been selected. For this, there needs to be found a causal link between the specific memes or practices being acted out in the behaviour observed and the features of the environment which have enhanced their relative reproductive fitness; and that in turn depends on finding the place down the chain of phenotypic effects where selective pressure has come to bear. Sociologists of all theoretical persuasions are well aware that unintended consequences can make more difference to what happens in the world of collective human behaviour than intended ones. But the extended phenotypic effects of information affecting phenotype can equally well be either. The populations which comparative sociologists have to analyse if they are to account for the evolved differences between cultures and societies are populations of items or packages of information (including, if they are deontic in logical form, instructions or strategies), not of the individual minds or the dyads of institutional

---

[1] Providential epidemiology has a history which not only goes back, in Europe, to pre-Christian convictions that plagues and other natural disasters are a punishment for offending the gods but forward to mid-nineteenth-century Britain and the Evangelicals' doctrine of 'Atonement'. Hilton (1988: 155, 113) quotes Thomas Watson's influential textbook of 1843, *Lectures on the Principles and Practices of Physic*, where he says that 'It is ours to know in how many instances, forming indeed a vast majority of the whole, bodily suffering and sickness are the natural fruits of evil courses', as well as the Rev. Charles Vansittart's *A Sermon on the Famine* of 1847, where he says that the Irish Famine is *'a visitation* – a chastisement for our national sins and crimes – for the grasping, gambling, monopolizing, covetous spirit, which of late has engrossed the minds of all ranks of classes and men'.

role-incumbents that are their carriers. It is then on the carriers interacting directly with the environment, not the information itself, that selective pressure presses. That is why they are sometimes referred to not as
'carriers' (or alternatively 'vehicles') but as 'interactors'. The process of
selection necessarily involves both the information reproduced and the
organisms, minds, or roles that carry it, and the same entities function
as both interactors and replicators. But in the application of selectionist
theory, as a leading evolutionary game theorist has aptly put it, 'it is the
strategies that come to the fore; the individuals that implement them on
various occasions recede from view' (Skyrms 1996: 10).

3

All selectionist explanations are 'just-so stories' in which the link between
selective pressure and evolutionary outcome is identified only in hindsight. The term 'just-so story' is commonly used in a pejorative sense,
which is perhaps why some philosophers of science prefer to talk about
'how possibly' explanations. But there is nothing inherently wrong with
asking how the elephant got his trunk. Thanks to the theory of natural
selection, the just-so story of how he really did get his trunk can be correctly told. Sometimes, selectionist hypotheses cannot be conclusively
validated because the evidence necessary to test them against possible
alternatives is unobtainable. Hypotheses grounded in the theory of cultural selection have to confront the inadequacy of the documentary and
archaeological record in the same way that hypotheses grounded in the
theory of natural selection have to confront the inadequacy of the fossil
record, while hypotheses grounded in the theory of social selection have
often to confront the problem of overdetermination by multiple selective
pressures all driving the evolution of a society's modes of production, persuasion, and coercion in the same direction. But the difficulty of finding
the evidence which will conclusively invalidate rival explanations is not an
argument against selectionist theory. The literature of comparative sociology cannot but be full of both more and less plausible just-so stories. But
a just-so story has always to be the right one, whether about how Protestant
Christianity evolved out of Catholic Christianity, or factory out of artisan production, or universal suffrage out of oligarchy, or Gothic out of
Romanesque architecture, or electronic out of electrical technology, or
pidgin out of standard English. Selectionist just-so stories combine theoretically grounded accounts of the mechanisms of transfer of information
affecting behaviour in the phenotype with narratives of path-dependent

sequences of historical events in which the relatively higher probability of reproduction and diffusion of one rather than another item or package of heritably variable information explains the outcome observed.

The just-so stories of selectionist sociology diverge most clearly from conventional historical narratives at the points where the deliberate choices and conscious objectives of individual agents are agreed by observers of all theoretical schools to have had a significant influence on the subsequent course of cultural or social evolution. Biographically told, as narrative historians commonly do, the story is likely to be seen by the agents themselves, and therefore by the narrator, as a succession of ingenious attempts to achieve the agents' chosen aims in either collaboration or conflict with other purposive agents. But although, in selectionist theory, it is explicitly recognized that successful innovations may contain, in the phrase of Herbert A. Simon (1990: 2), 'large components of conscious invention', when it comes to explaining how it is that cultures and societies come to be of the kinds that they are, innovators need to be seen as carriers of what might as well be random inputs into the ongoing process of heritable variation and competitive selection of information rather than as executants of master plans which are then helped or hindered by what might as well be random inputs from the environment. *Descriptively*, the second can hardly fail to give the more authentic account of what it feels like to reach a chosen goal despite the obstacles standing in the way: neither Julius Caesar nor Napoleon Bonaparte are likely to feel like, or think of themselves as being, chance intruders into the ongoing course of social evolution. But that is what they are. Although competitors for influence or power whose ambitions have been realized may present themselves as winners who have overcome these obstacles through their exceptional foresight and strength of will, to the selectionist sociologist they are initiators of variations in memes or practices whose extended phenotypic effects and long-term reproductive fitness they could no more predict than they could control. It explains nothing to say that a lasting population-level change in cultural or social behaviour-patterns accords with an individual decision-maker's aims unless and until it has been shown what selective pressures in the environment have caused those aims to be realized.

4

The psychologist John Bowlby (1969: 50) was the first person to make explicit the distinction between *evolutionary* adaptedness and *designed* adaptedness. But in either case, the right just-so stories will have to specify what it was in the environment which gave the critical mutations or recombinations of information their greater probability of reproduction and diffusion than their competitors. A novel strategy which turns out to have far-reaching population-level effects may have been adopted after careful trial-and-error, after diagnosis of the entrails of an animal sacrificed to the gods, after tossing a coin to decide between two available alternatives, or after taking advice from a management consultant. But the underlying process of heritable variation and competitive selection of information affecting phenotype is the same.

Nor does the neo-Darwinian paradigm presuppose, as its opponents persistently allege, that competitive selection brings about a Panglossian best of possible worlds. By definition, it produces winners and losers. But success is always relative, optimization is always to a local standard, and adaptation is always a matter of trade-offs. It is quite possible that for all the designed adaptedness of innovations introduced by medical researchers into the unending war against disease, both cultural and social evolution will one day come to an end because of the competitive advantage which natural selection gives to bacteria over human beings. But in that event, bacteria will have proved themselves 'better' than humans only in the trivial sense that they are still there and we are not. Likewise, it can readily be seen that some designs are 'better' than others, as much in the arms races of the natural world in which both predators and prey, such as cheetahs and antelopes, become more and more efficient at pursuing and being pursued, as in the arms races of the human world, in which lethal weapons become more and more ingeniously constructed and cost-effectively manufactured. But for all the ingenuity of the solutions to problems of design which are arrived at by natural, cultural, and social selection alike, the natural, cultural, and social worlds are full of demonstrable imperfections relative to the theoretical optimum. The degree of imperfection which is compatible with local reproductive success is a matter to be examined case by case, and the technique of reverse engineering which evolutionary biologists apply to the study of organisms and evolutionary psychologists to the study of the human brain can be no less profitably applied by evolutionary sociologists to the study of cultures and societies.

5

In sociology, as in biology, the resemblances generated by the evolutionary process can be as remarkable as the differences, and where they occur some means has to be found of establishing whether similar collective behaviour-patterns are the outcomes of convergent evolution, homologous descent, or lateral diffusion. Sometimes, the resemblances are the evident outcome of designed adaptedness and deliberate imposition: any story of the evolution of Japanese society after the Meiji Restoration of 1868 will include the determination of its rulers to follow the example set by the practices, roles, and institutions of what they saw as the more successful societies of the West. But no such story can account for the resemblances which the Spanish conquistadors discovered – to their surprise – between the institutions of the societies of the American continent and the institutions of their own. Similarly, the resemblances between the laws promulgated by the kings of Anglo-Saxon England and Hammurabi's law-code as promulgated in Babylonia two millennia earlier can only be explained as the convergent evolution under common selective pressures of wholly unrelated societies which were, however, remarkably similar in their modes of production, persuasion, and coercion alike. On the other hand, there are many law-codes which have been formulated in direct imitation of others, or even designed on request by a professional lawgiver like Philolaus of Corinth, who was expressly summoned for the purpose to Thebes (Aristotle, *Politics* 1274b). In cultural selection likewise, when the folktales handed down within seemingly separate cultural traditions look – as they often do – like identical reflections of universal human concerns evoked by common experience, it may nevertheless be unwise to rule out the possibility of lateral transmission for which the migration of a single carrier from one population to another can be enough. But the subsequent reproduction and diffusion of the imported memes will then depend on the receiving environment, which may favour them either because they have a selective cultural affinity with the indigenous tradition, or because they evoke a biologically adaptive self-protecting emotion (Heath *et al.* 2001), or both.

In natural selection, lateral gene transfer and hybridization are sufficiently unusual that the just-so stories of descent with modification normally start from the assumption that species are reproductively isolated. Cultures, by contrast, are much more permeable than species, and societies are always vulnerable to invasion by mutant practices exogenously imposed. But phylogenetic models borrowed from biology have been applied to good effect in the construction of trees of material artefacts as well as of languages, and in the absence of documentary records they can make it possible to test the consistency with the data of rival hypotheses about the vertical transmission of the information which finds expression in distinctive behaviour-patterns from carpet-weaving to bridewealth (Mace *et al.* 2005). If, as is theoretically possible, lateral transmission of either acquired or imposed information affecting phenotype were to be sufficiently continuous and extensive, it would call into question the whole idea of heritable variation and competitive selection: both cultures and societies would lose their internal coherence, no enduring cultural traditions or social institutions would become established, and comparative sociology would be reduced to the study of shifting networks of short-term interpersonal influence or institutional power. But both cultures and societies tend, for all their disanalogies with species, to be both stable and resilient. Although concepts, techniques, and life-styles, like organizational forms, codes of law, and systems of government, can all be borrowed from elsewhere, this is nearly always within and not in place of a pre-existing set of beliefs and attitudes and a pre-existing set of economic, ideological, and political institutions. I shall come back to the topic of 'punctuated equilibrium' in Chapter 4. But in both cultural and social evolution, partial modification is much more often than total extinction and comprehensive replacement the answer to 'just what is going on here?'

THREE LEVELS OF VARIATION AND SELECTION

6

In Section 3 of the Prologue, I used the example that sociologists of warfare are simultaneously observing three different kinds of behaviour: biologically *evoked*, culturally *acquired*, and socially *imposed*. The distinction applies no less to other equally longstanding sociological topics: in the comparative sociology of kinship and descent, for example, the differences between populations can be fully understood only if due attention is paid to genetic relatedness *and* cultural construction of kinship terms *and* social construction of inheritance practices. But the comparative sociology of warfare brings out particularly clearly the three separate levels at which the three different mechanisms of transmission from carrier to carrier of information affecting phenotype operate both in parallel and in interaction with one another to generate collective behaviour-patterns of distinctive kinds.

There is, as so often, a definitional problem. But it is not a serious one. Wars need to be distinguished from skirmishes, raids, ambushes, or feuds (to which I return in Section 9 of Chapter 2). Battles between bands of

hunters and gatherers are very different from battles between the professional armies of large sovereign states. But in each case, even if casualties
are deliberately kept low, there is organized lethal violence going on, and
its explanation does not depend on being able to specify what does or does
not amount to full-scale 'war'. Lethal violence is unmistakably discernible
not only among chimpanzees[2] and present-day hunter-gatherers but in
the evidence for pre-literate peoples (Keeley 1996). There is no prelapsar-
ian idyll in the history of the human species when it was unknown. The
archaeological record is full not only of clubs and daggers but of trophy
skulls, traces of spear-inflicted injuries, and so-called 'parry fractures',
and wherever face-to-face combat is studied directly, evoked behaviour
can be observed in immediate responses to direct physical threat, in spontaneous support for endangered comrades, and in instinctive retaliation
even at high personal risk – to say nothing of such readily understandable behaviour as the incorrigible edging to the right, vividly described by
Thucydides, of Greek infantry ranks whose stabbing weapons were carried by their right arms while their shields were carried on their left.

But even a cursory glance at the historical and ethnographic record
discloses the extent to which beliefs about, and attitudes to, warfare and
the resulting behaviour in which they find expression are acquired by imitation and learning from parents, mentors, peer-groups, and role-models.
Populations which are not only indistinguishable genetically but also share
a common ecological environment can be significantly more or less war-
like than one another. Even when reared in an exceptionally non-violent
culture, young adult males recruited into a foreign army may turn out
to fight as ferociously as the rest: a revealing example is the recruitment
of young males of the Malaysian Semai, who are one of the most peaceable peoples in the ethnographic record, by the British after the Second
World War in order to fight a Communist insurgency. But that could be
said to make it all the more striking that the Semai should have evolved
a culture in which the naturally selected aggressive dispositions of young
adult males are unusually effectively restrained. When the historical and
ethnographic record is surveyed overall, it reveals that in the overwhelming majority of places and at the overwhelming majority of times bravery
in battle is admired and cowardice condemned, successful combatants

---

[2] Chimpanzees, that is, of the kind first closely studied (Wrangham and Peterson 1996) and most
closely related to ourselves. Bonobos, although less peaceable than earlier thought (Dunbar 2004:
85–6), are significantly less aggressive than either *pan paniscus* or *homo sapiens*. De Waal (2005:
221) summarizes the position of *homo sapiens* by saying that 'Being both more systematically brutal than chimps and more empathic than bonobos, we are by far the most bipolar ape.'

are held up for admiration in history, fiction, and myth,[3] those who have died in battle are honoured and their memory preserved, conquests and annexations are both celebrated and legitimated, the killing of enemies is sanctioned by explicit moral codes, and the active deployment of the means of coercion against the hostile 'other' is taught to be both a right and a duty. But the variation both within and between different cultural traditions, from the Semai at one end to, say, the Aztecs at the other, cannot be accounted for except as the product not only of evoked responses to different environments but also of beliefs and attitudes acquired by imitation and learning within different cultural traditions with path-dependent histories of their own.

At the same time, however, no sociologist of warfare can be unaware of the power of the institutional inducements and sanctions enabling the roles through which societies control and exercise lethal violence to function as they do. In the early stages of the transition from culture to society, the inducements and sanctions are interpersonal only: friends or kinsmen are recruited ad hoc,[4] and cowards or deserters are punished, whether physically or by shame and ostracism, without there being any formal role to which disciplinary power is attached.[5] But societies lacking the roles constitutive of states cannot compete, if it does come to full-scale war, with societies in which practices defining institutionalized military roles enjoy an overwhelming advantage. Armies – to say nothing of navies and in due course air forces – are groups of a kind which shared cultural norms and purely interpersonal influence cannot sustain by themselves. The behaviour of the fighters in institutionalized armies, as opposed to the fighters in hostile gangs or feuding families, is 'imposed' not merely in the sense that their commanders' orders are backed by the state's monopoly of the means of coercion but in the sense that the roles into which recruitment takes place are defined by practices over which their

---

[3] The convergent evolution of a cultural tradition of heroism like that of ancient Greece among African populations where the proud and courageous warrior is likewise admired and extolled is documented in detail by Iliffe (2005).

[4] As, for example, by Telemachus in Homer's *Odyssey*. Although the example is fictional, it is symptomatic that when Telemachus has to find a crew with whom to set out for news of his father, he can only do so by calling on contemporaries who are also friends (III.363), and when Antinous asks him how he managed it (IV:642–4), the only alternative he puts forward is house servants of Telemachus' own. One way of putting the difference is to say that his crew are members of an 'association', in contrast to, for example, the crew of Nelson's *Victory*, who are members of an 'institution' – namely, the British navy.

[5] Thus among the Bergdama (Schapera 1956: 83), a band member might be singled out for physical punishment, but the decision would be 'reached casually round the campfire' and its execution entrusted for the occasion to the younger men.

incumbents have no say. Instructions which all recruits are required to follow now override whatever culturally transmitted beliefs and attitudes they bring with them to the soldierly roles which they occupy and perform. The patriotic volunteer brought up in a family with a long-standing cultural tradition of military service may fight more bravely than the reluctant conscript. But both are subject to a compulsory power different in kind from that of the gang leader or family head.

7

Once it is recognized that there are not two but three different mechanisms by which, and levels at which, the heritable variation of information affecting phenotype and the pressure of competitive selection on its extended phenotypic effects generate the observed resemblances and differences between human populations, it follows not only that the notion of 'socio-cultural' evolution needs, as I have insisted already, to be broken down into its two separate components, but that the notion of 'gene-culture co-evolution', which has become a standard term in the vocabulary of the neo-Darwinian paradigm, needs to be supplemented by both 'gene-society co-evolution' and 'culture-society co-evolution'. The terminology is discretionary. Either 'nature-culture' or 'gene-meme' – or 'meme-gene' (Bull *et al.* 2001) – co-evolution would be a more logical formulation than 'gene-culture'. But the distinction is fundamental, however worded,[6] and however frequently glossed over by sociologists analysing the workings of large and complex societies with long 'sociocultural' histories behind them. Selectionist theory has the wide-ranging implications for comparative sociology that it does precisely because the idea that all behaviour is the acting-out of information transmitted through the process of heritable variation and competitive selection applies no less when the behaviour is the acting-out of information institutionally imposed than when the

---

[6] The problem created by different sociologists' different definitions of 'institution', to which I referred in the opening Section of the Prologue, is further compounded by the distinction, significant as it is, drawn by the philosopher John Searle between 'brute' and 'institutional' facts (1995: Ch. 2). For example: the physical properties of gold are a 'brute' fact, whereas the uses to which it is put by human beings are an 'institutional' one; but the value attached to it as personal adornment ('jewellery') is a *cultural* construction, whereas its function as a bullion reserve in the vaults of a central bank is a *social* construction. In an influential game-theoretic analysis of self-reinforcing equilibrium in medieval merchant guilds by the economic historian Avner Greif (2006: Ch. 4), meme-practice co-evolution is clearly at work, but Greif's chosen definition of an 'institution' lumps rules, beliefs, norms, and organizations together as the generators of regularities of collective behaviour.

information has been interpersonally acquired by imitation or learning independently of the practices encoded in the agents' social roles.

A by now textbook example of 'gene-culture' (i.e. gene-meme) co-evolution is adult lactose absorption (Durham 1991: Ch. 5; Holden and Mace 1997). Contrary to what was for many years an untested assumption of medical research, milk-drinking is far from universal among human populations. Instead, the physiological capacity to absorb lactose has evolved to high frequencies in populations where an ecological environment in which vitamin D and metabolic calcium are lacking is combined with a long cultural tradition of dairying. The gene involved in the metabolism of lactose has been identified, and its high frequency in Northwest Europe, as among the East African Tutsis, demonstrated. The precise relation between the cultural information encouraging milk-drinking and the genetic information permitting lactose absorption is not easy to disentangle, but the cross-cultural evidence strongly suggests that the necessary genetic modifications were driven at least in part by the continuing transmission by imitation and learning of packages of information in which milk was positively evaluated as a source of well-being – a conclusion supported by comparative analysis of the folklore and creation myths of cultures which do and don't have a norm of milk-drinking. Then, however, as social selection also comes into play, the institutional practices and roles of the dairy industry combine with culturally constructed representations of cows to cause consumers in market economies to buy more and more dairy products (Wiley 2007).

Adult milk-drinking and the genetic modification that it requires are, however, a long way away from the topics in the world of armies, banks, temples, courts (in both senses), taxation, conscription, bureaucracy, churches, businesses, governments, and so on with which sociologists are accustomed to deal. With these, we are confronted by behaviour-patterns generated by large-scale, long-lasting, and wide-ranging institutional, and nor merely intra-familial or intra-associational, inequalities of power. Conformity is no longer a matter of cultural conventions and personal sanctions, but of obedience to rules imposed by the incumbents of roles to which there attaches formal entitlement to punish infringement or deviation. The transmission of information through imitation and learning still continues, as it must. The people who are to occupy and perform their interacting roles as generals and soldiers, priests and parishioners, masters and slaves, parliamentarians and electors, professors and students, capitalists and wage-labourers, judges and plaintiffs, or tax-collectors and tax-payers all have to get into their heads and retain there the correct information about what to *do* in order to *be* what – institutionally speaking – they are. But what they do when they are is no longer just a matter of imitation or learning. The difference is not that social, as opposed to cultural, rules *have* to be followed, since even where rulers' commands are backed by overwhelming physical force recalcitrant individuals may choose incarceration or death rather than obedience. The difference is that the information encoded in institutional practices makes a society's roles what they are independently of how their successive incumbents have come to learn to perform them or what their individual motives are for doing so. To sign a labour contract, do military service, pay a poll tax, render dues to a manorial lord, stand trial for witchcraft, manage a coal-mine or a shipyard or a factory, run for elective office, or sue a fellow citizen for damages is to do something different in kind from following a recipe for cake-making, playing a tune on the violin, wearing a copper amulet as a palliative for rheumatism, or laying flowers on your mother's grave.

Why then is it that the difference has been ignored to the extent that it has in the literature on 'sociocultural' evolution? Durham, for example, in the book just cited, explicitly allowed that behaviour can be 'imposed' in the sense that agents' otherwise free choices can be subject to the decision of others more powerful than they, but treated this simply as an unexplained externality which from time to time redirects what would otherwise be the course of cultural evolution. It is not in dispute that such effects can be a matter of purely interpersonal inequalities between the older and the younger, or the eloquent and the inarticulate, or the skilful and the incompetent, or the physically strong and the physically weak. But in the world of economic, ideological, and political institutions, behaviour is imposed through the practices which define the relationship between dyads of complementary social roles and the systacts – classes, orders, age-sets, castes, status-groups, and so on – which they form. The resulting differences between one society and another are just as much the outcome of a process of heritable variation and competitive selection irreducible to cultural evolution as the beliefs and attitudes which distinguish one culture from another are the outcomes of a process of heritable variation and competitive selection irreducible to biological evolution. In cultural evolution, mutant memes emerge through *reinterpretation* in the minds that carry them. In social evolution, mutant practices emerge through *renegotiation* between the incumbents of interacting roles.

8

The distinction between cultural and social selection is both analytic and historical. Analytically, one way to bring it out is to consider just what is going on when Captain Bligh and his companions are cast off from the *Bounty* by Fletcher Christian and the mutineers. Bligh is deprived at a stroke of the institutional inducements and sanctions which sustained his role as 'Captain': he can no more grant a favoured subordinate promotion than he can order a recalcitrant one to be court-martialled. His companions entrust him with the steering since it is on his navigational skills that their survival will depend. But if for any reason they decide to replace him at the tiller by another of their number he will be powerless to prevent them. So far as food is concerned, they now offer a textbook instance of 'immediate-return' (which is adaptive for hunter-gatherers), as opposed to 'delayed-return' (which is adaptive for agriculturalists), behaviour. These are just the circumstances for which was devised the game of fair division known in the British navy as 'Who shall have this?' In this game, when a fish or sea-bird has been caught, it is divided up in the sight of everyone into as near-equal portions as feasible. One person chosen at random then goes into the bows of the lifeboat, looks straight ahead and calls out the names of the complement in a random sequence, while another in the stern holds up the pieces in what is likewise a random sequence. It may well be Captain Bligh or someone like him who organizes the game and teaches his companions its rules. But in doing so, he is behaving no differently from the informal, ad hoc leader of a band of hunters and foragers whose advice is followed about where to look for a water-hole where there may be a chance of finding game. It is only when the lifeboat has safely reached Australia that Captain Bligh once again becomes, as he instantly does, 'Captain Bligh'.

Historically, the transition from acquired to imposed behaviour has taken place wherever and whenever interpersonal relations conceptualized as leader/follower, senior/junior, mentor/novice, or foreigner/indigene have been supplemented by, or converted into, formal relations between institutional role-incumbents explicitly recognized as such in the natives' language. It can be effected either by agreement or under compulsion. Its first occurrence did not depend on agriculture, although agriculture and the domestication of animals as well as plants gave it a powerful impetus. It did not require literacy, which only emerged several millennia later. It did require language, but language long predated it – by how much, nobody knows. It may have been many tens of thousands of years after the evolution of art, ritual, and myth that there evolved economic, ideological, and political institutions of societies thereby distinguishable as such. In the absence of written records, sociological reconstruction depends on such inferences as can be drawn from the archaeological record. But the evidence from the area between the Eastern Mediterranean littoral and the Syro-Arabian desert (Bar-Yosef 2001) is more than adequate to underwrite a story of sedentary or semi-sedentary foragers who during a period of local warming lasting from about 14,500 to 12,800 years ago began to live in permanent or at least seasonal hamlets or villages, to domesticate plants and animals, to harvest wild grains with sickles, to manufacture baskets, fish-hooks, decorated bone implements and kitchen equipment, and to bury their dead with grave offerings which include pet dogs. Sedentism can be both limited and reversible, and agriculture, when it becomes an option, is not necessarily a more attractive way of life than hunting and gathering. Nor are hunter-gatherers without well-established conventions of behaviour, consistent intra- and extra-familial relationships, division of labour, and organized collaboration for common purposes as well as ritual activities informed by jointly accepted attitudes and beliefs. But once material resources begin to be accumulated and stored and families or households to settle at designated locations which their members regard as their own, the necessary conditions for the transition from acquired to imposed behaviour are in place. As settlement sizes become larger, face-to-face relationships more tenuous, and problems of social control more severe, the need for institutional roles by which repeated interactions can be made predictable independently of purely personal characteristics becomes increasingly pressing. Discipline of children within the face-to-face group and informal coalitions of like-minded adults against free-riders, defectors, and self-aggrandizers are no longer enough to keep the peace. Since we have no way of knowing just what 'they' were saying to one another, we have no way of knowing what the first such roles actually were. Perhaps the plaster-covered rounded bench found in a small Natufian building at Ain Mallaha (Bar-Yosef 1998: 163) was sat on by one or more people in whom formal power like that of a judge or magistrate or chief had been vested. Or perhaps those who sat on it were not distinguished from others in any way which went beyond some immediate short-term purpose or need. But whatever the answer, by the time of the 10-hectare, 1,000-person settlements of the period known as 'Pre-pottery Neolithic B', let alone the 20,000-strong Sumerian cities, their populations could not have cohered and reproduced themselves without institutionalized political, economic, and ideological roles of a kind unthought of by their hunting and foraging forbears. It is a matter of continuing debate among archaeologists whether it is appropriate to speak of a 'Neolithic Revolution'. If the question at issue is about cognition and material culture and the relation between the two, the answer would appear to be no: there was a gradual ongoing cultural evolution of a classic Darwinian kind. But sociologically, the answer would appear to be yes: the culture-to-society transition (Runciman 2001b) was a revolutionary transformation of interpersonal relationships and consequential behaviour-patterns without precedent in the earlier history of the human species.

In the vocabulary of present-day hunters and gatherers, the presence or absence of words for institutional as opposed to personal roles in the vernacular terminology is a visible symptom of the difference. Thus, the !Kung San are reported by Lee (1979: 344) as applying to themselves, as opposed to Bantu headmen, the word for 'chief' only 'in a derisory manner', and among the Batek the Malay word for 'headman' (*penghulu*) had to be imposed on their informal leaders by the Department of Aboriginal Affairs (Endicott 1988: 123). The terminology may be fluid and ambiguous, and it is not to be supposed that the first transition from culture to society happened overnight. But if a representative member of the population is asked by a visiting anthropologist, 'Why do you behave towards so-and-so as co-operatively you do?', the answer 'Because he is my friend' or 'Because he is a courageous fighter' is different in kind from 'Because he is our hereditary monarch' or 'Because we have just elected him to be our commander-in-chief'.

Somebody has to have been the first incumbent of any novel institutional role, just as somebody has to have been the first person to have a novel belief or attitude inside their head. But a person can, for example, have the hitherto unknown idea of drawing in the sand or on the wall of a cave an object or person or animal and therefore introducing 'art' into their culture without initial reference to anyone else. In social evolution, by contrast, the behaviour is necessarily a two-sided affair. An artist can be an artist without a public, but a capitalist employer can't be a capitalist employer without a market in labour. Back in the Palaeolithic, there may have been many occasions when a successful claimant to supernatural insight sought recognition as permanent head of an ongoing following of disciples, or a household head controlling more stored foodstuffs than others tried to become the acknowledged collector and distributor of a community's surplus, or a successful leader in skirmishes with other groups or bands tried to assume formal authority over all activities connected with warfare. Or perhaps there were communities in which 'elders', having at first been no more than males living beyond a certain age, became credited with economic, ideological, and political powers entitling them to control hunting and the distribution of game, to deploy supernatural sanctions against deviants, and to order young men into battle without taking part in the fighting themselves. In later and more complex societies, too, there are many borderline cases. Is the Greek *kolax*, or 'flatterer', the incumbent of a social role (Millett 1989: 32), or is his relation to his rich patron personal rather than institutional? Later still, under the Roman Empire, the 'sycophants' dining at the tables of great men might be not just personal cronies but carriers of publicly recognized practices which functioned to channel political influence both upwards and downwards between rulers and ruled. But only after the line has been crossed do children start to grow up in a world not merely of parents, friends, mentors, siblings, and culturally defined exemplars but of roles whose incumbents wield economic, ideological, and political power which attaches to them independently of occupancy by any particular person.[7] Then, but only then, does *social mobility* – the inter- and/or intra-generational upward or downward movement of individuals from one to another institutional role located in three-dimensional social space – become a standard topic on the sociological agenda. Individual rank-orderings are familiar from other species as well as from human groups. But the alpha male in a chimpanzee troop is not, except metaphorically, its 'king', any more than the most admired female in a rank-order of personal prestige based on physical appearance is, except metaphorically, a 'beauty-queen'.

9

Although no direct inference can be drawn from the vocabularies of the hunters and foragers documented in the ethnographic record to the peoples whose culture has to be inferred from the archaeological record, there are many well-documented peoples whose vernacular terminology illustrates the transition from culture to society. Radcliffe-Brown, for example, noticed long ago that in the North Andaman language men of outstanding personal qualities were spoken of simply as 'big'. But among the South American

---

[7] Institutional roles can also exist without incumbents, as most obviously in interregna. In a strictly hereditary monarchy, succession is instant: *le roi est mort, vive le roi!* But there was a ten-year interregnum in the Lombard kingship during an early stage of their occupation of Italy (Paul the Deacon, *History of the Lombards* III.16).

Achuar, the *juunt*, who is literally a 'great man', is a household head who is also a 'war herald' (*chicharu*) whose role empowers him to organize defence against, or negotiation with, potential enemies (Descola 1996: 290). Some Inuit call an informal leader 'he who thinks', but the 'knowledge-able one' (*nindibuga*) of the Australian Mardujarra does not merely offer advice but trades his esoteric knowledge for a share of the young men's meat (Tonkinson 1988: 157). A good example of a transitional designation is the Alaskan *umialik* or *umealaq* – a family head of some personal wealth who is a boat-builder and captain of its crew and who is allotted a larger share of the catch in recognition of his greater responsibility (Halstead and O'Shea 1989: 18). In twentieth-century Papua New Guinea, a successful war leader (*watenge*) could control 'vast' amounts of wealth flowing in exchange net-works (Feil 1987: 249), and the position became heritable. In a borderline case, it has to be established whether or not the designation implies that there are recognized inducements and sanctions attaching to it which are transferred, whether automatically or after an interval, to a successor: thus, among the Cree hunters of Northern Quebec, the *uuchimaau* is the leader of an extended kin-group who controls a hunting ground and the animals on it and will be replaced by another if he fails in the management of the resources for which he is held responsible (Scott 1988: 39–40).

Just as, however, there are anthropologists who underestimate bio-logical influences on cultural evolution, so are there sociologists who underestimate cultural influences on social evolution. Consider what happens when money and the institutions which it brings with it displace gift, barter, and customary exchange. For Marx, in particular, money was a destructive innovation which undermines social solidarity and substi-tutes exploitative practices and roles for non-market transactions in kind. Such effects do undoubtedly occur: on any theory, it is unsurprising that, for example, among the Kinnaurese of the Western Himalayas the intro-duction of cash and a market economy modified the centuries-old *binana* system of customary work exchange between different castes (Raha 1978). But the range of variation is much wider than Marx allowed for. It has often been found that 'the meanings with which money is invested are quite as much a product of the cultural matrix into which it is incorpo-rated as of the economic functions it performs as a medium of exchange, unit of account, store of value, and so on' (Parry and Bloch 1989: 21). All over the world, from India to the Andes and from the Roman Empire[8]

---

[8] In the later empire, the wealth which entered the establishment of a Christian 'holy man' would be symbolically cleansed by 'a dramatic story in which the original giver of the wealth had first been "taught a lesson" by the saint' (Brown 1995: 64), like the twentieth-century Lebanese lord

to twentieth-century Madagascar, detailed analysis of the ways in which monetary practices and the roles of their carriers are interpreted and symbolized reveals meme-practice co-evolution at work, with the consequence that money as a potentially disruptive social force is culturally purified and tamed.

The dependence of institutional practices on culturally transmitted beliefs and attitudes is easiest to see in societies' modes of persuasion. A collective behaviour-pattern in which deference is paid to superiors in social status in an ideological hierarchy of honour and respect is self-evidently vulnerable to a memetic mutation which causes the sanctions underpinning it to lose their force. But reproduction of the practices defining economic roles through which material goods are exchanged according to institutional rules is equally vulnerable to a refusal to accept those rules as valid. So too is reproduction of the practices defining political roles to a refusal to be intimidated by the sanctions encoded in law and enforced by soldiers or police. Practices in all three dimensions of social space are always at the mercy of the fragility of the cultural constructions on which all social constructions depend. What the French sociologist Pierre Bourdieu calls the 'habitus' – the set of conventions dictating appropriate behavioural strategies which the members of a common culture derive from their observation of each other's behaviour – is usually sufficiently robust to sustain the economic, ideological, and political institutions which they occupy and within which they perform their roles. But it cannot be taken for granted, as prudent rulers even of long-established and seemingly well-disciplined societies are well aware.

10

Given that there are three levels of selection, there are by definition three levels of adaptation. The concept of adaptation has long been controversial in evolutionary theory, partly because it can be used to cover any kind of re-equilibrating systemic response to exogenous disturbance, partly because of its mistakenly alleged implication of Panglossian optimization, partly because of the need to distinguish biological adaptedness from cultural or social adaptedness, and partly because adaptive

'taught a lesson' by the sheikh whose disinterested distributions of largesse are in large part funded by the lord (Gilsenan 2000: 102–3). Among present-day Swedish conservative Protestants, even the most seemingly commoditized monetary transaction 'partakes of a sacred quality in that it contributes to the global Faith nexus of production, distribution, and associated missionary activities' (Coleman 2004: 431).

behaviour may or may not be an adaptation so designed as to be adaptive in a particular local environment. Selectionist theory accommodates both maladaptations and 'exaptations' where the genes, memes, or practices of which they are the phenotypic effects are adaptive in their present environment for reasons other than those for which they were selected in an earlier one. But it is always a matter of relative advantage: a mutation or recombination of information affecting behaviour in the phenotype, whether biologically, culturally, or socially transmitted, is adaptive to the extent that its probability of reproduction within the relevant population is greater than that of its competitors. The just-so stories of how cultures and societies have come to be of the kinds that they are are stories about how the impact of their environment on the phenotypic effects of their constitutive memes and practices has benefited not, or not necessarily, their carriers, but themselves. Variation can also be adaptive at one level and not another, so that the problem becomes one of finding some way to establish which is the stronger evolutionary force. Moreover, there is the further complication, although a terminological rather than a substantive one, that 'natural selection' can be used to refer either to genetic selection or to selection which comes about through the extraneous winnowing or even extinction of the population of carriers. When, for example, Chindasuinth succeeded to the kingship of Visigothic Spain in 462 CE and, according to the chronicler known as 'Fredegar' (IV.82), put to death 700 of the Gothic aristocracy, this was selection of the same kind as when a species is driven extinct not by maladaptive genetic variation but by a climate change resulting in a catastrophic shortage of the foodstuffs on which its members depend for their survival.

A vivid example of how a culturally adaptive mutation can be biologically maladaptive is the red trouser (*pantalon rouge*) worn by French infantry soldiers at the outset of the First World War (Tuchman 1962: 48). It cost many of its wearers their lives in the environment in which they went into battle. But it encoded an emotionally resonant patriotic symbol ('*le pantalon rouge, c'est la France!*') whose potential encouragement of in-group loyalty was transmitted down successive generations of recruits as a part of their initiation into the culture of the army they had joined. Before long – before, that is, the population of potentially reproductive red-trousered recruits had been winnowed by their more effectively camouflaged German opponents – the higher command imposed a change. But it was a change which in the summer of 1914 had been unthinkable.

That cultural mutations can be biologically maladaptive may be too obvious to require illustration: to take the extreme case of the Shakers, if a whole population is converted to the view that it is wrong to procreate there will soon be nobody left to pass on their genes at all. But a more widespread setback for natural selection is the persistent decline in fertility in modern human populations to levels well below what they could be. This topic has a long history in the study of both animal and human behaviour, and it is well recognized both that reproductive fitness is not a matter of numbers in a single generation and that quality of offspring is as important as quantity. But the global data on present-day human populations do not endorse the expectation that parents who invest more in a smaller number of healthier children will have more grandchildren. Just what explains the difference between relatively undifferentiated agricultural or horticultural societies in which parents have as many children as they can and are admired for doing to and industrial societies in which (with Roman Catholic and some other sub-cultural exceptions) they prefer to restrict their number of children far below the theoretical maximum is uncertain: it is not a function only of mortality rates or differential fertility among inbred or outbred populations or levels of disposable income. But for the present, at any rate, in the competition between natural and cultural selection, cultural selection is winning in more affluent and better-educated populations. In countries like the one in which this book has been written, parents are deciding (or imitating other parents who have so decided) to behave in a way which does little or nothing to maximize the probability of ongoing replication of their descendants' genes, whatever it may do for their children's average quality of life or, for that matter, their own. And then there is the further possibility that the behaviour is neither evoked nor acquired but imposed by institutional sanctions, like the 'one-child' policy of the rulers of twentieth-century China, so that gene-practice co-evolution supplements gene-meme co-evolution. Behavioural ecologists are not wrong to point to well-researched cases where predictions derived from their models are confirmed (e.g. Borgerhoff Mulder 2000). But comparative sociologists are not wrong to point to demographic fluctuations of whose evolutionary significance they are fully aware but whose explanation may depend on both cultural and social influences which override the innate disposition to maximize inclusive reproductive fitness, as among middle-class families in Victorian Britain (Banks 1981).

Just as cultural selection can compete directly with natural selection, so can social selection compete directly with cultural selection. A well-documented example is the introduction of the practice of wage-labour into societies whose mode of production has hitherto been constituted by practices defining the roles of slaves, clients, sharecroppers, pawns, domestic workers, or junior kin. Sometimes, the competition between alternative practices is acted out entirely at the level of social selection: an entrepreneur in a pre-capitalist economy who is the first to assemble and supervise a body of wage-workers and then market a finished product directly to a growing number of consumers thereby raises his turnover sufficiently to be able to lower his prices and leave his rivals reliant on putting-out and domestic production no choice but to follow suit or go out of business. But sometimes, wage-labour fails to displace its competitors for reasons which are cultural, not social. Among the Baoule of the Ivory Coast, for example, young men regarded wage-labour as demeaning and therefore refused to undertake it in their own home territories, although they were willing to migrate seasonally in order to work for wages elsewhere (Iliffe 1983: 55). Where the employer's role is underwritten by sufficiently powerful institutional sanctions, the outcome may depend solely on the employer's calculation of self-interest and the practice will be imposed directly. Roman landowners often supplemented slaves with wage-labourers at certain times of year or for certain kinds of farmwork: Varro (*De Re Rustica* I.xvii.3) is explicit about the advantages of being able to chose them for their age and physical suitability and to interview them in person about their experience with previous employers. But prospective employers as well as employees may have acquired by imitation and learning beliefs and attitudes which dispose them against the practice of wage-labour even on terms economically advantageous to both individual members of the role-dyad carrying it.

There is wide scope for designed as well as evolutionary adaptedness at all three levels. At the biological level, the breeders of animals with whom Darwin so assiduously corresponded are the obvious example. But the advertisers in a capitalist economy who market-test their clients' products before they are launched into the population of prospective consumers are doing much the same, and rulers of newly subordinated populations can deliberately exploit their cultural traditions for the rulers' own social purposes. In the culture of pre-Inca Peru, a norm of generalized reciprocity was widely diffused among both the local descent-groups and the regional lords who provided the corvée labourers drawn from the descent-groups with food, beer, cuttings, and seed. Under the institutions imposed by the Inca, the agricultural surplus was systematically extracted for the benefit of rulers holding an effective monopoly of the means of coercion. But the rituals and routines of the local descent-groups were scrupulously respected and the food and beer continued to be distributed to the corvée labourers just as if nothing had changed (Murra 1980). Manipulation of this kind can extend also to evoked behaviour, as in the deliberate attempt of the promoters of the Catholic Counter-Reformation to arouse the desired emotions in susceptible congregations by vivid and sumptuous sights and sounds[9] in addition to formal readings or teachings or standard devotional rituals. But the effects of such manipulation will be what the designers intend only if its environment is favourable to the mutations in information affecting phenotype which the designers have introduced. Attempts by the rulers of Soviet Russia to use purpose-designed material structures to move the beliefs and attitudes of its citizens in the direction that they wished were notably unsuccessful (Humphrey 2005).

II

It is an all too well-known impediment to the testing of rival hypotheses in comparative sociology that controlled experimentation is impossible. A biologist can knock out a chosen gene in an experimentally engineered population of mice, but neither memes nor practices are susceptible to similar treatment. A sociologist can't knock out of the Roman Catholic Church the memes encoded in a papal encyclical in order to see what difference that would have made to the behaviour of the faithful or knock out the practices encoded in an amendment to the American Constitution in order to see what difference that would have made to the behaviour of American judges and politicians. At best, the evidence for some specific cultural or social innovation, or some specific change in the ecological or demographic environment, will enable its impact to be traced to the point of suggesting a plausible answer to the kind of 'what if?' question which comparative sociologists would always like to be in a position to answer. For example: an observer of the Kachin of Upper Burma who saw how their conical clan structure and communal ownership of land in an environment where population growth came regularly up against the ecological barrier of the fallow cycle generated a succession of regular transitions from egalitarianism to hierarchy and back again (Friedman 1975) might well wish to engineer the transfer of some segment of the Kachin population into a different environment in order to see what difference it would make to the practices

---

[9] Responses evoked by the manipulation of light have a history which goes back from the massed searchlights of Nazi party rallies through the oil-lamps in the basilicas of early medieval Gaul and the oil-lamps and pine torches 'casting all manner of shadows and reflections inside the gloomy Mithraea' of the Roman Empire (Clauss 2000: 125) to the tallow lamps flickering on the drawings on the walls of the Altamira and Lascaux caves.

defining the roles constitutive of their modes of production, persuasion, and coercion. In the event, that is just what happened when some Kachin groups moved down from the highlands into the plains of Assam: they evolved into small, class-based states. Similarly, the Maori emigrants from the same founding population who colonized the Chatham Islands provide a 'natural experiment' (Diamond 1997: 55) in which the climate and ecology of the Chatham Islands gave the Moriori, as they were called, no option but to revert from farming to hunting and gathering.

There is also the occasional possibility of following culturally dissimilar populations into near-identical environments. Richerson and Boyd (2005: 21) cite a study by the rural sociologist Sonya Salamon (1985) as an example whose 'essential elements' make it tantamount to a 'real experiment'. The descendants of German-born immigrants who settled in a part of Illinois subsequently settled also by immigrants from other parts of the United States preserved a distinctive set of cultural traits despite there being no difference between the adjoining areas in the quality of the soil. The German-Americans retain what Salamon calls the 'yeoman' values which lead them to pressure their children to remain on the land and to mix arable farming with labour-intensive dairying and livestock rearing in a way which supports a larger number of family members on a more limited acreage. Notice that the contrast between them and their more profit-hungry 'Yankee' neighbours does not merely illustrate the adaptedness of a pattern of acquired behaviour not modified by a shared ecological environment which might have been expected to evoke a common set of strategies. It also illustrates the capacity of an acquired behaviour-pattern to resist the selective pressure of a capitalist mode of production which would impose on the German-Americans the same practices of selling and renting as those approaching fixation among the 'Yankees'.

A further difficulty in assessing the relative evolutionary force of biological, cultural, and social selection is the timescale required for the genetic composition of a human population to undergo significant change. Recent research suggests that it may be shorter than used to be thought. But there is one well-known population where for many generations strict endogamy has been combined with higher birth-rates among families of relatively high status, extensive nepotism and in-group altruism, religious and linguistic separatism within which proselytizing is targeted principally at the rich and talented, high levels of parental investment and control, cultural selection against apostasy, social selection of practices defining intellectually demanding academic and mercantile roles, and a hostile external environment which constrained participation in alternative activities and reinforced in-group conformism: the Jews (MacDonald 1993). As MacDonald is well aware (1993: viii), 'Jewish history ... has been to a considerable extent a social construction performed by highly interested parties bent on vindicating very basic moral and philosophical beliefs about the nature of Judaism, Christianity, and gentile society generally.' But evidence for the part played by natural selection in the cultural and social history of Judaism has become stronger since then, and at the time of writing the hypothesis of a three-way interaction, although not definitively confirmed, looks increasingly plausible. Ashkenazi Jews, in particular, whose low rates of marrying out are confirmed by genetic analysis, are known both to score above the mean level in intelligence tests and to be likelier than others to suffer from genetic diseases such as Tay-Sachs which can, along with other symptoms, improve the linkages between brain cells. If this does turn out to be what has been going on for over 2,000 years, there could hardly be a clearer illustration of how genes, memes, and practices can co-evolve within the same population to distinctive effect.

SELECTION OF WHAT?

12

The question of just what the process of selection is actually selecting has been controversial since Darwin's day. It makes equal sense to say that it selects phenotypes (the Galapagos finches with the longer beaks), phenotypic effects (the beaks themselves), or genes 'for' longer beaks. In the wake of the 'new synthesis' of evolutionary theory and population genetics and the subsequent discoveries of molecular biology, it has become widely accepted that genes and their interaction with their own immediate environment are the answer which best helps to explain just what is going on. But genes work in different ways – they can split or overlap or be nested in one another – and other mechanisms besides replication of DNA are involved in natural selection, including 'epigenetic' inheritance involving cells with the same genotype but different phenotypes which transmit their phenotypes to their descendants (Jablonka and Lamb 1995).

In the study of cultural selection, argument has largely revolved around the requirement that memes, as presumptive replicators, should be discrete units capable of copying themselves independently of the phenotypic effects through which their adaptedness is decided. But sociologists have no need to be committed to the view that 'genuine' replicators must create strictly accurate copies of themselves and persist intact for a sufficient length of time to be able to do so. In the first place, in both cultural and social evolution, selection is often blended rather than particulate;[10] and in the second, both memes and practices are continually modified throughout the lives of the individuals who carry the reinterpretable memes in their minds and the renegotiable practices in their roles. Moreover, evolutionary sociologists are free to identify different combinations of information at different levels of complexity as objects of selection in the same way that evolutionary linguists can identity phonemes or syllables or words or even grammars as the objects of selection out of which languages are formed, or evolutionary economists can identify organizational routines or techniques of production as the objects of selection of which competing business firms are the carriers. It might be argued that if information is what is being selected it is by definition reducible to binary discriminations, and these are therefore 'the' units of mutation, transmission, and selection alike. But to suggest that biologists, let alone sociologists, ought to pitch their explanatory hypotheses at that level would be like suggesting that chemists ought to pitch their hypotheses at the level of sub-atomic particles. Identification of the critical memes and practices whose transfer from carrier to carrier makes different cultures and societies into what they are is not an exercise in particle-hunting. In the evolution of cultural artefacts, for example, the critical objects of selection are not 'primitive' units of information but packages of 'techno-memes' (Stankiewicz 2000: 230) assembled in a design space which generates the domain of possibilities open to innovators searching for locally optimal solutions.[11]

It is possible also for the same information affecting phenotype to be selected at either the biological or the cultural or the social level. In evolutionary game theory, the object of selection is by definition a strategy. Strategies come in many forms, and games are of many kinds. But consider the classic 'Hawk-Dove' game analysed by Maynard Smith (1982) in which, where animals are contesting for territory in a habitat favourable for breeding, 'Hawks' escalate and continue until injured or the opponent

---

[10] Where it *is* blended, the familiar image of the ever-branching evolutionary tree is no longer accurate: it is then as if branches could grow into as well as out of one another, so that a better image is accordingly a 'braided stream, with different channels flowing into one another and then splitting again' (Shennan 2002: 84).

[11] Techno-memes are sometimes, as in the early stages of industrialization in eighteenth-century Britain, encoded not in any verbal or written instructions at all but in the 'know-how' of experienced artisans, with the consequence that they can be diffused only by the migration – which employers may well seek to prevent – of the exceptionally skilled workmen who carry the know-how inside their heads (Matthias 1979: Ch. 2). Cipolla (1972: 50–1) reports a case where some Swedish workmen were literally kidnapped in the 1660s and transported in stages to France, where Colbert wanted to start an iron industry on the Swedish model.

retreats while 'Doves' display but retreat at once if the opponent escalates. In the real world, simple pairwise contests between animals who always behave the same way are much less likely than contests in which there is a wider choice of possible strategies, the contestants sometimes follow one and sometimes another, and the payoff in fitness to the individual contestant depends not on the strategies of successive individual opponents but on some average property of the population as a whole. But in the context of comparative sociology, the interest of the strategies of 'Hawk' and 'Dove' is that they can equally well be observed in the behaviour of human beings contesting for territory, and in such cases the resulting behaviour-pattern can be either acquired or imposed rather than evoked. To borrow from Avital and Jablonka (2000: 95), 'The crucial point, therefore, is not the precise mechanism for acquiring a new preference or pattern of behaviour, but the circumstances that allow the transmission of this information in a way that ensures its transgenerational [to which add lateral, as well as vertical] reproduction.'

13

The word 'meme' is disliked as much by the ultra-Darwinians on the one side as by the anti-Darwinians on the other: to the ultra-Darwinians, it implies a much closer analogy between natural and cultural selection than can in fact be sustained, while to the anti-Darwinians it implies that human beings are not as different from other species in their mental capacities as they are. But once it has been recognized that culture can evolve through heritable variation and competitive selection independently of natural selection acting on genes, it is a matter of simple convenience to have a word to stand for whatever items or packages of information make up the messages transmitted from mind to mind through imitation or learning by which behaviour in the phenotype is affected.[12] 'Meme' also has the advantage that in the years since Richard Dawkins coined it[13] it

---

[12] Richerson and Boyd (2005), who originally drafted their book using 'meme' throughout, then decided to replace it with 'cultural variant' (although it survives on their page 244, where they say that 'Modern societies, by vastly enlarging the scope for nonparental transmission, have also magnified the chance of choosing maladaptive memes'). But 'cultural variant' not only de-emphasizes the critical connection with the idea of information transfer from mind to mind; it also invites the response from anti-Darwinian cultural anthropologists that that is what they have been studying all along.

[13] The fundamental idea behind it was set out the year before by F. T. Cloak, Jr, who argued that 'The survival value of a cultural institution is the same as its function; it is its value for the survival/replication of itself or its replica(s)' (1975: 72).

has displaced its competitors sufficiently successfully to be cited as itself an example of an adaptive meme (Ball 1984). Provided, therefore, that it carries no pre-emptive implication about just how cultural selection works and acknowledges that memes are being continuously reinterpreted and reconstructed in the course of their carriers' development, sociologists have no good reason for refusing to accept it into their standard vocabulary.

One plausible way of looking at memes is to see them as the software of the hard-wired human brain. But although psychologists may one day discover just what is going on inside the natives' heads between the time when information transmitted by imitation or learning is first heard or read or inferred from observation and the time when it is acted out in phenotypic behaviour, sociologists have for the time being to go on treating the brains of the members of the populations whose shared beliefs and attitudes they are studying as black, or very nearly black, boxes. The information has gone into the natives' heads, and the consequential behaviour is subsequently observed, but we don't know just how information received is turned into the acting-out of a collective behaviour-pattern different from the one which preceded it, or just which are the items or packages of information whose adaptedness has been critical. There the natives are, sacrificing (let us say) to a tutelary deity to protect their community from harm. Assume that we can be sure that they are not just unthinking conformists doing whatever their neighbours do, or Machiavellian hypocrites in pursuit of personal advantage, and that they are neither re-enacting an empty ritual for the benefit of tourists or film-makers or doing what they do under compulsion from rulers or their agents. The extended phenotypic effects of the memes of which they are the carriers can be observed in the altars at which the sacrifices are made, the music to which the prayers are set, the supplicatory gestures of the officiating priest, and so forth. But we simply do not know just what is going on as the interaction between the carriers and the environment enhances or diminishes the adaptiveness of some relative to other memes in the minds of the carrying population. We can only say that there is a complex of co-adapted memes which has displaced its competitors and is being acted out in the same sort of way that a machine acts out its software program.

Suppose, to give a notional example, that a sociologist comes across a culture in which the natives all carefully wash their hands before every meal. (I say 'notional' not because table manners aren't a serious topic in comparative sociology, but because I don't propose to enter into serious discussion of them here. Hand-washing will reappear in passing in Chapter 5.) It explains nothing to say that the natives carry inside their heads a meme which enjoins the washing of hands before meals. One possible answer to the 'just what is going on here?' question is an instrumental, external, just-so story: the critical meme has the form of a conviction that diseases caused by the ingestion of contaminated food[14] can attach to unwashed hands, and the natives therefore punish by ridicule, insult, and refusal of commensalism anyone who eats without using the hand-basins which are provided in every eating-place. But another possible answer is an expressive, internal just-so story: the critical meme differentiates the ritually pure in-group from the stigmatized 'other' by symbolizing a notional decontamination which has nothing whatever to do with physical health. The least plausible hypothesis is individual trial-and-error learning: in no culture do children work out for themselves that washing their hands before meals is a good thing to do in the way that they work out how to get their food into their mouths without spilling it all over their faces. But some method has to be found without the benefit of controlled experimentation to establish which just-so story is the right one.

This is not made any easier by the volume of information – the 'memetic bombardment', as it is sometimes called – to which children in all cultures are subjected from infancy onwards. Think how much information is acquired by British children from parents, mentors, and peer-group members about anything from the rules of 'Noughts and Crosses' to the tune of 'Pop Goes the Weasel'. Neither of these is likely to feature prominently in sociologists' just-so stories of the evolution of the distinctive sub-cultures among which the British population is distributed. But what about beliefs about, and attitudes towards, the Russian Revolution or the life and sayings of Jesus of Nazareth? The problem is as familiar to historians studying the influence of the printed word as it is to anthropologists studying that of the oral traditions of pre-literate peoples or psychologists that of rumours spread laterally across a population of contemporaries. Suppose a historian of nineteenth-century Europe studying the evolution of a culture in which there has emerged a bourgeois norm of cleanliness discovers that an etiquette-book which enjoins, among other things, the washing of hands before meals has gone though innumerable editions over many decades and has enjoyed a consistently high level of sales. What reason is

---

[14] Food taboos have in fact been observed much more frequently in relation to meats, with their inbuilt risk of pathogenic infection, than fruits (Fessler and Navarrete 2003).

there to suppose that the memes encoded in the etiquette-book explain the conformity to the bourgeois norm of purity and not precepts being inculcated in any case by both instruction and example down successive generations of hand-washing bourgeois parents and like-minded school-teachers? The historian Robert Darnton has remarked that it is impossible 'to argue from the sales patterns of books to the behaviour patterns of human beings' (1979: 40), and that 'we still have only a vague sense of how readers construed texts' (1996: 184). Yet Darnton's own research has shown that successive editions of Diderot's *Encyclopédie* sold well to readers of the kind who voiced radical opinions in 1789. Nobody is going to argue from this that without the *Encyclopédie* the French Revolution (to which I return in Chapter 4) would not have taken place. But it is a clear example of a time-lag effect where memes encoded in books find subsequent phenotypic expression in an environment which has changed in such a way as to enhance their adaptedness. Etiquette-books, like sermons, tracts, manuals, newspaper editorials, or readings from holy writ, may simply be repeating instructions with which those who receive them are familiar already, and many recipients may be no more likely to follow them in consequence than they were in any case. But the behaviour-patterns which distinguish both literate and non-literate cultures from one another would not be what they are if the memes encoded in their written texts and oral traditions had no phenotypic effects whatever on which selective pressure came to bear. As another historian has said of the moralizing novelettes of Harriet Martineau, which in the estimate of her publisher were each being read by some 140,000 people in the mid-1830s, 'the message was so intrusive, the moral assumptions so pervasive, that it is difficult to see how even the most casual reader could have escaped from them' (Himmelfarb 1984: 169). The trouble is that we have no way of finding out in retrospect just how many readers' behaviour was actually modified in consequence. When Tom Paine's *Rights of Man* in a sixpenny format and Hannah Moore's anti-revolutionary tracts priced at about a penny were alike being bought in their hundreds of thousands, perhaps their readers all agreed with the author already. Since we can't experiment, we just don't know.

14

I have talked up to now about the transmission of memes from mind to mind as if the concept of social, as opposed to individual, learning was less problematic than it is. But as researchers into animal behaviour well know, it is often difficult to distinguish empirically between 'true' imitation on the one hand and learning through some form of social influence on the other. From one point of view, imitation is a kind of learning: the learner learns what to do by copying other people who are washing their hands, reading encyclopaedias, and so forth. But then so can learning by instruction be said to be a kind of imitation, the difference being that now the learner copies the behaviour by following the mentor's verbal or written instructions rather than mimicking the mentor's behaviour directly. 'Do as I do' is one form of instruction and 'do as I say' another. The hymns sung by the church choir on Sundays may be sung either because the singers sing what they have heard other people singing or because a choirmaster has taught them how to read the printed score. A contradiction may arise when, as often happens, instructions given by parents or teachers are at variance with the behaviour of the parents and teachers themselves: 'You tell me to do what I'm told, but you often refuse to do what you're told yourself.' But this is merely a special case of the competition between rival memes which is going on all the time inside every native's head. For the purposes of comparative sociology, the question is why the winning memes which distinguish one culture from another at population level *are* the winners, whether their reproduction and diffusion came about by instruction from teachers to learners, by imitation of role-models who are not even aware of being imitated, by a combination of both, or by something in between.

The more important difference between imitation and learning is that learning is notoriously costly. Individual trial-and-error learning is particularly so: that is why it has as little to offer comparative sociology as it does, even though cultural evolution would slow to a halt without the heritable variations which individual innovators provide. Cultural traditions will be more likely to persist unchanged among populations where individual learning is costly, and in a population consisting entirely of unreflective imitators and social learners there would be no escape from cultural inertia. But social learning, even if more efficient than learning by individual trial-and-error, still imposes a cost on both teacher and pupil which learning by direct imitation of a mentor's observed behaviour does not. Evolutionary game theorists are able to model in detail conditions under which 'imitate the most successful strategy' will itself be the most successful strategy. There are obvious advantages to the naive individual player in imitating perceived success rather than trying to learn the programme that the most successful players are following, let alone trying out a range of alternative possible strategies and seeing which one does best. Under some conditions, formal instruction will despite this be favoured over informal exhortation and simple example. But this is likely to be in an environment of social as well as cultural selection, where practices defining the roles of teachers remunerated by public or private employers are transmitted down successive generations within institutions where students, novices, or apprentices are being formally trained to occupy specialized economic, ideological, or political roles.

The distinction between imitation and learning is particularly problematic in relation to artefacts, given how difficult it can be to infer by simple inspection the essential features of their design. They contain the critical memes in the sense in which an instruction manual contains them in its own different form, but not in the sense in which genes are contained in organisms. The problems of reverse engineering faced by archaeologists studying pots, pictures, monumental architecture, statuary, the lay-out of houses and workplaces, gardens, weapons, musical instruments and so forth may seem of only marginal relevance to comparative sociologists concerned with large-scale differences between cultures and societies of different kinds and long-term qualitative changes from one kind to another. But all these are a part of what differentiates one culture or sub-culture from another, and they all come into existence through the transmission of information from mind to mind by imitation and/or learning. So: just what is going on here?

The answer is that artefacts are extended phenotypic effects of techno-memes which at the same time encode them. When archaeologists 'digging for memes' (Lake 1998) detect in the morphology of buried artefacts a sequence of variations culminating in a locally stable design, they are recovering from objects which are themselves a medium of transmission information previously handed down by imitation or learning from one to another generation of artificers. They are thereby enabled to undertake an exercise in reverse engineering which reads back from the material objects they have unearthed to the memes which were inside the heads of their designers, whether the reading-back is an exercise in inferring the assembly-instructions from study of a finished mechanical contrivance or in inferring the allegorical symbolism from study of a finished work of art. The important difference is between genuine imitation, whether by following what the mentor does or learning to do what the mentor says, and uncomprehending copying. It is quite possible to envisage, for example, a native artist copying pictures of the crucifixion of Jesus without the least idea of what it represents and thereby unwittingly reproducing an image which, when subsequently decoded by others, turns out to be adaptive in an environment of active Christian proselytization. But this would be no more than a special case of indirect transmission of information affecting phenotype from mind to mind which in itself is unproblematic. The printers of the bibles which the missionaries are distributing to the natives don't have to have marked, learned, and inwardly digested, as opposed to merely seen, the words which they reproduced while their minds were on other and lower things.

15

When the objects of selection are practices rather than memes, it is not to be assumed that rules encoded in legislation about institutionalized roles necessarily determine phenotypic behaviour on the ground. To quote the medieval historian Chris Wickham, 'we have to abandon the legal history paradigm, and do it quite consciously. Instead, we have to confront the harder talk of comparing, not rules, but the sets of local practices that constituted whole societies' (Wickham 1994: 207).

Since the carriers of the information affecting phenotype are now dyads of interacting roles, it follows that the individual incumbents of both must share not only an understanding of its meaning but an acceptance of the inducements and sanctions which underwrite its implications for how they are to behave towards one another. The landlords and tenants, or priests and parishioners, or generals and soldiers have not only, as I put it in Section 7, to know what to do in order to be what they are; they have also to accept that the practices which make them so, renegotiable as they may be, are not theirs to alter at will. Consider what goes on in a Catholic country where some male adolescents grow up with the ambition of entering the priesthood. It is not enough for them to inform themselves about Christian doctrine, study the text of the Bible, and adhere to the norms of Christian conduct. Nor is it enough for them to learn what priests do (how a mass is conducted, what is involved in administering extreme unction, and so forth). They have to be institutionally qualified and assigned to a parish where their qualifications are accepted by their parishioners as carrying the ideological authority of the Roman Church. Admittedly, the doctrine of sanctity of clergy may lead ordinands to continue to regard themselves as priests even if they so behave as to be defrocked: 'Not all the water in the rough, rude sea Can wash the balm from an anointed king.' But I cannot resist repeating (from Runciman 1983: 60) the Jewish joke about the mother who is telling her friend about 'my son the captain': sure enough, there is the son parading around in nautical dress with his talk of 'abaft' and 'astern' and 'belay there!'; but the friend says, 'So to you, he's a captain; to me, he's a captain; but to captains, is he a captain?'

All the same, it is always possible that both cultural and social selection are simultaneously determining the form taken by a collective behaviour-pattern. Consider the practice of sharecropping. It is sometimes but by no means always found in an exploitative relationship in which the landlord's control of the means of production imposes it on the tenant irrespective of whether the tenant believes it to be advantageous or feels it to be fair. In such environments, the adaptedness of the practice is a joint function of the local ecology and the relative bargaining power attaching to the landlord's and tenants' roles: in nineteenth-century France, for example, landlords used sharecropping contracts not only to realize economies of scale in livestock rearing but at the same time take advantage of family labour at a time of rising wages (Carmona 2006: 237). Conversely, the balance of negotiating power can be in the sharecropper's favour where able-bodied young men work the land for elderly proprietors unable to work it for themselves in exchange for not only a share of the produce but inheritance of the land itself on the proprietor's death (Robertson 1980). But cultural selection can at the same time be at work in favouring one rather than other type of sharecropping contract. Richerson and Boyd (2005: 85), drawing now on a study by Burke and Young (2001) of Illinois farmers, offer an example in which the division of the crop between landlords and tenants converges on a small number of simple ratios which are freely chosen through imitation or learning (or, it might be, individual learning and rational choice). Variations of this kind are a clear illustration of how cultural reinterpretations can influence the outcome of negotiations conducted within an established social institution. Cultural selection is not swamped by social selection simply because the transition from culture to society generates inequalities of economic, ideological, or political power attaching to interacting roles and systacts.

16

There remains the vexed question whether selective pressure bears only on individuals as the carriers of information affecting phenotype, or whether it bears also on groups as such. Discussion of this topic was for a long time dominated by the arguments of biologists who were held to have conclusively refuted the view that self-sacrificing altruism on the part of individual members of a group, including limitation on number of offspring, could be explained by its contribution to the greater good of the group rather than its function in maximizing the prospects of reproduction of the genes of the altruist (or the altruist's kin). The revisionists did not, however, argue that there are no conditions under which natural selection operates on competition between groups rather than between individuals. They only insisted that, as W. D. Hamilton put it in demonstrating formally the characteristically greater power of individual selection for altruism when grouping is random, or nearly random, 'we have to consider whether the population can get into the specified state, and, if it can, whether its present trend will continue' (1996 [1975]: 333). If, for example, a species is divided into several separate populations established by different founders, then competition for territory and resources between one group and another may be a stronger influence on the probability of reproduction of their members' genes than within-group competition between individuals. But once there is migration between groups, individual competition will again come to the fore. It would accordingly be a mistake for sociologists to assume that at the biological, let alone the cultural or social, level group selection has been shown to be incapable of acting as a significant evolutionary force. On the contrary: there are good reasons for thinking that intra-group cooperation was favoured by inter-group selection throughout the entire course of hominid evolution.

The possibility of cultural group selection was explicitly envisaged by Darwin himself in an often-quoted passage of the *Descent* (1882: 132). He argued that groups with a higher proportion of members motivated by a sense of 'glory' to sacrifice themselves for the good of the rest will have a competitive advantage over groups with a lower proportion, by which he appears to have had in mind (not that he could have put it that way) gene-meme co-evolution in which the memes in the heads of the members of the first group would make them more likely to reproduce their genes successfully than the members of the second group. The time which it will take for a group to be driven to extinction by its competitors is difficult to calculate. Soltis *et al.* (1995), using data on local group extinctions among the small warrior societies of Papua New Guinea prior to pacification, estimated that without acceleration by individual choice it might take a thousand years for the replacement of the relevant traits in a metapopulation. But once cultural selection is operating alongside natural selection, migration between groups does not pose the same difficulty for group selection, since imitation and learning enable migrants to acquire the memes which are dominant in the group they have joined and the cultural traditions of different groups are likely to be sufficiently stable for individual variation within them to be relatively low. Furthermore, memes themselves can outreproduce their competitors through cultural group selection whether or not they enhance the reproductive potential of the population of the group.

At the level of social selection, competition between institutionally structured groups such as armies or business enterprises or political parties is so familiar to sociologists that the extinction of the losers could almost be said to be a routine observation. It may be that the behaviour of the winning group is no more than a statistical effect of the traits of its individual members (the winning army wins purely because it has a larger proportion of more courageous soldiers). But often it is because the outcome depends on the successful integration of different packages of information carried by different individuals or role-dyads which is acted out in active collaboration consequential on communal decision-making. Many traits predicable only of groups, but not of their individual members, can make the memes and the practices carried by the winning group mutually co-adaptive. Consider the account of the much-studied Nuer/Dinka relationship given by the anthropologist Raymond Kelly (1985), which Sober and Wilson (1998: 191) cite as 'a smoking gun of group selection in action'. The domination of the Nuer over the Dinka, with whom they originally shared a common ancestry and a common ecology, is attributed by Kelly to a critical mutation in the nature and scale of bridewealth payments. The difference in the minimum acceptable level of these was sustained by phenotypic effects which extended to herd management, grazing requirements, and herd sizes. The tribes with comparatively high ideal bridewealth payments were then those whose practices generated a form of military organization which the Dinka were unable to counter. The outcome cannot be explained either by demographic differences or by attributing to the Dinka a reluctance to fight. If Kelly's just-so story is the right one, then, whatever scope there may be for disagreement over its details, there can be no doubt that group selection through heritable variation and competitive selection of both memes and practices was just what was going on.

The arguments over individual versus group selection are in some ways reminiscent of the arguments over 'Individualism' versus 'Holism' on which much intellectual energy was expended by both sociologists and philosophers during much of the twentieth century. In both cases, the issues at stake were apt to be obscured by mutual accusations of bias. Individualists could find themselves charged by Holists with condoning the evils of capitalist property relations and encouraging the uninhibited pursuit of self-interest, while Holists could find themselves charged by Individualists with implicitly advocating totalitarian forms of government and the curtailment of freedom. But 'Individualists' are not committed to denying that individual behaviour has to be placed in its social context or that groups have properties not predicable of their individual members, and 'Holists' are not committed to positing metaphysical entities to which are attributed properties of individual minds or to explaining the course of social evolution by reference only to the properties of groups, communities, and systacts (or even societies, empires, and civilizations). There is nothing contentious in the observation that cooperative groups can secure for their members advantages which the individual members could not secure for themselves and that some groups not only exploit but alter their environments more effectively than others through what evolutionary biologists call 'niche construction' (Laland *et al.* 2000), so that their members' genes, memes, and practices alike are all more likely to be reproduced – with the continuing possibility of further mutations – as a result.

Lastly, there is no need for comparative sociologists to be concerned over different definitions of what constitutes a 'group'. Since institutional practices depend on interaction between the incumbents of two complementary roles, social evolution could be said to be a matter of group selection by definition. But it makes no difference whether selection is thought of as operating on populations of individual role-incumbents or metapopulations of role-dyads. These are merely two different ways of reporting the same thing. In the evolution of economically, ideologically, and politically stratified societies out of hunting and foraging bands (or 'band-clusters'), it is entirely plausible to suppose that 'proto-households' (Bergucki 1999: 152) competing with one another for resources were better fitted to exploit their environment by risking-taking initiatives than were individual hunters and foragers. In large and complex capitalist industrial societies, technological innovations are subject to selective pressures from the research community and the market which act on both the individual traits of risk-taking technologists and on the structural properties of the laboratories, firms, and institutes within which they work. Hitherto adaptive techno-memes and the practices associated with them can then be driven to extinction either by the invasion of the team, laboratory, firm, or institute by rival mutants or by the extinction of the laboratory, firm, or institute through loss of funding or personnel. Whatever the right just-so-story, it can be told either as a story about laboratories, firms and institutes or as a story about technologists. There is no need to complicate the formulation and test of a proffered explanation by argument over whether one way of phrasing it is to be preferred over another a priori.

CHAPTER 2

Natural selection and evoked behaviour

DISPOSITIONS, CAPACITIES, AND SUSCEPTIBILITIES

I

Since we – human beings, that is – are the surviving one among many hominid species all descended from primordial apes, it is not surprising that the explanation of much of our behaviour can be traced as far back as it can in our biological inheritance – with the corollary, among others, that if we had been descended from monkeys we would have had female kin-bonding in our evolved past of the kind which is lacking among apes. The similarities between our behaviour and that of the chimpanzees in the Gombe rain forest, the Arnhem zoo, and the Yerkes field station are unmistakable: there they are, fighting, playing, imitating, seducing, grieving, deceiving, collaborating, and showing off just as human beings in all cultures and societies do. But how much does that help us to explain the similarities and differences between cultures and societies with which comparative sociologists are concerned?

The standard response of twentieth-century sociologists was to insist that since our innate dispositions can be radically diverted, refined, encouraged, modified, or suppressed in different ways in different groups, communities, cultures, and societies, they are of no more relevance to comparative sociology than that human beings in all cultures and societies laugh, cry, yawn, dream, and express their emotions in facial expressions which Darwin correctly hypothesized to be naturally rather than cultur-ally selected (although they can, at the same time, be simulated with the intent to deceive). But more to the point are first, the many examples where deliberate attempts to modify behaviour – notably where the upbringing of children is concerned – are frustrated by evoked responses which owe nothing to either culture or society; and second, the many instances in the ethnographic and historical record where a similar pattern of evoked behaviour can be observed in widely different cultural and social environments. Cultural and social selection both drive different human populations down one rather than another of a wide range of different evolutionary pathways. But not even the most intransigent anti-Darwinian can deny that there are some innate, species-wide dispositions, capacities, and susceptibilities which impose some inescapable limits on the possible extent of variation between one culture or society and another.

The paradox is that our biological inheritance includes both the innate constraints which mean that not just anything is thinkable or doable, any more than just anything is digestible, and the innate capacities which enable us to display a far greater variety of behaviour than any other species. As it has been aptly put by Ernest Gellner (1989: 516), 'Question: how can a species genetically granted by Nature such remarkable freedom and licence, nevertheless observe such restraint, such narrowly defined limits, in its actual conduct?' The diversity is not merely between groups or between individuals within groups but within individuals themselves, as memorably described with characteristic insight by Montaigne in his essay 'On the Inconstancy of our Actions'. The incumbents of even the most tightly structured institutional roles are still the 'irrational, disorderly, unpredictable, and spontaneous' persons which all of us are (Coleman 1990: 197). Yet the diversity of cultures is a diversity of stable combinations of memes acquired by imitation and learning, and the diversity of societies is a diversity of stable sets of practices defining the roles constitutive of the ongoing modes of production, persuasion, and coercion which are comparative sociology's stock-in-trade. How can this be? At population level, evolution somehow favours relatively stable equilibria, and consistency within a far from unlimited range of collective behaviour-patterns is maintained over most of the world for most of the time.

2

Whatever surprises future research on the human mind may hold, the distinction which folk psychology makes between attitudes and beliefs (or, if you prefer, between passion and reason, or the heart and the head) remains as self-evident in theory and indispensable in practice as it has always been. Whatever the relation, under the heading of 'attitude', between preferences, norms, and values, and whatever the criteria by which the strength and consistency of beliefs are to be judged, a contrast between the two is rightly taken for granted by sociologists of all theoretical persuasions. But that does not in itself make the relative stability of our collective behaviour-patterns any easier to explain, since our brains have not evolved in such a way as either to give our intellectual superegos mastery over our emotional ids or, conversely, to subordinate reason to the point of becoming, in Hume's celebrated phrase, the 'slave' of the passions. It is rather a matter of 'the parallel operation of the emotional and the rational brain within every human being', with the ventromedial prefrontal cortex providing an interface between them (Massey 2002: 24). Nor has natural selection designed us to be as good as we might like to suppose at either logical thought or consistent emotion: for all our psychological advantages over our primate cousins, we are as careless in our reasoning – particularly our statistical reasoning – as we are impulsive in our feelings. Yet the beliefs (however weakly held) and attitudes (however erratically felt) which coexist inside all of our heads work together in such a way that stable collective behaviour-patterns persist over successive generations. However exactly it came about, our ancestors' larger brains with their proportionately larger neo-cortices enabled them to become more skilled at interacting with one another than their primate cousins and thereby preventing the aggregation of unrelated strangers into larger and larger groups from leading to either ungovernable anarchy or headlong fragmentation.

Thus despite our individual irrationality, disorderliness, unpredictability, and spontaneity, the human species appears to have an innate predisposition to conformity. When a leading theorist of rational choice says that the 'main reason habitual behaviour permeates most aspects of life is that habits have an advantage in the biological evolution of human traits' (Becker 1996: 9), he is implicitly appealing to evolutionary psychology as well as explicitly appealing, as he does, to Aristotle and Adam Smith. The study of both the reasons and the passions continues to be fraught with conceptual as well as empirical difficulties. But all human beings have them both, and can recognize them in others. We all have a naturally selected capacity for quick intuitive evaluation (Haidt 2001) as well as for 'fast and frugal' (Gigerenzer and Goldstein 1996) ratiocination. Moreover, we are all, whatever the culture in which we are reared, not only 'theory-*inventors*' trying to make sense of the world around us but 'theory-*retainers*' (Carey 1985: 914). Readiness to subject acquired beliefs to lengthy and careful test is a late and limited product of cultural, not natural, selection. Although we are all aware that other people cling with equal conviction to beliefs as well as attitudes incompatible with our own, we are reluctant to take as seriously as might be expected of us the possibility that they, not we, might be right. Ask yourself how often you have ever actually won (or lost) an argument with anyone about religion or history or politics. All beliefs are rational to the people who hold them, however unconvincing their reasons to the members of other cultures or other members of their own.[1] Our innate desire to be relieved from uncertainty makes us at the same time explanatorily voracious, theoretically credulous, and obstinately loyal to the fellow members of our local sub-culture.

Once, therefore, a package of co-adapted memes acquired, from whatever source, by imitation or learning has made the workings of the immediate environment more manageable, the natives in all cultures and societies are predisposed to keep it in their heads, whether they are Roman litigants convinced that their failure to win their case must be due to their opponents' recourse to a binding spell, or Shang Chinese soothsayers heating animal bones in order to read the future from the resulting T-shaped cracks, or Egyptian priests 'partial to exegesis on the worst possible etymological principles' (Kirk 1980: 203), or chartists in a stockbroking office claiming to have anticipated a downturn in the equity market, or astrologers impervious to the suggestion that their occasional successful predictions could be due to coincidence, or laboratory experimentalists adept at finding reasons to ignore results which conflict with their favourite hypotheses. As theory-retainers, we not only use reasoned argument to justify rather than challenge convictions already held but display 'a prevalent, and disturbing, tendency to assimilate any new information to existing theories' (Kuhn 1991: 268). As is illustrated as well by the belief in witchcraft among early modern Europeans as among Evans-Pritchard's Azande or the Etoro of Papua New Guinea or the population of 'ancient' Rome, it is not intellectual argument which will of itself drive to extinction the memes whose phenotypic effects the historian or anthropologist has observed. 'How can you behave as if you believed such nonsense?' is as ineffective a question addressed to worldly judges and learned divines in a self-consciously sophisticated intellectual culture as it is to illiterate peasants living at the margins of subsistence. The arguments deployed against the persecution of witches in Britain by Francis Hutchinson in 1718, which found ready acceptance, were much the same as those offered by Thomas Ady in 1656 and Reginald Scot in 1584, which had been treated as 'part of the radical fringe' (Bostridge 1997: 3). Not all conformity to conventional wisdom is to be explained as directly evoked by situational cues or motivated by an inbuilt desire to behave like other

---

[1] That general statement is not invalidated by professions of 'faith'. *Credo quia impossibile* is an appeal to a higher-order criterion of rationality, not an expression of epistemological nihilism. Sociologists, unlike philosophers, have no grounds for dismissing as 'irrational' beliefs whose justification they do not themselves accept (Runciman 1991).

people. But reflective assessment of alternative courses of future action is rarely to be observed except when motives conflict in ways which make self-conscious decision-making inescapable.

It was not, therefore, Popperian hypothesis-testing which held together the hunting and foraging bands dispersing out of Africa from whose members we are all descended, even if conjecture and refutation played some part in their choice of techniques for, among other things, evading predators or tracking prey. It was more a disposition to defer to received beliefs and conform to shared attitudes coupled with a capacity and will-ingness to imitate or learn from the carriers of mutant memes without recourse to individual trial-and-error. In the course of cultural evolution (Henrich and McElreath 2003), the arbitrary symbols by which our dis-tant ancestors differentiated themselves from one another came to vary increasingly widely: a prodigious range of markers, decorations, idioms, dialects, totems, signals, gestures, and taboos evolved to express the mutual recognition and attachment of in-group members and their self-differentiation from groups perceived as 'other'. There is abundant experi-mental as well as ethnographic and historical evidence to show just how easily mutual recognition and attachment can be engineered between arbitrarily differentiated human groups, whether soldiers recruited into regiments, schoolchildren assigned to classes, or players of sports and games and their audiences organized into teams and supporting cliques. But the diverse cultural forms which this behaviour takes, although the product of heritable variation and competitive selection of memes, not genes, are at the same time evoked expressions of dispositions, capacities, and susceptibilities formed by natural, not cultural, selection.

The same holds for the disposition not merely to categorize but to dis-associate from out-groups in accordance with culturally acquired criteria. The defensive self-circumscription of the small groups of anatomically and psychologically modern humans spreading out into an increasingly wide range of local environments was a biologically adaptive response evoked in consequence of it. The stereotyping of strangers with whom part-cooperative, part-competitive relationships had somehow to be formed and sustained was an adaptive strategy for making necessary discriminations in an environment where relevant information was imperfect and diffi-cult to obtain (van den Berghe 1997; Gil-White 2001). The stigmatizing of the members of groups seen as potentially unreliable exchange partners or carriers of pathogens reduced the frequency of interactions differen-tially likely to impose fitness costs (Kurzban and Leary 2001). The range of cultural forms which relations with out-groups took thereafter among different hunting and foraging peoples at different times and in different places (Kelly 1995) is not an argument against the biological inheritance of capacities, dispositions, and susceptibilities which underlie them all. The widely different ways in which 'otherness' is culturally defined are not in contradiction with the claim of E. O. Wilson that 'Our brains do appear to be programmed to the following extent: we are inclined to partition other people into friends and aliens in the same way that birds are inclined to learn territorial songs and to navigate by the polar constellations' (1978: 119). We do not know just when or under just what selective pressures they were so programmed. But they were. Natural selection doesn't dictate what particular people, or on what ostensible grounds, you will designate as 'other', any more than it dictates what language you will learn. But it does dictate that you will designate some people as such, just as it dictates that you will, unless reared without human contact, grow up speaking at least one language. And it dictates that you will have inside your head some moral attitudes and some metaphysical beliefs, although it is cultural selection which dictates what particular standard of conduct you subscribe to and what particular presumptive effects you link to what particular presumptive causes as you try to make sense of the workings of the world in the course of your individual development.

3

Some sociologists may still wish to insist that once cultural, and subsequently social, selection are under way, natural selection can explain nothing more about the differences with which comparative sociology is concerned than the extent to which collective behaviour-patterns are 'ultimately', or 'at the end of the day', constrained by the design of the human brain on one side and the drive to sustain inclusive reproductive fitness on the other. They will refuse to accept that, to take an obvious example, both a creed which enjoins holy war against all unbelievers and a creed which prohibits the waging of war in any form are nothing more than alternative expressions of the same innate predispositions evoked by different local environments. True as it may be that the 'so-called moral sense' is a product of natural selection and that what we call 'conscience' was biologically adaptive for our remote forebears, some human beings think it a sacred duty for fathers to kill daughters who have dishonoured their families by an illegitimate pregnancy while others think it a sacred duty to refrain from killing not only fellow humans but animals likewise. How can natural selection account for that?

The answer to that question is that no neo-Darwinian sociologist is committed to claiming that it can. But research needs to be designed for the purpose of finding out just how far the behaviour in question which might, in the environment in question, be the acting-out of an innate predisposition of a universal kind is or isn't a product of natural rather than cultural or social selection. If, for example, the members of a non-literate population of hunter-horticulturalists in the Ecuadorian Amazon perform no differently in a test of conditional reasoning from Harvard undergraduates (Sugiyama, Tooby, and Cosmides 2002), are we to conclude that there is a similar cheater-detection mechanism in the natives' heads in all the cultures and societies in the historical and ethnographic record? A comparative study designed to test whether norms of fairness and reciprocity override the pursuit of economic self-interest in the same way in fifteen small-scale societies (Henrich *et al.* 2004) found that, although there was much more inter-group variation than in experiments with students as subjects, in none of them was the experimental behaviour consistent with the rational-choice model of the economics textbooks. When the one-shot, two-person Ultimatum Game (in which both proposer and respondent earn nothing if the responder refuses the offer of a proportion of a fixed sum of money) was played by the Machiguinga of the Peruvian Amazon forest, the mean offer was 28 per cent as against 48 per cent among graduate students in Los Angeles, and Machiguinga respondents almost always accepted offers below 20 per cent which the Los Angeles sample almost never made in the first place. In Papua New Guinea, by contrast, where a gift is likely to be culturally construed by the recipient as a strategy designed to enhance the status of the donor and place the donee under a potentially unwelcome obligation, generous offers of more than half the money were often rejected; and where social selection comes to bear, the offers of players in societies integrated into the practices and roles of a market for goods and labour were likely to be significantly higher than the offers of players who were not. The inescapable conclusion is that the different degrees of selfishness and unselfishness displayed by the members of different populations in experiments which model real-life strategic choices reflect the simultaneous workings of natural *and* cultural *and* social selection.[2]

---

[2] Similarly suggestive is an experimental study of anti-social punishment (i.e. punishment of cooperators) among university undergraduates in sixteen countries in which it was found that 'antisocial punishment is harsher in participant pools from societies with weak norms of civic cooperation and a weak rule of law' (Hermann *et al.* 2008: 1366).

BEHAVIOURAL UNIVERSALS

4

Disagreements about the scope, nature, and significance of presumptively innate species-wide determinants of behaviour are a longstanding feature of the literature on so-called 'universals' observable in any and all cultures and societies. No comparative sociologist will dispute that there are some behaviour-patterns which are common to all members of the human species – food is procured, infants are nurtured, languages are learned, and utensils are made. But what does this tell us about the relative strength of the forces of natural, cultural, and social selection? A universal behaviour-pattern may or may not be innate, and an innate behaviour-pattern may or may not be universal.

Surprisingly long lists of supposed universals are compiled from time to time only to invite the objection that unless they are made to hold good by pre-emptive definition there are always exceptions to be found somewhere in the ethnographic or historical record – or, alternatively, that where they do hold good, they are of no more than trivial interest, since what matters is the difference in the ways that different people in different cultures and societies do these commonplace things. But the universal most important for comparative sociology is the one which sociologists (unlike both brain scientists and philosophers[3]) most often take for granted: the universal comprehensibility of the terms in which the members of different human populations represent themselves as such. No anthropologist has ever returned from the field reporting the existence of a human community about which nothing more can be said than that its members interact with one another in an apparently non-random yet wholly baffling way. Not only can all physiologically normal human beings learn to speak a language, but they can all learn to talk to each other between as well as within languages about their different culturally transmitted beliefs and attitudes, contested as these may then turn out to be.[4]

---

[3] Wittgenstein, for all his insistence on the distinctiveness of different 'forms of life', is explicit that a researcher in a strange country with a wholly alien language who wonders how to tell whether the natives are really giving, receiving, understanding, obeying, and rebelling against orders has to rely on mankind's universal mode of behaviour (*Handlungsweise*) as the system of relevance (*Bezugssystem*) for doing so (*Philosophical Investigations* §206).

[4] To go so far as to say that 'any language can be used to convey any proposition, from theological parables to military directives' (Pinker 2002: 37) is to invite Evans-Pritchard's rhetorical question 'How do you render into Amerindian language "In the beginning was the Word"?' (1965: 14). The

It is therefore not only an ethnographic but a biological fact that whatever items or packages of information find phenotypic expression in the cultural or social behaviour-patterns of any human population chosen for study, they can in principle be decoded, whatever the mechanism or the route by which they have been evoked, acquired, or imposed. In practice, it may be that they can't, whether because of aberrant genes inherited or brain-damage suffered by the chosen native informant or for the social, rather than (or perhaps as well as) cultural, reasons for which some 'secret societies' do indeed remain secret. Rare as they may be, there are cases of individual linguistic behaviour which is incomprehensible alike to the visiting observer and to the fellow members of the speaker's own culture (and may well, therefore, lead to the speaker's behaviour being clinically explained as 'pathological' and pejoratively described as 'mad'). But consistent patterns of collective behaviour are never incomprehensible in this way. Distinctive, culturally selected complexes of representations, attitudes, and beliefs, like distinctive, socially selected modes of production, persuasion, and coercion, presuppose both a shared underlying ontology and a shared underlying acceptance of meaning without which the necessary minimum of consistency and stability of behaviour wouldn't be achievable at all ('understanding' in the descriptive, phenomenological sense of 'what it really feels like' to be one of 'them' being, as always, a separate but not unrelated matter).

Dispositions, capacities, and susceptibilities do not, however, find expression of their own accord in solitude. It is another universal that they have to be activated by social contact. Just how this comes about is a controversial question in cognitive science, where some psychologists assert but others deny that 'protoconcepts' are innately encoded in the neural structure of the human brain. If our brains are modular rather than general-purpose in design, locally variable behaviour-patterns may be more likely to be evoked than acquired. But sociologists do not need to take sides on this contested issue. They need only to recognize that there are some universal understandings of number, time, space, movement, and physical bodies, some conceptual universals in interpersonal language, and some universal intuitions about purposive artefacts. There are also some universals in 'fundamental motivational mechanisms' (Heckhamen and Schultz 1999) and 'behavioural development' (Bateson and Martin

---

answer is that of course you can't do it in one move. But languages can be extended to incorporate parts of other languages – it happens all the time – and in due course Amerindian speakers can be taught to understand 'In the beginning was the Word' as well (or badly) as English speakers can be taught to understand 'ΕΝ ΑΡΧΗ ΗΝ Ο ΛΟΓΟΣ' or, for that matter, the vocabulary of Amerindian cosmology.

1999), and a universal capacity for 'empathy' (Hoffman 1981). Moreover, just as there are some behavioural universals whose sociological relevance is undeniable, so are there some conceivable behaviour-patterns which are nowhere to be found in the ethnographic or historical record. There are no human populations in which infants are all freely traded as marketable commodities any more than there are populations where Hamilton's Rule is stood on its head – unconditional cooperation with outsiders but ruthless egoism towards close genetic kin.

Anthropologists are, as a rule, more disposed than other behavioural scientists to insist on the magnitude of the cultural differences which our shared biological inheritance permits. Look (they will say) at how differently time itself is conceptualized by the Nuer or the Mursi or whoever by comparison with 'us' and our clocks and calendars and schedules and routines geared to the exigencies of our parochial social institutions, or how differently space is conceptualized not only by people who live in different ecological environments (forest, jungle, savannah, desert) but by people with different poetical and mythical traditions, or how differently humanity itself is conceptualized in animistic or totemistic cultures from a 'naturalistic' culture like the anthropologist's own (Descola 2005). There have been, and still are, very many people in the world whose ideas about, and behaviour towards, what 'we' call 'nature' are radically different from our own, and to whom the distinction deployed in this book between the natural, the cultural, and the social would be entirely alien. But anthropologists are equally concerned to insist on the common humanity of themselves and the peoples whose beliefs and attitudes they document. This can sometimes look uncomfortably like having it both ways, particularly when the aim in view is to privilege the culture being studied at the expense of the anthropologist's own. But there need not be any inconsistency. Reportage, let alone explanation or description, of the diversity of beliefs and attitudes documented in the ethnographic record depends on the application of terms which reflect the universal biological inheritance which makes it possible to report them in the first place. The more the culture which the anthropologist has been studying is different from the anthropologist's own, the more the anthropologist's success in elucidating the difference testifies to an innate species-wide psychological inheritance shared between 'us' and 'them'.

5

Unarguable as the evidence is for a universal human psychology, the equally unarguable range of cultural variations which it makes possible continues to pose some longstanding conceptual questions which are no less problematic for selectionist sociologists than for any others. How far is 'love' as observed in ancient Athens the same as in present-day Beijing? How far is 'anger' as observed among the Hopi Indians the same as among the English bourgeoisie? And so on. The languages of different people are full of words for emotions which are unique to themselves: what, to go no further afield, is the English equivalent of the German *angst*? But neither the differences in the way in which what 'we' call 'love' and 'anger' are conceptualized nor the conventions governing their appropriate behavioural manifestations in different cultures entail the conclusion that there is nothing which deserves to be called 'love' or 'anger' to be found inside the heads of the natives in all cultures and societies. It is necessary only to recognize that 'If we want to posit universal human emotions, we must identify them in terms of a language-independent metalanguage, not in terms of English folk words for emotions' (Wierzbicka 1992: 120). There is no reason for selectionist sociologists to deny that there are local ethnopsychological variations in meaning (Mallon and Stich 2000) or that love and anger are differently manifested in outward behaviour, as well as differently classified and prioritized, in different human populations. But however fluid the vernacular terminology, and however ambiguous the exchange of phenomenological descriptions of subjective experience between the members of different cultures, no anthropologist has ever found one so peculiarly distinctive that neither love nor anger can be attributed to the natives unless those words are given a meaning applicable to nobody other than themselves. Love and anger are demonstrably being felt by infants still too young for memes acquired by imitation and learning, let alone institutionally imposed practices, to account for it, just as they demonstrably make and act on presumptive connections between things observed in the world whereby one occurrence is held to be produced by another, antecedent one. In no physiologically normal infant's brain is the amygdala not activated by whatever in its environment evokes a response recognizable as fear. Nor is there anywhere in the world where children are so reared that all of their behaviour is either solipsistically utilitarian or else part of an indefinite series of existential *actes gratuites*.

Beliefs and attitudes which are susceptible to intersubjective understanding, intrinsically connected to one another, and acted out in distinctive collective behaviour-patterns can now be detected inside the natives' heads in any and all human populations not only through their verbal reports which anyone who has learned their language can understand but by the application of neurological and chemical techniques such as positron emission tomography which locate them in the brain. Such techniques will not by themselves resolve the difficulties of comparative sociologists confronted with behaviour which raises the question whether, as one anthropologist has put it, 'a forgotten message, or a sign that betrays some meaning, or a message that no-one understands, is an example of communication, in any strict sense. To say that people in the society continue to do it because they feel an obscure appropriateness or satisfaction in what they do is to speak in terms of stimulation and response rather than in terms of communication and message' (Lewis 1980: 37). But in all cultures, whatever exactly is going on inside the natives' heads, the memes whose phenotypic effects have been acted out are not totally undetectable. The observer of an initially baffling behaviour-pattern is still able to infer something about the attitudes to which it gives expression, and to decipher something about the beliefs which it implies – which is just what Lewis himself proceeds to do for the Gnau of New Guinea whom he has been studying in the field. The observer may conclude that the appropriate parallel is with musical rather than verbal meaning (Baranowski 1998), or that if the natives are unable to give an answer when asked for a specific symbolic meaning it is precisely because a verbal expression of its meaning is 'not necessary to the communicative function of the ritual acts' (Arno 2003: 808–9), or that the meaning to be derived from the concatenation of the significata of a ritual is so abstract, complex, and at the same time emotionally charged as to be 'ineffable' (Rappaport 1999: 256). But in none of these cases are the anthropologists telling their readers that the natives' behaviour has no meaning whatever. Their own interpretations of the evidence they report are themselves evidence for the universal, innate human capacity to go beyond information explicitly given – not (*pace* Steven Pinker) to the point that its meaning can be extracted and translated directly and in full into the anthropologist's own language, but to the point that the anthropologist can, by talking to the natives in their own language, establish what additions to the anthropologist's own language that would require.

6

The innate human capacity for calculation of individual self-interest continues likewise to be problematic for comparative sociology. But that is not because to attribute rationality to actions is of no explanatory value so much as because some sociologists think that other sociologists think that the appeal to 'rational choice' explains much more than it actually does

(Zafirovski 1999). Rational choice theory has even been criticized as 'pre-Darwinian' in its explanatory logic (Vanberg 2002: 25), and as having an 'ontological framework' into which the well-attested phenomenon of fellow-feeling cannot be fitted at all (Sugden 2002: 63). Evolutionary game theorists can demonstrate formally how, for example, strategies of commitment can escape extinction even where they fail the test of modular rationality (Skyrms 1996: 44), and behavioural game theorists can supply convincing experimental evidence for systematically irrational choices (Camerer 2003). Brain scientists applying transcranial magnetic stimulation to players of experimentally constructed games can see just what is going on inside the players' heads when norms of fairness override calculations of pecuniary self-interest. But it is as plain that human beings in all cultures and societies have an innate capacity for making choices in accordance with their assessment of the probability of more or less satisfaction to themselves from the outcome as it is that the individual choices which they make are often driven by motives which can be labelled 'rationally self-interested' only by stretching the definitions of 'rationality' and 'self-interest' so widely that the differences between memes of the one and the other kind have to be reinstated within it in other terms.[5] It does not matter for the purposes of comparative sociology whether the competing memes are then categorized as 'rational' versus 'normative', or as rational in one sense ('purpose-rational') as opposed to rational in another ('value-rational'). Selective pressures sometimes favour the one and sometimes the other, and both result from what natural selection has done for our brains.

It is only to be expected, therefore, that the ethnographic record will be full of cultures where there is no 'functional or utilitarian reason' which can explain, for example, the plants and trees used in the making of Wala canoes (Tilley 1999: 109).[6] But it is equally to be expected that there are cultures in which 'people approach religion in the way that they approach other objects of choice. They evaluate its costs and benefits and act so as to maximize their utility' (Iannacone 1995: 172) – a claim supported, in the case of the United States of America, by the evidence for hypotheses derived from rational-choice theory on denominational mobility, conversion ages, and patterns of denominational intermarriage.

---

[5] Yair (2007) argues that James S. Coleman, although a leading proponent of rational choice theory as the paradigm for sociological explanation, relies in his own empirical studies on expressive motivation to impel rational agents to seek to maximize their short-term utility.

[6] In the archaeological record there are similar examples, as in pre-Hispanic Andean metallurgy, where gold and silver were incorporated into the body of an object at high cost in time and labour instead of being plated on its surface (Dobres and Hoffman 1994: 218).

No comparative sociologist seriously supposes either that the choice of materials for building canoes is nowhere made for functional or utilitarian reasons at all, or that religious affiliation is everywhere a matter of cost-benefit calculation alone. Nor, in any case, is it always rational to act 'rationally': if playing to win leads to peer-group hostility and institutional demotion, is it not rational to play (sometimes) to lose? It can be just as mistaken for sociologists to assume that the information affecting phenotype to which a particular environment gives selective advantage must be of the form presupposed by rational choice theory as to assume that it can't be when, however indignantly the natives themselves may deny it, that is just what it turns out to be.

7

What, then, about the innate disposition to 'probe the social order for weaknesses and look for openings to improve one's standing', as Frans de Waal puts it (1996: 102)? Before the transition from culture to society, the 'social order' is a system of interpersonal ranking only. But the motivation to rise in rank within such an order can be just as strong as in a system of institutional roles and inter-systactic conflicts. If the sociology of our Palaeolithic ancestors was similar to that of the ethnographically documented hunting and foraging bands, self-aggrandizers were held in check by joking, teasing, enforced sharing, vigilant monitoring, counter-dominant coalitions, and occasional assassinations. But it does not follow that would-be self-aggrandizers were not present in every successive generation (Hayden 1998: 18). Leaders were unable to turn themselves into rulers, but that is not a reason to assume that they would not have done so if they could. The behaviour which restrains the aggression of the self-aggrandizers is itself aggressive behaviour.

It is not impossible that natural selection worked to reduce the reproductive success of the self-aggrandizers. If the resentment which they provoked led to the formation of coalitions whose members cooperated in punishing them, and if the punishment took the form of depriving them, whether by assassination, exile, or denial of access to nubile women, of the opportunity to have children, then perhaps 'the imperative for authoritarianism was somehow cleansed from the genes of our pre-human ancestors, only to be revived in relatively recent history as a *cultural* adaptation to the need to domesticate plants and animals in response to population pressures' (Binmore 2001: 162, citing Knauft 1991). There was ample time during the long millennia of the Pleistocene for significant changes in the human genome. But how then account for the evidence of the archaeological record which overwhelmingly supports the conclusion that 'hereditary social status will develop everywhere the economic and social circumstances will allow it' (Maschner and Patton 1996: 101)? It does not require market towns or agricultural estates or public works. Sustainable aquatic resources are quite enough, as illustrated by the Kwakiutl of the Northwest Pacific Coast with their chiefs and slaves and their celebrated 'potlatches'. It is true that the transition from culture to society need not lead to the emergence of a role to which there attaches the quasi-despotic power of an alpha male chimpanzee. There are 'covenants without the sword' (Ostrom *et al.* 1992). Cooperation can be imposed among competitors for limited resources by a role whose authority derives, in game-theoretic terms, from the addition to the players' decision-free of a parameter representing the cost of self-financed monitoring and a strategy for negotiated agreement (Ostrom 1990: 16). Nor need females be carriers of the same strategies as males. But that still does not make Palaeolithic sociology a just-so story of gene-meme co-evolution in which the previously inherited disposition to 'look for openings to improve one's standing' was bred out of our ancestors only to be culturally reselected many millennia later.

Although we cannot be sure that the results of present-day psychological experiments are a reliable guide to what was going on inside our Palaeolithic ancestors' heads, one of the first things to look for would be an innate desire to punish cheats who flout the terms of an implicit social contract (Cosmides and Tooby 1992; Fehr and Gachter 2002). Among the members of hunting and foraging bands in continuous face-to-face contact with one another, a mutation which turned anger into righteous anger could hardly fail to be adaptive. Furthermore, whenever our ancestors first began to speculate about the existence of supra-human agencies responsible for the workings of the world in which they found themselves, the idea of reciprocity could readily be projected from the inter-human onto the human/supra-human level. Propitiation, compensation, and sacrifice are all deep in our evolutionary past (Burkert 1996), and could be as readily evoked in reaction to what was perceived as interference in human affairs by presumptive supra-human agencies as by the behaviour of fellow human beings, whether the supra-human agents are thought to be well-disposed towards human beings or not (or, as 'Dualists' have not unreasonably hypothesized, the world is a battleground in which forces working for harmony and good are fighting it out with forces working for chaos and evil).

The biological inheritance of the hunters and foragers of the Pleistocene did not, therefore, make their interpersonal relationships a world of endemic mutual hostility and physical violence any more than of continuous cooperation and undisturbed harmony. But their relationships were no more relationships of strict equality than their motives were authentically egalitarian. Enforced sharing might eliminate virtually all differences between them in material possessions, but an individual marginally disadvantaged in access to food could suffer as badly as a member of an impoverished underclass in a stratified society. Differences in personal prestige might be slight and evanescent, but an individual consistently less well-regarded than others could suffer as much in disesteem as the member of a socially stigmatized caste. Counter-dominant coalitions might prevent any individual from dominating the rest of the band by force or the threat of force, but a deviant singled out for punishment could be as unpleasantly treated as one institutionally convicted of criminality in a society with law-courts, police, and prisons. The standard measure of inequality – the Gini coefficient – can be as high in a group in which one person alone has a symbolically valued possession – say, a gold necklace or a jade axe – as in a market society much of whose abundant wealth is concentrated in the ownership of a relatively small number of exceptionally rich families or households. Contests between cheats, defectors, free-riders, and self-aggrandizers and the strong reciprocators determined to punish them are waged at all levels of inequality and in all ecological and demographic environments.

EVOLUTIONARY ADAPTEDNESS

8

The environment in which our Pleistocene ancestors hunted and foraged for many millennia was anything but uniform (Foley 1996; Irons 1999). Far from there being a stable 'Environment of Evolutionary Adaptedness', there was continuous modification of the ancestral environment both by large variations in climate and ecology and by the niche-constructing behaviour of our ancestors themselves. The successive mutations in the design of their brains gave them the capacity to react to dangerously unpredictable environments in whatever ways might enhance their reproductive fitness in face of them. Thereafter, not only do biologically inherited dispositions, capacities, and susceptibilities persist under conditions in which they may have ceased to be adaptive, but they become adaptive for other reasons and in other ways.

Consider the example of the 'sweet tooth'. It is often cited as an example of a physiological trait which, having evolved in an environment where it was manifestly adaptive as promoting ingestion of a nutritional source of energy, survives into a different environment where it ceases to be so. It has not yet been explained as authoritatively as adult lactose absorption has been. We do not know just when, where, or why it evolved. But once it had, its interest to comparative sociology lies in, among other things, its connection with the institution of slavery. 'Who says sugar, says slavery', from the Normans and Venetians in Sicily, Cyprus, and Crete through the Portuguese colonization of the Atlantic Islands to the point where, in the mid-eighteenth century, 1.4 million of slaves in the Americas – 40 per cent of the total – are to be found working on sugar plantations (Klein 1986: 60).[7] Culture was part of the story too, particularly in the fast-spreading fashion for drinking chocolate (and also the taste for drinking rum). But the prodigious demand for sugar in Europe was an evoked response traceable to a biologically inherited trait which was then, in the environment of much later times, reinforced by cultural selection and satisfied by the social selection of the practices constitutive of the institution of slavery (about which I shall have more to say in Chapter 4).

Another example is the universal response to rhythm. The sensations evoked by the beating of drums, the chanting of songs in unison, the propulsion of boats or canoes through water by coordinated rowing or paddling, and the performance in step of dancing or marching are documented across an extremely wide range of places and times. But in the context of warfare between the infantry armies of the European states of the seventeenth century, 'Military drill, as developed by Maurice of Nassau and thousands of European drillmasters after him, tapped this primitive reservoir of sociality directly' (McNeill 1982: 131),[8] with the consequence that group selection favoured those armies of foot-soldiers which parade-ground training had welded into more effective fighting units than their competitors. As a just-so story so phrased, this one has

---

[7] The United States is, as its historians well know, very different in this respect: 'Even at its antebellum peak, sugar was never more than a minor Southern crop that utilized less than 10 per cent of the slave labor force' (Fogel 1989: 29). It does not follow from 'who says sugar says slavery' that 'who says slavery says sugar'. Mines are as important to the history of slavery as plantations. But it is a plausible conjecture that if the Romans had known about sugar they would have used slaves to produce it, and rich Romans would have consumed it in quantity.

[8] McNeill also quotes from the Maréchal de Saxe: 'I shall be told, perhaps, that many men have no ear for music. This is false; movement to music is natural and automatic. I have often noticed, while the drums were beating for the colours, that all the soldiers marched in cadence without intention and without realizing it. Nature and instinct did it for them' (1982: 133 n.12).

to be modified to allow for the objection that foot, as opposed to arms, drill could not become institutionally established until the era of artificially levelled parade grounds and macadamized roads: seventeenth-century armies were under much the same environmental constraint as the proverbially militaristic Spartans had been who, although they advanced into battle in close formation and were trained in quite complex infantry manoeuvres, weren't, and effectively couldn't be, taught to manoeuvre strictly in step given the nature of the terrain on which they fought. But that is not an argument against the universal bonding effect of close-order drill which McNeill himself experienced as an infantry recruit in the Second World War.

The possibility of deliberately exploiting innate dispositions and susceptibilities has long been recognized by the people who do it. Orators are often aware of their ability, as Albert Speer put it in reminiscing about Hitler and Goebbels, 'to unleash mass instincts' (1970: 47), and the success of professional teachers of rhetoric from the Greek and Roman world through the Renaissance to the present day is testimony at once to those instincts and to what can be learned and taught about how to channel them into patterns of evoked behaviour.[9] Those whose behaviour is influenced in this way may be unlikely so to explain it to themselves. They may even be actively resistant to the suggestion, just as many people become angry when told that close and long-lasting friendships between fellow humans are an evolutionary product of the reproductive advantages under ancestral conditions of readiness to engage in reciprocal exchange of favours (Tooby and Cosmides 1996: 131). Soldiers writing home from the battlefront about their willingness to die for the 'fatherland' or 'motherland' may be no more able to account for the appeal to them of the symbolic equation of nation with family than children frightened of animals or the dark are aware that they are responding instinctively to what Bowlby called 'natural clues' (1973: 161). But that is what is going on, whether they realize it or not. Politicians appealing to party loyalty and corporate executives denouncing whistle-blowers are practising applied evolutionary psychology no less than are the advertisers who use photographs of sexually attractive women to sell sports cars to prospective purchasers presumed to be male.

---

[9] Darwin was, once again, there already: 'The impassioned bard, orator, or musician, when with his varied tones and cadences he excites the strongest emotions in his hearers, little suspects that he uses the same means by which his half-human ancestors long ago aroused each other's ardent passions, during their courtship and rivalry' (1882: 573).

Evoked behaviour has, moreover, an importance in warfare which goes beyond the immediate self-protective responses evoked in face-to-face combat to the bonding effects of sustained companionship under conditions of stress. Richerson and Boyd (1999) concluded from studying the evidence for the comparative performance of the American and German armies in the Second World War that German soldiers who were recruited from the same town or district, were kept together during training, joined the same platoons or companies, were led into battle by the same officers who had commanded them as recruits, and when withdrawn from the front were retrained by those same officers fought much more effectively than American soldiers who were trained in temporary groups, were sent to the front individually, and joined large divisions composed of strangers within which casualties were replaced piecemeal. This conclusion would, admittedly, have surprised neither Xenophon nor Frederick the Great. Xenophon's writings about Greek infantry warfare consistently emphasize the value of comradeship as opposed to instruction, and Frederick the Great more than once recorded his conviction that recruits drawn, as his were, from the same cantons were more likely than others to support each other automatically in battle and encourage each other's willingness to put their lives at risk. The difference in performance is not to be explained in terms of evoked behaviour alone: as I remarked in Section 6 of Chapter 2, cultural and social selection are both at work also in differentiating the performance of armies and thereby influencing the subsequent reproduction and diffusion of the memes and practices of which they are the carriers. But McNeill's 'tapping' of the 'primitive reservoir of sociality' can confer a marginal advantage on one army over another which is potentially as decisive as either warrior norms acquired through imitation and learning or military discipline imposed by institutional sanctions.

9

It should not, however, be supposed that evoked behaviour is 'instinctive' in a sense that would imply that its motivation always comes from the emotional rather than the rational brain. Since human beings have inherited an intellectual repertory which, limited as it may be, still makes us potential Bayesians and potential game-theorists, these capacities too must have been adaptive in the millennia during which they were naturally selected in parallel with our repertory of emotions.

The idea that Bayes's theorem models an inferential process biologically inherited from our remote ancestral environment is apt to be queried for two reasons: first, because Bayesian reasoning is excessively dependent on unascertainable prior probabilities of the evidence given only the background knowledge; and second, because the computations which the theorem requires are beyond the capacity of human beings to carry them out inside their heads when confronted with real-life choices in complex environments. But *a* part of the human psychological repertory is an ability to modify a belief in the recognition that the probability of its being true depends on the probability of later evidence for that probability being true. The cultural inertia too easily attributed by some sociologists to 'peasant' communities does not totally inhibit cultivators from studying the yields which their neighbours obtain from their plots and modifying their own techniques in consequence, just as seemingly unreflective working-class adolescents in industrial societies have been shown to modify their educational aspirations in the light of what they observe about their prospects of upward social mobility. Bayesian decision-takers may be less often found, and may make the mean behaviour of the present population less different from the mean behaviour of the previous population when they are, than unthinking imitators of prestigious role-models or of the majority of what they regard as their peer-group. But a recognizably Bayesian response triggered by a changed environment does sometimes provide the explanation of differentiated behaviour-patterns where pre-existing memes and practices are becoming relatively less adaptive. To accept that natural selection has not equipped the human brain to do probability problems at all well is not to deny that it has given it a capacity for modification of initial beliefs in the light of observed outcomes without an explicit calculation of probabilities having to be carried out as such.

Similarly, collective behaviour can conform to game-theoretic models without its being assumed that the natives are consciously applying a pay-off matrix which they have been carrying around as such inside their heads. Coleman, in analysing escape panics, shows how they differ from the classic Prisoner's Dilemma because of the possibility of coordination conditional on the responses of others over an initial period of time following the response immediately evoked by obvious physical danger: the dilemma is that to delay running for the exit as soon as the fire breaks out in an enclosed area both increases the opportunity for coordination which would benefit everyone and heightens the risk that if others start to run survival will turn out to depend on having been among the first to do so. Such panics, which pre-game-theoretic authors were apt to attribute to collective consciousness, mob psychology, herd instinct, or quasi-hypnotic suggestion, are an obvious example of evoked behaviour set off by the universal instinct for survival, with the consequence, as Coleman argues (1990: 214 n.7), that the emotion labelled 'panic' is created by the high cost of taking time before making the potentially fatal decision to run or not to run for the exit. In examples like this, rational choice theory and evolutionary psychology combine to produce some of the most plausible just-so stories of all.

10

One of the standard topics in comparative sociology which invites analysis along these lines is the feud.

Feuding is abundantly documented in the ethnographic and historical record across a range of times and places from pre-Islamic Arabia to medieval France to the Southern United States, the Peloponnese, Corsica, Andalusia, Algeria, East Africa, Montenegro, Albania, and others besides. The melodramatic tales culturally transmitted in song and story, whether in the *gestes* of the minstrels, the Icelandic sagas, the Spanish *cantars*, or simply the folk memory of kin-groups nurturing their culturally inherited hatreds of one another, reflect behaviour-patterns with which their audiences were all familiar. The 'highly structured poetic genre' exemplified in particular in the Icelandic sagas (Fentress and Wickham 1992: 167; Dunbar *et al.* 1995) reflects both the structure of the feuds and the relations of kinship among killers and killed. It is striking how often the stories mirror Hamilton's Rule directly: the intensity of the desire for vengeance is proportionate to the genetic proximity of avenger to victim, compensation is accepted in settlement only when the scale of it corresponds to the closeness of the relationship, and importance is particularly attached to the chastity of nubile female relatives which, if violated, requires young adult males to seek out and kill the violator. To borrow McNeill's metaphor about the bonding effect of close-order infantry drill, the feud 'taps a primitive reservoir' of kin-based solidarity and masculine aggression. In principle, moreover, feuds can continue for as long as the memory of injuries not fully avenged. A feud is 'not a finite series of hostile acts which can be said to have both a beginning and an end' (Black-Michaud 1975: 37). Even where settled by arbitration or negotiation of some kind, or seeming to peter out over time or across physical distance, feuds can be evoked all over again by a chance face-to-face encounter, or an accidentally reawakened territorial dispute. But the feud is a distinctive behaviour-pattern which persists only under a specific range of environmental conditions in which evoked *and* acquired *and* imposed behaviour all play a part.

One of the more frequently observed of these conditions is the absence of a strong central state – that is, of practices defining roles to which there attaches the power to impose a monopoly of the means of coercion on the feuding parties. But no lawlike generalization to that effect can be framed – feuding persists in some strong states, and is absent in some weak ones. Similarly, there is a positive correlation between pastoral economies and the feud, but some village-dwelling agriculturalists engage in feuding. The feud is a textbook example of convergent evolution where different cultures and societies in which it is found have just-so stories which are unique in some respects to themselves but at the same time point to similar selective pressures at work. The biologically inherited readiness of young men to go out and kill the killers of their kin is supported by memes enjoining defence of familial honour handed down by imitation and learning in an environment of institutional practices and roles which are always permissive of, and sometimes positively favourable to, it. Feuds cannot be explained in the same way as wars – they involve the killing of fellow members of the same society, not of others, in ways that conform to certain specific rules. As has been said of the society depicted in the sagas, 'The social and governmental order that the advocacy system reinforced made Icelandic feud possible' (Byock 1982: 38). Or as Evans-Pritchard said of the Nuer, 'Blood feuds are a tribal institution, for they can only occur where a breach of law is recognized, for they are the way in which reparation is obtained' (1940: 150). Variations in this common behaviour-pattern are explicable by reference to local selective pressures which derive, for example, from the dispersal of fraternal interest-groups through non-patrilocal residence (Kang 1979), or the relation of compensation in blood-money to the institutions of a market economy (Otterbein 2000). As it is put in a study of the feud in nineteenth-century Corsica, where court records provide an unusually reliable source for the precise number and nature of the killings, the participants 'were highly strategic even as they sacrificed individual interests for collective action. They reliably reproduced a feuding system not because of a commitment to a society-wide system of values or out of purely individual self-interest, but out of devotion to their own family units – a devotion on which they acted in a highly strategic way' (Gould 2000: 700).

A thoroughly researched just-so story about interpersonal violence which rests on a co-evolutionary explanation at all three levels is the analysis of the 'culture of honor' in the American South by

Richard E. Nisbett and Dev Cohen, who in their Preface explicitly endorse the principles underlying evolutionary psychology as 'an emerging metatheoretical base for the social sciences that is particularly relevant to cultural studies' (1996: xvii). The readiness of white, non-Hispanic Southern males to respond with lethal violence to personal insults or threats to their families and property is amply evidenced in the homicide rates disaggregated by Nisbett and Cohen from US Department of Justice records. Particularly striking are the correlations with rural residence in herding as opposed to farming regions. Furthermore, the regional differences between the South and Southwest on the one hand and the non-South on the other are significantly more marked in the case of 'argument-related' than of 'felony-related' homicide. The ecological correlations are underpinned by both survey data and experimental results, and alternative hypotheses convincingly disposed of. The descendants of the Scotch-Irish immigrants who settled on the frontier herding territories have inherited a culture enjoining violence in the protection of property, physical retaliation against personal insult, distrust of public authority, and unquestioning loyalty to family and kin. In this they differ from non-white Southerners as much as they do from Northern whites. But their attitudes are coherently formulated and consistently expressed, and they pursue their families' interests as strategically as anyone else. The explanation is not to be sought in behaviour genetics: there is no reason to suppose that they are innately predisposed to violence to a significantly greater degree than the generality of young adult males. But a biologically inherited potential has come to be evoked to an extent that it is not elsewhere because of the selective pressures which have favoured a co-evolution of memes and practices through which feuding persists.

HUMAN SOCIOLOGY AS PRIMATE SOCIOLOGY

II

The science writer Matt Ridley has described (1996: 159) the sense of uncanny familiarity with which he responded to an account of the Wars of the Roses which he happened to read shortly after reading de Waal's account in *Chimpanzee Politics* of the goings-on in the Arnhem zoo: here were Margaret of Anjou, Edward the Fourth, and Warwick the Kingmaker behaving just like Luit, Nikki, and Yeroen in their struggles for place and power. Parallels of this extended kind between human and animal behaviour have a long history in literary and philosophical discussion of human nature. But the combination of advances in neo-Darwinian theory with the findings of primatologists working in the field has given them greater precision as well as point. We now have book titles like not merely *The Naked Ape* and *The Third Chimpanzee* but *The Arbitrary Ape*, *The Thinking Ape*, *The Ape That Spoke*, *The Protean Primate*, *The Promising Primate*, and even *Primates in the Classroom: An Evolutionary Perspective on Children's Education*. There is thus a sense in which comparative sociology might be called one among other sub-disciplines of comparative primatology. On what grounds is 'chimpanzee politics' a less legitimate term of behavioural science than 'vigilant monitoring among hunter-gatherers' or 'kingship in Sub-Saharan Africa' or 'the capitalist state'?

Sociologists may protest that this example is too easy. Struggles for personal dominance among a small number of contenders within a close-knit transitive rank-order are a different matter from the varied and continuous movements of persons between roles, and of roles themselves in three-dimensional social space, of the kind familiar from human societies with complex systactic structures and long histories of evolving modes of production, persuasion, and coercion. But I recently had an experience very similar to Ridley's on rereading a classic study of English politics in the period from 1675 to 1725 (Plumb 1967). The players in that game were contending for power in an institutional environment dominated by a royal court and a bicameral parliament in one part of which replacement of representatives of one party or faction by another in periodic elections could be decisive for the maintenance or loss of status. It is a world yet further away from the Arnhem zoo than the Wars of the Roses. But the favours given and received among the politicians and their supporters still correspond to the mutual grooming of the chimpanzees; the monetary emoluments – or bribes, if you will – correspond to the chimpanzees' gifts or exchanges of food; the votes cast at the hustings or in parliament correspond to the support which chimpanzees give to one another in circumstances of actual or potential conflict; the higher-ranking males in both cases enjoy pickings and perquisites from which the lower-ranking are excluded; coalitions form and reform among both with equal ease and speed; rituals of submission are performed at court or in parliament as they are in the Arnhem zoo; in both cases, ties of kinship, reciprocal altruism, and 'Machiavellian' social manipulation are equally visible; and in both cases, there can be discerned differences in cultural traditions shared by sub-groups within the population as a whole.

No less striking are the parallels in the details of evoked face-to-face behaviour. Stereotypical gestures, facial expressions, the keeping of physical distance, and actions such as bending and bowing (or alternatively rising upright) are readily observable in humans and chimpanzees alike. So too is the emotional instability manifested in abrupt reversals in conduct. Humans and chimpanzees alike switch from defiance to submission. Both make sudden displays of sympathy or affection, both intervene unexpectedly as either participants or mediators in conflicts previously watched with apparent detachment, and both are prone to outbursts of collective anger. The vocalizations of chimpanzees (laughter included) carry meaning,[10] and their lack of vocabulary, grammar, and syntax does not prevent them from having some sense of their own identity and attributing some degree of knowledge and intention to others (including humans). They not only retaliate immediately against their enemies but take delayed revenge. They recognize allies as allies and rivals as rivals over extended periods of time. They jointly patrol the boundaries of territories which they regard as their own. They often quarrel, but often become reconciled with those with whom they have quarreled. They tend each other when sick or injured. If two chimpanzees consistently groom each other, help each other, play with each other, pay attention to each other, huddle up with each other, and share with each other, what more do they have to do before the primatologist studying them is allowed to talk of them as 'friends' who, as Aristotle stipulates (*Nicomachean Ethics* 1156a 3–4), want to do good to each other and are conscious that the other does the same?

12

But chimpanzees are still ... well, chimpanzees. Luit, Nikki, and Yeroen can't sit down round a conference table to renegotiate their roles in the way that Margaret of Anjou, Edward the Fourth, and Warwick the Kingmaker can. If a primatologist came back from the field having found a chimpanzee population with monumental architecture, an ancestral mythology, and a council of elders, it wouldn't be a chimpanzee population. It would be a population of other primates, however exactly to be classified, with a critical difference, whatever exactly it might be, in their genetic inheritance and the design of their brains. This would, as in our own case, have taken many generations since the last common ancestor. But it would be no less a difference of kind. As Darwin allowed, 'no animal is self-conscious, if by this term it is implied that he reflects on

---

[10] To an extent that those of vervets, for example, do not (Cheney and Seyfarth 1990); by comparison with chimpanzees, vervets can almost be labelled solipsists.

such points as whence he comes or whither he will go, or what is life and death, and so forth' (1882: 83). But that is just what human beings can't help doing. We are not just a loving and hating and playing and fighting and cooperating and dissembling and grieving and rejoicing primate but a narrating and speculating and sacralizing one. However important it is that sociologists should recognize both that evoked behaviour is pervasive in all human societies and that acquired behaviour is not unique to the human species, none of the research which has vindicated Darwin's alleged anthropomorphism has gone beyond the reservations which he himself explicitly made.

From the perspective of comparative sociology, therefore, the way to put it is to say that somewhere down the evolutionary sequence which leads to 'us' primatologists have to turn into anthropologists. We do not know, and may never know, just when our ancestors started to talk to each other. If, as the anatomical evidence suggests, they had the physical capacity to do so by about 300,000 years ago, they may have used it to shout, growl, laugh, sing, and cheer long before they used it to debate what to do tomorrow or reminisce about what happened last week. But at some unascertainable time, they started to exchange moralizing judgements and metaphysical speculations as well as sharing practical information, agreeing plans for the future, and comparing recollections of the past. They began to ask each other such questions as 'How can you excuse such bad behaviour?' and 'Do you think the spirits of our ancestors are watching us?' The anthropologist who tracked them down in the field could infer their beliefs and attitudes not only by observing their outward actions, but also by learning their language, hearing what they thought about their actions, and discussing with them what they meant in talking about them as they did.

Thereafter, there is no escape from the perennially troublesome disjunction between the natives' and the observer's conceptualizations of their behaviour. No primatologist at the Arnhem zoo or the Yerkes field station or in the Gombe rain forest is concerned with a conflict between 'their' account of their behaviour and 'ours'. But every anthropologist is concerned with it from the first day of fieldwork, whether 'they' are speakers of a language which the anthropologist has to learn from scratch or of a language which is also the anthropologist's own. The procedural maxim which follows from the distinction drawn in Section 5 of the Prologue between intentions and motives remains as relevant as ever: the natives' reports of what it is that they are doing are privileged over the observer's at the same time as the observer's explanation of why they are doing it is privileged over the natives'. But once the natives are willing to answer questions about their own subjective experiences, the anthropologist observing them has both the benefits and the attendant risks of access to evidence about what they are doing and why which not even the most intelligent chimpanzee, dolphin, or elephant can provide.

Primatologists whose experiences in the field have enabled them to detect the differences in temperament and personality between one chimpanzee and another may, like Darwin himself, refuse to accept that their subjective mental states are indistinguishable, and still less that they have none. Might there not after all be a chimpanzee phenomenology (to say nothing of a dolphin or elephant phenomenology)? Why shouldn't the subjective experiences of Luit, Nikki, and Yeroen lend themselves to incorporation into a novel as persuasive as William Golding's *The Inheritors*, in which the encounter between Neanderthals and humans is narrated from the perspective of a hypothetical Neanderthal protagonist whose 'cloudy, static, non-abstract awareness of life' is a world 'where neither action nor its corollary, speech, contains any subordinate clauses' (Green 1963: 46)? Authentic accounts of what other people's experience is like for them don't require the account to be given in words which are there inside their heads. Vivid and illuminating descriptions of mental states can be phrased in language which couldn't possibly have been used by 'them', whether a child (or a chimpanzee) in a state of boiling rage who doesn't know what 'boiling' is, or a Machiavellian ruler (or the alpha male at the head of a chimpanzee troop) who ruled long before Machiavelli was born, or a Palaeolithic Neanderthal (or chimpanzee) Othello consumed by sexual jealousy who has never seen a performance of Shakespeare. But the critical difference remains that humans can, but chimpanzees can't, have put to them by the observer the suggestion that the proffered description of what is going on inside their heads does authentically fit their case.

There is no evidence, after decades of field and laboratory research, that chimpanzees have the capacity for meta-representations. 'Machiavellian' chimpanzees who, like Darwin's decoy elephants, 'well know what they are about' still cannot to be taken to be conducting an interior monologue about what they are about of the kind that human beings do. Chimpanzees are able to exchange information with one another to a greater degree than used to be believed. But no primatologist has found a chimpanzee who has, to quote Darwin again, developed a power of reasoning to the point of speculating, even 'vaguely', on 'his own existence' (1882: 94). When Frans de Waal observes two unruly female teenage chimpanzees being punished by the rest of the colony in the Arnhem zoo for refusing to enter their sleeping quarters and thereby delaying everybody else's evening meal (1996: 89), it is difficult to resist the inference that something very like 'serve 'em right!' is going on inside the punishers' heads. But that still doesn't license a further inference to Darwin's 'so-called moral sense'. Subsequent experiments by de Waal and others have shown that not only chimpanzees but capuchins (Brosnan and de Waal 2003) register awareness of a difference between equitable and unequitable exchanges. But evoked responses to 'unfair' rewards or 'grabbing' instead of sharing of food still fall short of self-consciously virtuous restraint of the impulse to grab, assignation of value to a sense of fairness as such, assessment of the relative strength of a claim of need as against a claim of desert, and judgement on the behaviour of both self and others as a violation of a specifically moral norm. Among chimpanzees, tolerance for inequity may increase with social closeness (Brosnan *et al.* 2005), but they do not exhibit the other-regarding preferences and concern for the welfare of unrelated group members found in humans (Silk *et al.* 2005).

Some readers, including particularly dog-owners, may respond by saying that they have seen animals display unmistakable signs of guilt at having disobeyed a command. But that is to confuse guilt with shame. Guilt presupposes the violation of a norm for which the violator is aware of deserving to be punished because the norm carries an inherent moral obligation to conform (keeping a promise when it is personally disadvantageous to do so) as opposed to a norm which does not (speaking the vernacular language correctly). There is, moreover, a parallel between the so-called moral and the so-called aesthetic sense. Just as chimpanzees can be observed responding with what might be thought to approach righteous anger at the behaviour of unruly teenagers who delay the evening meal, so can they be observed responding to the sight of a fire or a waterfall with what might be thought to approach aesthetic appreciation. But to borrow from Kant (despite my remark about him at the end of Section 6 of the Prologue), to say that something is beautiful is to say that everyone else ought to approve of it too. The chimpanzees standing awe-struck in front of a fire or a waterfall do not have the same thing going on inside their heads as Henry Adams standing awe-struck in front of Chartres Cathedral (and then deciding to tell the rest of us how deserving of admiration it is). Only among primates who can talk to each other can cultural selection begin to generate out of a naturally selected moral sense the diversity of both moral and aesthetic attitudes which, like the diversity of causal beliefs about the workings of the world, is for comparative sociologists, not cultural primatologists, to explain.

CHAPTER 3

Cultural selection and acquired behaviour

BELIEFS AND ATTITUDES

I

How then should comparative sociologists proceed when contrasting one human culture or sub-culture with another? What kind of just-so story will best explain why *these* and not *those* memes are the ones being acquired and acted out?

However the process of heritable variation and competitive selection of memes is modelled, it will have to be estimated as accurately as possible just how widely the distinctive beliefs and attitudes and the representations underlying them are distributed among the population of carriers. Obvious as this may be, there are more instances than there should be in the historical and ethnographic literature where an author implies without sufficient qualification that the members of the culture chosen for study were all carrying much the same bundles of memes inside their heads. It might turn out that some representations, at least, are shared with only insignificant differences between the information in one native's head and another's. Perhaps every Hellene shares a broadly similar representation of Zeus, every Navajo a broadly similar representation of *hozho* (harmony, beauty), and every Polynesian a broadly similar representation of *mana*. But the ideal type of a traditional culture, in which every native holds exactly the same beliefs and shares exactly the same attitudes, has never been more than that. Not only does there have to be an explanation of how an allegedly unquestioned set of inherited memes came to be selected in the first place, but the capacity of the human mind actively to reinterpret or reconstruct any inherited meme means that any complex of memes by which the natives' collective behaviour is guided is likely to be challenged by at least some of the members of each successive generation. This is so even if the behaviour-pattern is the product of meme-practice co-evolution and an imposed ideology is underwritten by institutional sanctions attaching to the roles of elders or priests or literati or schoolteachers or party cadres. It is true that there are (or at any rate, have been) cultures whose members are unaware of any other cultures different from their own. But that does not mean that the culture in question did not evolve out of an earlier one in the past or will never evolve into another one in the future, even if it remains shielded from invasion by the memes of any other.

Nor should it be assumed that beliefs, any more than attitudes, are carried inside the natives' heads without vacillation or ambivalence,[1] even where a widely shared belief is of a self-evidently practical rather than metaphysical kind. Quesalid, Franz Boas's Kwakiutl shaman, is proud of his successes, but he is well aware how much trickery he and his fellow-sorcerers administer (Lévi-Strauss 1963: 175–8), just as Zande witch-doctors 'know that their extraction of objects from the bodies of their patients is a fake, but they believe that they cure them by the medicine they administer' (Evans-Pritchard 1937: 255). In matters of health and sickness, it is only to be expected that uncertainty will be felt, if not always admitted, both by shamans, sorcerers, oneiromancers, faith-healers, astrologers, and doctors on the one side and by their patients and clients on the other. It is not surprising in any culture to come across the advice given by Samuel Johnson in a letter to his friend Bennett Langton dated 17 April 1775: 'My opinion of alternative medicine is not high, but *quid tentasse nocebit?*' – what harm will it do to have given it a try? The anthropologist Mary Douglas, having reported the !Kung Bushmen as laughing out of court the suggestion that they believe that their rain rituals cause rain, also reports of the Dinka that 'Of course they hope that rain rituals will cause rain' (1966: 58, 68), while Evans-Pritchard reports of the Nuer that 'they are little interested in ritual for bringing rain and even think it presumptuous to think of asking God for rain before sowing' (1956: 200). The elder Pliny, in his rambling, encyclopaedic *Natural History*, at one point denounces 'magic' as 'the most fraudulent of arts' (XXX.1) but at another (XXVIII.4) concedes that it works. There is no human population whose members have no beliefs whatever inside their heads. But not

---

[1] 'Half-belief' in the sense of uncertainty needs to be distinguished from 'half-belief' in the sense that the natives follow a rule such as 'never walk under a ladder' despite disavowing the 'superstition' behind it (Campbell 1996). Does the congregation 'really' believe in purgatory? Do the voters 'really' believe that the performance of the national economy will be significantly improved by a change of government? Perhaps not. But what matters to comparative sociology is whether, in the culture or society under study, they behave as if they do.

even the most vehement protestations of belief are a guarantee that the protester is immune to the possibility of doubt.

Since, however, comparative sociology is concerned only with the reproduction and diffusion of information which does demonstrably affect population-level behaviour-patterns, this means, in cultural evolution, the displacement of one set of memes by another which reaches the point that the later one has phenotypic effects sufficiently consistent, widespread, and distinctive for sociologists of all persuasions to agree that a new culture (or sub-culture) has emerged. There will always be scoffers and sceptics like Diagoras of Melos, who responded, according to Diogenes Laertius (VI.59), to the sight of the votive dedications in a temple of the sea-god Poseidon with the remark that there would be many more of them if those who had been drowned had been able to do the same. But the temple and the dedications were there for Diagoras to be sceptical about, and they were part of the complex of memes and their extended phenotypic effects covered by the conventional designation 'Greek religion'. It is also possible for competing memes to co-exist side by side in the same heads, with the result that, for example, an Anglo-Saxon king keeps a pagan altar alongside a Christian one (Bede, *Ecclesiastical History* II.15). But once a large-scale qualitative change in a previously stable cultural behaviour-pattern is reported as having occurred, its explanation depends on finding out where, down the chain of extended phenotypic effects, selective pressure has come to bear in such a way as to favour what have turned out to be the more reproductively successful mutations and combinations of the particular memes to which the behaviour-pattern is giving phenotypic expression.

It is not to be expected that the natives will all agree in their beliefs about, let alone their attitudes to, the past any more than the present. The anthropologist Robert Borofsky, doing fieldwork on the Polynesian atoll of Pukapuka from 1977 to 1981, was astonished to find in operation a traditional form of social organization which had been deliberately revived shortly before but on the evidence of previous anthropologists, as well as of missionaries and government officials, appeared never to have existed at all. Extensive interviews with elderly informants revealed that there had indeed existed more than once in the past a two-village, as opposed to three-village, form of social organization, but previous outside observers had failed to ask the questions which would have revealed it, and the informants' views of just what went on, let alone just when and why, differed significantly among themselves (1987: Ch. 1). But that is itself just what goes on when, for example, the recollections of strikes and protests among the members of working-class communities in Europe and the United States are studied in the same way (Fentress and Wickham 1992: Ch. 3). All cultural traditions are inventions in the sense that somebody has to have been the first person to put together the package of memes which is reproduced in recognizably similar form down subsequent generations of readers or listeners. The inherited histories or folktales or myths by which the natives' behaviour is affected do not need to have been selected for the degree of their correspondence with observations which have been tested for their accuracy. It is true that in any culture, there are numerous beliefs about the past which are no more disputed than the beliefs transmitted by formal learning down successive generations of British schoolchildren about the dates of the battles of Hastings and Trafalgar. But 'traditional' representations of the past become such wherever, whenever, and in whatever way the environment in which they are handed down has enhanced the adaptiveness of their constituent memes, whether or not they have a demonstrated correspondence with 'the facts'.

2

Although the naturally selected capacity for fast and frugal reasoning and quick intuitive evaluation does not exclude second-order reflection about the possible merits of other competing theories, such reflection is, as I suggested in Section 2 of Chapter 2, rarely found outside of, and not always within, sub-cultures where norms of disinterested enquiry and test of received opinion are among the memes routinely acquired from teachers by their pupils. The Fijian chief who said to the Protestant missionary 'muskets and gunpowder are true, and your religion must be true' (Sahlins 1983: 519) may have been speaking with a touch of irony. But as Donald T. Campbell remarked in one of his articles, 'Priests can be as ignorant as the superstitious populations they dominate of the true adaptive functions of the belief-systems they perpetuate' (1975: 1107).

In general, memes which find expression in stable collective behaviour-patterns are more likely to have been inherited by imitation than by learning, and if by learning less by individual trial-and-error than by initially passive social learning from parents and mentors. Once a change is under way, frequency-dependence is sometimes a sufficient explanation by itself. But time and again, there is an exemplary carrier of a mutation who is imitated by others on the basis of personal prestige, not only in cases of religious (or, for that matter, political) conversion but across the whole spectrum of phenotypic effects from burial customs to natural-scientific research. In France, it was the precedent set by a pious daughter of Pepin the First which diffused the replacement of the Merovingian custom of burying the dead with their accoutrements by the Christian custom of unfurnished graves a whole two centuries after the Franks had become Christian (Fletcher 1997: 259). In England, the success of the memes constitutive of the program of experimental science was significantly advanced by the invasion of the sub-culture of natural philosophy by the 'conventions, codes, and values of gentlemanly conversation' (Shapin 1994: xvii) of which Robert Boyle was an exemplary carrier. And sociologists studying the formation of 'public opinion' in the mid-twentieth-century United States found that the relevant information was transmitted in a 'two-step flow' from leaders to followers within their local communities (Katz and Lazarsfeld 1955).

Such deference to prestige is no guarantee that the memes transmitted will be advantageous to their individual carriers, if acted on, in the way that the imitators themselves may suppose. It is likely enough that once prestige no longer attaches to the conspicuous burial of valuable material goods alongside the body of the deceased the heirs will gain materially by retaining them, that once experimental methods become demonstrably effective natural philosophers will help to further their careers if they adopt them, and that the implicit presumption on the part of followers of opinion that the articulate leaders have access to information which they do not is at least as likely to benefit them as the assumption, in a textbook example, of diners who, when they see queues for places in two externally indistinguishable restaurants, conclude that those in the longer queue are in it because it is for the one that has been found by experience to be the better of the two. Once, however, social as well as cultural selection is involved, the distribution of institutional power may be more important, evolutionarily speaking, than that of beliefs and attitudes, and memes which would otherwise have been better adapted than their competitors become less so. It is true that the incumbents of roles to which there attaches institutional power cannot force other people to believe things they regard as untrue or approve of things which they regard as repugnant, even with muskets and gunpowder: as Kant said, it is the body, not the mind, that bows to a superior, and willingness to die for strongly held convictions is as well documented for the sectarians of the Eternal Mother cult in Qing China as for the early Christian martyrs. Nor can conversion be achieved simply by attacking, as would-be reformers so often do, the extended phenotypic effects of the offending memes. Although books can be burned, statues smashed, altars desecrated, and churches or temples pulled down, this may entrench the offending memes instead of extirpating them. Sociologists of religion have often observed that small, strict sectarian communities can be stronger and longer-lasting than larger and less restrictive ones. But in a society whose practices include institutional sanctions deployed by the incumbents of the topmost roles against anyone suspected of adherence to a prohibited creed, doubters, opportunists, and lukewarm conformists are not only more likely to conceal their convictions and refrain from behaviour which might attract the attention of the authorities, but also less likely to pass the offending memes down to their children. As in natural selection, the criterion of adaptedness is not the size of the population of carriers.[2] But social selection is likely to be a stronger evolutionary force than cultural selection in populations where commitment is limited to what A. D. Nock, in his classic study of conversion, called 'mere adhesion' (1933: 7). The changed institutional environment then has the same effect in winnowing the strong from the weak as does a changed ecological environment where biological rather than cultural survival is at stake.

To the extent that the distribution of memes is demonstrably correlated with the economic, ideological, or political power attaching to their carriers' roles, something therefore needs to be retained within neo-Darwinian sociology from what used to be called, somewhat misleadingly, the 'sociology of knowledge'. The causal impact of the carrier's role may be either positive, in the sense that a systactic interest is directly served, or negative, as when, to borrow an example from Karl Mannheim (1936: 175), the memes constitutive of the Christian idea of brotherly love run up against the practices constitutive of the institution of serfdom: the medieval knight can be a committed adherent of the Church, loyal to his superiors, courteous to his equals, and generous to his inferiors, but he cannot act out a strategy of unconditional cooperation with his fellow human beings without abandoning his role. The appeal of different doctrines of salvation to the members of different systacts has been a commonplace among sociologists of religion since Weber, and the answer to the 'just what is going on here?' question has to include the extent to which memetic mutations or combinations which modify an existing norm of conduct are on average more likely to be reproduced and diffused among carriers whose roles are of one rather than another kind. Just as Methodism in nineteenth-century England appealed to tradesmen and artisans more than to

---

[2] As George C. Williams rhetorically asks, 'Is a fox population less successful than the more numerous rabbits on which it feeds?' (1966: 104).

other people not simply through the inherent persuasiveness of the theology expounded by its charismatic preachers, so did Christian Science appeal to middle-class professionals in twentieth-century England more than to other people not simply through the inherent persuasiveness of Mrs Baker Eddy's beliefs about spiritual health. It is true that in both cases, the converts were making a choice. But they were not (to echo Section 13 of Chapter 1) *deciding* what to believe about either this world or the next. They were deciding what kinds of people to associate with, what attitudes of theirs to be prepared to act in accordance with, and what beliefs of theirs to take provisionally on trust. Sub-cultural variations like these are not directly predictable from the individual converts' roles. But nor can they be fully explained except by a just-so story which takes account of the higher probability of diffusion of memes in the minds of people whose roles are located in one rather than another region of social space. In selectionist theory, for 'sociology of knowledge' read 'meme-practice co-evolution'.

3

Cross-cultural comparisons in shared attitudes and beliefs are made no easier by the lack of agreement among both the participants and the researchers who report them about the terminology for doing so. There is not only the familiar question touched on in Section 5 of Chapter 2 whether it is legitimate to apply to the memes in other people's heads terms to which there are no corresponding terms in their own vernacular language. There is also, even within the population whose vocabulary is the same as the observer's own, the problem of whether to assign to a familiar conventional category the same set of beliefs and attitudes that the natives do. In the culture within which this book is written, it is easy to point to collective behaviour-patterns which both the academic observer and the natives can agree to be 'religious': there are the worshippers singing hymns on Sunday, the theologians expounding the Old and New Testaments, the mourners at the burial service voicing their faith in an afterlife, and so on. But what about civil weddings, the national anthem, taboos on the eating of domestic pets, fortune-telling, faith-healing, Christmas presents, initiation rituals, 'New Age' spirituality, reverence for Nature, and commemoration of the war dead on Armistice Day?

   The selectionist response to that question is not to argue over the definition of 'religion' but to identify the co-adaptive memes being acted out in the behaviour-patterns of the members of the culture or sub-culture under study which are phenotypic effects of either beliefs in supra-human agencies on the one hand or sacralizing attitudes on the other. As soon as that is done, some of what is conventionally labelled 'religion' begins to look increasingly like some of what is conventionally labelled 'science', and some of what is conventionally excluded from 'religion' begins to look increasingly like a part of it. A causal belief, however hesitantly or ambivalently accepted as a guide to action, is no less a causal belief if the agency held to operate on what goes on in the world is an invisible quasi-personal being or an invisible impersonal force. When the emperor Marcus Aurelius (*Meditations* XII.38) said that we know that gods exist because we experience their power, he was voicing what countless human beings over many millennia have accepted as a truism: somehow or other the world works in many ways independent of human choice or intervention, and the fact that it *does* work, however mysteriously, makes it plausible to suppose that somebody or something is making it work as it does.[3] In many cultures, the local ontology allows for impersonal and quasi-personal forces in, so to speak, the same breath: when, to take a Roman example, Livy (III.vii.1–2) reports the abatement of a plague, he is frankly open-minded about whether the cause was divine intervention or an improvement in the weather. To Newton's successor as Lucasian Professor at Cambridge, the existence of 'demons' was 'no more to be denied, because we cannot, at present, give a direct solution of them, than are Mr Boyle's experiments about the elasticity of the air' (Clark 1997: 306). This is just as 'scientific' a belief as when the Fang people of Cameroon tell a visiting anthropologist that those of them who are particularly successful in oratory, business, horticulture, or witchcraft have been born with an internal organ called *evur* which cannot be detected directly (Boyer 2001: 76). It may turn out in further discussion that the Fang have different standards of evidence and proof from 'us'. But their beliefs about *evur* are no less beliefs about how the world works than are our beliefs about genes and chromosomes and Newton's successor's beliefs about demons.

Where the memes acted out in the behaviour-pattern observed are traced to the emotional rather than the rational brain, it is equally

---

[3] A belief that the workings of the world are under the control of one or more quasi-personal agencies benevolently disposed to human beings is, on the other hand, anything but a truism. To the contrary, when one of Aristophanes' comic slaves (*Knights*, line 32) asks another why he believes in gods and is told 'because they've got it in for me, don't you see?', the questioner finds the answer entirely convincing. Cf. Cohn (1993: 50) on the culture of Mesopotamia: 'As servants of the gods the Mesopotamians knew better than to trust in the goodwill of their masters. That gods could act ruthlessly, could even be wantonly destructive and cruel – that was obvious already in the

misleading to assume that the adaptedness of 'religious' attitudes is to be differently explained from the adaptedness of attitudes unconnected with beliefs about quasi-personal superhuman agents. Durkheim's distinction between the sacred and the profane, although deployed by him in support of his much criticized conception of religion as the worship of society by itself, captures the universality of the urge to attach intrinsic value to culturally constructed kinds independently of any instrumental value as a means to some practical end. Sacralizing memes which are acted out in rituals of veneration are easily discernible in 'irreligious' sub-cultures in such fields of human activity as art, sport, and politics.[4] It may be that their probability of continuing reproduction is enhanced where they are combined with memes constitutive of a belief that the behaviour they dictate is approved by a god, or a saint, or the spirits of the ancestral dead. But sacralizing memes can make an atheistic soldier on the field of battle as ready to die to keep a regimental flag out of the hands of the enemy as a Christian martyr thrown to the lions to die rather than abjure.

Where the memes located in the rational brain and those located in the emotional brain are mutually adaptive, it makes no difference whether the design of the combination is deliberate or unconscious. It doesn't matter whether or not Joseph Smith, the founder of Mormonism, mixed a cocktail of beliefs drawn from Protestantism, Freemasonry, and Hermeticism and then cunningly laced it with attitudes of approval of higher education and polygamy because he decided, after careful reflection, that that was how he would have the best chance of winning the largest number of prospective converts. The right just-so story has to show, whatever Joseph Smith thought he was doing, what it was about that combination which accounts for Mormonism's rate of diffusion of 40 per cent per decade for a hundred years. Marxism offers a similar example, despite – or, perhaps, because of – Marx's explicit repudiation of conventional 'religious' doctrine. Many commentators – Joseph Schumpeter, Karl Popper, and Leszek Kolakowski included – have remarked on the traits which Marxism, or Marxism-Leninism, shares with the Christian culture to which it is ostensibly opposed – a combination of hypotheses about why the world is as it is with eschatological prophecies, charismatic leaders, sacred texts, ritual initiations, ceremonial processions, annual festivals, and not least

---

days of the Sumerian city-states, and it remained obvious so long as Mesopotamian civilisation existed.'

[4] Their adaptedness may well have been deliberately designed, as for example in the appropriation of Roman symbols in the myths and rituals of Fascist Italy (Gentile 1996). The similar appropriation of the Roman past during the French Revolution is briefly discussed in Chapter 4.

Lenin's mausoleum as 'the symbolic centre, the "holy shrine"' (Lane 1981: 80). The extended phenotypic effects of the memes which the rulers of the Soviet Union wished to diffuse among the Russian and other subordinate populations may not be a reliable guide to what was in fact going on in the natives' heads: if the public expression of dissent is sufficiently effectively repressed, both rulers and dissenters may mistakenly believe that the memes prescribed by the ruling ideology are more widely diffused than in fact they are (Kuran 1995). But belief in the inevitability of Communism and disapproval of the ethos of capitalism are likely to enhance the rate of diffusion of each other. The temptation to be resisted, here as elsewhere, is the Fallacy of Elective Affinity – that is, the assumption that a conceptual affinity is a causal one when it isn't. However plausible the connection in the observer's mind, it may not be there in the natives' heads at all. A fatal flaw in Weber's initial formulation of his celebrated thesis about the 'Protestant Ethic' was his attribution to the Calvinist idea of predestination the motivation which drove 'inner-worldly ascetic' entrepreneurs to reinvest their hard-won profits in their businesses rather than spend them on self-indulgent private consumption or ostentatious public display. So stated, the thesis fails because neither Weber nor anyone else has produced the evidence to show that Protestant entrepreneurs were in fact motivated by beliefs about predestination to behave in a way that Catholic entrepreneurs did not and they themselves would not otherwise have done. That does not rule out the possibility of a co-adaptedness of other Protestant – or, more accurately, Puritan – memes and certain of the practices which Weber regarded as critical to the evolution of 'modern' capitalism. But that is a very different just-so story from the one that he advanced in 1904, and I shall return to it at the end of this chapter.

4

The range of beliefs about how the world works, wide as it is, is far from unlimited, and the resemblances between them down the ages and across the globe are too marked to be attributable solely to chance. But the reverse engineer who is looking for the memes whose combination forms the locally optimal design will time and again find that its probability of continuing retention in the natives' heads is highest where a belief which is not straightforwardly obvious is combined with an attitude which is strongly felt. The appeal of what are defined by the local culture as 'miracles' is that they at the same time invite assent to some violation of conventional assumptions about causes and effects and generate abnormally heightened feelings of veneration or repugnance. When an anthropologist comment-ing on Brazilian millenarism says that the ability of a charismatic leader to 'create a performance that showcases his divine power and teachings', when combined with 'the development of miracle stories by his devotees', is critical to the process of sacralization (Pessar 2004: 46), the same could equally be said not only of the charismatic instigators of secular political uprisings and charismatic healers who defy the predictions of orthodox practitioners of medicine but of charismatic arbiters of fashion. The young men-about-town who see 'Beau' Brummell walking down St James's Street with his cravat *un*tied are at the same time led to believe that their status will be enhanced rather than diminished by violating accepted sartorial convention and encouraged in their disdain for those whom they regard as too timid or too obstinate to follow Brummell's example.

The search for the critical memes being acted out in the emergence of a novel culture or sub-culture sometimes leads to the formulation of a just-so story of immediate plausibility. The novel beliefs so clearly approxi-mate to what psychologists define as a 'cognitive optimum', and the atti-tudes with which they have a selective (as opposed to elective) affinity so obviously enhance the self-esteem of the believers, that their reproductive success is virtually guaranteed. But sometimes, the disciples and converts are attracted to beliefs which are not only extravagantly counter-intuitive but difficult to comprehend and to attitudes which involve the sacral-ization of rituals and life-styles which are not only eccentric but pain-ful. This seeming paradox is addressed by the anthropologist Harvey Whitehouse in terms of the distinction which he draws between 'doctri-nal' and 'imagistic' modes. He himself restricts it to 'religion', defined for his purpose in terms of 'any set of shared beliefs and actions appealing to supernatural agency' (2004: 2), and he avoids the word 'meme' because he wishes to adopt a position intermediate between the memeticists' emphasis on population-level frequencies of discrete, culturally selected units on the one hand and the cognitivists' emphasis on innate, gen-etically selected biases on the other. But he is explicit that 'The theory advanced here operates on principles of selection' (2004: 74), and there is no reason not to extend it to cover 'religions' which have no 'gods'. 'Doctrinal' memes depend for their reproductive success on semantic memory, routinization, and standardization of authoritative teaching, where 'imagistic' memes depend on episodic memory, infrequent per-formance, and high arousal in groups without centralized leadership. The two are not mutually exclusive.[5] The search, as always, is for the memes

---

[5] Historically it may be that in Palaeolithic Europe, at any rate, an imagistic mode preceded the doctrinal mode, and the emergence of a doctrinal mode required political and priestly roles and

which combine in a co-adaptive complex, and the right just-so story has, as always, to estimate the trade-offs. In the 'doctrinal' mode, routinization confers a selective advantage on orthodox over heretical variants of the crititical memes, and the trade-off is that routinization succeeds at the cost of diminished motivation. In the 'imagistic' mode, the trade-off is between the intense cohesion generated by rare climactic rituals and the reduced probability of diffusion to other groups without radical mutation of the critical memes in the course of transmission. But many successful movements, parties, denominations, and sects are successful precisely because their distinctive behaviour-patterns are a phenotypic effect of a combination of co-adaptive doctrinal and imagistic memes.

Behind the selective reproduction and diffusion of the most successful memetic combinations there can always be discerned the innate disposition to form teams and cliques differentiated by cultural markers. As I remarked in Section 2 of Chapter 2, there is abundant experimental as well as ethnographic and historical evidence for the ease with which the commitment of recruits to such deliberately constructed groups can be engineered. But there is also much experimental as well as ethnographic and historical evidence for the degree to which this commitment can be reinforced by rituals of initiation.[6] In the culture within which this book is written, rites of passage extend all the way from elaborate public ceremonials like the coronation of kings or queens through secret rites like those of the Freemasons to the initiation by symbolic humiliation of new members of schools or street gangs or army regiments. It is sometimes possible for the same result to be achieved simply by the shared experience which is a function of the roles occupied and performed by the members of the group: the 'baptism of fire' undergone by soldiers who have not previously been ordered into battle is enough by itself to bind them to their companions-in-arms in the way discussed in Section 8 of Chapter 2. But the reverse engineer will look for designs which combine 'doctrinal' memes which are easily understood and frequently repeated with 'imagistic' memes whose esoteric and internally generated meaning is encoded in an infrequent but highly emotive performance difficult to

---

perhaps literacy. But on this point, 'Whitehouse's theory is weakened by the fact that the pre-literate societies for which an imagistic mode of relation is proposed encompass an immense degree of economic and political variability, which, in Western Asia for instance, ranged from small-scale, egalitarian, highly mobile hunter-gatherers, to hierarchically organized, sedentary hunter-gatherers, to farmers living in permanent villages with two-storey mud-brick architecture' (Mithen 2004: 20).

[6] In an intriguing early example, Aronson and Miles (1959) showed by administering an 'embarrassment test' to American college women who had volunteered for the experiment that severity of initiation was positively related to group preference after holding constant motivation for admission.

forget. Conformity can then be reinforced by meme-practice co-evolution through the institutional sanctions which attach to the roles of the elders, priests, or officials who control and deploy the means of persuasion in the society concerned.

It requires, accordingly, a just-so story of selection at all three levels to account for how it is that, as Macaulay put it, 'The experience of many ages proves that men may be ready to fight to the death, and to persecute without pity, for a religion whose creed they do not understand, and whose precepts they habitually disobey.' Consider the massacre of its prisoners, women and children included, by the Covenanting army after the Battle of Philiphaugh in 1645 (Smout 1969: 64) to the cry of 'Jesus and no quarter!' What can possibly explain the butchery of these innocents, who posed no conceivable threat to their killers, in the name of the preacher of the Sermon on the Mount? It is not enough to appeal to evolutionary psychology for the proposition that just about anything will serve as a rallying-cry by which to evoke collective behaviour, even if, for example, soldiers in English armies who responded automatically to the invocation of 'St George for England!' had no idea who St George (if he ever existed) actually was. Nor is it enough to cite the Monophysites who walked about the streets of fifth-century Alexandria shouting, 'Cry the name of Jesus!' to startled bystanders, or the 'Honk if you love Jesus!' stickers displayed by car-drivers in the North American 'Bible Belt'. The naturally selected traits which predispose adult males to lethal violence against out-groups were combined, in this instance, with culturally selected memes drawn from an Old Testament conception of a God who enjoined his followers to smite the enemy in His name, and socially selected practices imposing soldierly obedience to orders from above. The rank-and-file of the Covenanting army may have been less motivated than the Covenanting ministers by the prospect of purging the Scottish church of prelacy in the name of 'King Jesus'. But they obeyed them readily enough. It is a clear example of an exaptation where a mutant meme initially diffused among the disciples of a charismatic founder come to be acted out in the subsequent course of cultural and social evolution in a phenotypic behaviour-pattern directly contrary to what the charismatic founder had in mind.

5

Memes acted out in patterns of acquired behaviour can also be adaptive when they take the form of beliefs which make the believers' environment, as they see it, more manageable for them even though their behaviour is stigmatized by the fellow-members of their own culture and punished by the rulers of their own society. This takes us to the category of behaviour conventionally labeled 'magic'. As with 'religion', no useful purpose is served by arguing over its definition. But it is another of the words – there are more to come in Chapter 4 – which it seems that sociologists cannot do without, even though they may be as much of a hindrance as a help in the identification of the critical memes or practices whose adaptedness explains the behaviour observed.

Any attempt at comparison across different cultures has to reckon not only with the scepticism of an anthropologist like Edmund Leach, who claimed that he had 'almost reached the conclusion that the word has no meaning whatever' (1982: 133), but with that of a historian for whom 'magic, as a definable and consistent category of human experience, simply does not exist' (Gager 1992: 24). But it can be asked about any culture or sub-culture whether its members draw a distinction between knowledge and related skills regarded as open, legitimate, and accessible, and knowledge and related skills regarded as secret, illegitimate, and accessible only to initiates. Forms of knowledge and skill accepted as legitimate may also be believed to be accessible only to disciples who have undergone prolonged training or are endowed with exceptional talent, like Freudian psychoanalysts or Ndembu 'doctor-adepts',[7] or apprentices who have mastered the 'mysteries' of their craft. But when a Greek *agyrtēs* and a Visigothic sorcerer both lay claim to a mysterious ability to control the weather, or African and Roman farmers alike complain that their neighbours' crop-yields are due to their surreptitious invocation of a suprahuman power, or 'witches' (whatever the vernacular term) are believed to be inflicting otherwise inexplicable misfortunes on their neighbours by supernatural means in Europe, the Americas, sub-Saharan Africa, India, Madagascar, and Papua New Guinea, these different cultures all have in common a distinction between 'good' knowledge and 'bad'. The practitioners may continue to be disapproved of even when the knowledge becomes generally accessible. But they then cease to be 'magicians'.[8]

---

[7] The parallel extends to the requirement that the female Ndembu doctors 'must at some time have been patients (*ayeji*) themselves, and may not become practitioners until they are generally regarded as having been cured after undergoing the ritual' (Turner 1968: 57).

[8] In some cases where the word is used, it is questionable whether the 'magician's' esoteric knowledge or skill is culturally stigmatized at all: 'magic' was 'by no means illegal or socially deviant in Egypt' (Rigner 1995: 53). In early colonial Ghana, by contrast, a pejorative general ethnonym was applied to outsiders stigmatized as 'uncouth primitives' who were nevertheless believed to 'possess access to an array of the most potent ritual powers, together with the esoteric knowledge necessary to mobilize them in defence of the cultural order' (Parker 2004: 401).

Thus, poisoning is explicitly associated with magic in Cicero's (as before him in Plato's) writings and in the *Lex Cornelia de sicariis et veneficis* of 81 BCE, and the rumours surrounding the death of Germanicus (Tacitus, *Annals* II.69) are echoed by those surrounding the *affaire des poisons* at the court of Louis XIV (Somerset 2003). But in a cultural environment which includes an accepted pharmacology, poisoning loses its occult status (even if it is still not as easy to detect as police and prosecutors would like). Conversely, technological expertise can continue to be suspected as 'magic', as it often was in Renaissance Europe, until its efficacy, however difficult for the uninitiated to explain, comes to be taken for granted as part of everyday routine.

Once the reproduction and diffusion of 'magical' memes is approached in this way, the confusion which bedevilled much of the earlier literature between behaviour which is the phenotypic effect of 'instrumental' and 'expressive' memes is dissolved. Nineteenth- and early twentieth-century anthropologists and sociologists were often too ready to designate as 'magic' behaviour-patterns which are the phenotypic effects of memes involving no belief one way or the other about the effectiveness of the behaviour in enlisting or manipulating occult agencies. Sometimes, admittedly, it is difficult to get far enough inside the natives' heads to tell. When Malinowski (1935: 101) reports the Trobriand *talala* ('we make to flower') rite as 'meant to impart fertility to the soil', on what evidence can he be sure whether the Trobrianders are celebrating a process which they know will succeed as a matter of course, seeking to persuade an unseen quasi-personal agency to ensure that it does, or acting out a strongly felt wish that the soil should be as fertile as it can be made? But where wax is melted in an 'execration ceremony' (Faraone 1993: 63), the wish thereby symbolized, although it may have the perlocutionary effect of frightening those against whom it is directed, is no more the acting-out of a package of memes which includes a causal belief than is, for example, the carving of an inscription in fourteenth-century Andhara which threatens that 'He who steals endowed land ... will be reborn as a maggot in excrement for 60,000 years' (Talbot 2001: 12).[9] There are also performative, as opposed to either instrumental or expressive, rituals. When the Roman

---

[9] The surviving Anglo-Saxon charters are similarly full of threats to the effect that, for example, 'if anyone is so presumptuous towards God as to desire to alter this, God Almighty shall remove him from the bliss of heaven to the abyss of hell, unless before his death he make amends as fully as possible' (Robertson 1939: LXXXV). Did the bishops and earls who witnessed the document really believe that? Selectionist theory suggests that what is going on here is not an affirmation of belief but the signalling of a presumptively costly commitment to cooperation (Sosis 2003; Sosis and Alcorta 2003).

fetial priests threw a spear into enemy territory – or, if the border was a long way away, into a piece of land near the temple of Bellona which by a deliberate legal fiction was designated as such (Beard *et al.* 1998: 132–3) – they thereby transformed a state of peace into a state of war in exactly the same way that the Maring, by hanging 'fighting stones' from the central poles of their houses, transform opponents into enemies to be engaged in full-scale battle with lethal weapons (Rappaport 1999: 75). But in these cases, the memes in the natives' heads are not to be equated with the memes encoded in charms, spells, or incantations which are believed to cure a sickness, excite the passion of a lover, safeguard a valued possession, frustrate a competitor, or appease the ghosts of the unburied dead. If the critical memes acted out in the observed behaviour have not been correctly identified at the outset, the selectionist just-so story of their reproduction and diffusion will be in danger of generating an explanation of something which was not going on at all.

In practice, the reverse engineer trying to infer from the ethnographic or historical evidence the essential features of an adaptive memetic design will often find that its successful reproduction depends on a combination of beliefs and attitudes of which some are locally defined as magical at the same time that others are not. 'Magical' memes can often be detected in among both the routine, down-to-earth precepts of doctors, farmers, or technicians on the one side and the abstruse, high-flown speculations of preachers, theologians, or mystics on the other. The competition for adherents is often a competition between rival bundles of memes in which the adaptedness of claims to acquaintance with questionably acceptable occult agencies accessible only to initiates depends on their combination with straightforwardly legitimate claims of practical efficacy. When Bishop Hincmar of Rheims recommended *medicinae ecclesiasticae* as a cure for sexual impotence (Flint 1991: 294) he was linking a claim to reputable authority to what might otherwise be thought a suspect claim to disreputable expertise, just as the self-styled 'occultists' of nineteenth-century England linked the prestige of Victorian science to what might otherwise be thought a suspect claim to have discovered a hidden, supra-sensible world (Owen 2004) – a claim which some eminent contemporary practitioners of 'science' were willing, at least provisionally, to entertain (Lamont 2004). There is no reason to suppose that either Bishop Hincmar or Sir William Crookes (President of the Royal Society) were cynical confectioners of whatever combinations of memes they thought likeliest to appeal to the largest number of people. But whether they were or not, they might as well have been – as were, for example, the well-dressed, smooth-talking, self-appointed Bemba witch-finders observed by the anthropologist Audrey Richards in what was then Northern Rhodesia, whose ritual for the detection and cure of sorcery was the phenotypic effect of a judiciously concocted combination of traditional and Christian memes (Richards 1935).

One of the more successful examples on record which has time and again emerged at different times and places is the so-called 'evil eye'. Like the feud, it is a product of natural as well as both cultural and social selection. The anxiety aroused by a fixed and prolonged stare can be traced far back in our evolutionary past (Burkert 1996: 43), and 'the attribution of suspicion to eye-to-eye contact, a straight look, is so widespread – and not restricted to human populations – that it does not require exaggeration to say that a psychological universal may explain why the concept is specifically the evil *eye*' (Spooner 1976: 284). In the Norse sagas, when a magician is apprehended a sack is at once put over his head for fear of it (Kieckhefer 1989: 50). But the evil eye is not found worldwide. It is not unknown in Islam, but it is not found in China. It is less common in Anglophone than in Hispanic America (*mal ojo*), and less common in India than in Mediterranean Europe. It was generally recognized in the worlds not only of 'Ancient' Greece and Rome but of Byzantium. The remedies prescribed for it typically involve expressive or performative effects as well as, or as part of, instrumental techniques (Herzfeld 1986). In the Graeco-Roman world, there is a lack of archaeological evidence for it to match the extensive literary evidence, but this can plausibly be explained by reliance either on words and gestures to counter it or on amulets or charms made of perishable substances (Dickie 2001: 97). After the advent of Christianity, the Church might, as in Byzantium, seek to replace the 'pagan' conception of it with the idea of saintly intervention in favour of the all-seeing eye of God (Maguire 1994), or, as in modern Greece, denounce folk remedies as sinful and stipulate the use of holy water in their place (du Boulay 1974: 66). As with the feud, no lawlike cross-cultural generalization can be framed from which its incidence could be predicted in advance. But the environments most favourable to the probability of its continuing reproduction are relatively small communities relatively little differentiated in social distance between roles where feelings of envy are readily evoked and relative good or ill fortune held to call for special explanation (Schoek 1969: 261; Limberis 1991: 171; Ogden 2001: 107; Boyer 2001: 222). Each just-so story has distinctive features of its own. But the appearance of the evil eye in widely separate cultures under similar environmental pressures is as clear-cut an example of convergent evolution as the convergent evolution in different species of the eye itself.

ENCODED WHERE? TRANSMITTED HOW?

6

There is a bewildering diversity of places where memes can be encoded and routes by which they can be transmitted from mind to mind. This in itself is one obvious reason why the transmission of information from one carrier to another by imitation or learning is so different from the biological transmission from one carrier to another of information passively copied in the receiving organism with only the possibility of occasional and limited mutation. But from the perspective of comparative sociology, the coherence and stability of widely different cultures and sub-cultures is evidence for the remarkable capacity of functionally equivalent memetic combinations to reproduce those of their component units of information which affect behaviour in the phenotype despite the information loss and intentional or unintentional distortion and reconstruction which, except in such cases of stock formulation as the Christian 'Lord's Prayer' or the hymns of the Indian *Rig Veda*, is always more likely than perfect copying. Even when a norm of conduct is transmitted from parent to child, or mentor to pupil in strict deontic form ('cremate the dead', 'blow the trumpets at the new moon', 'abstain from pork and alcohol', 'give your mother a present on her birthday'), there is scope for alternative interpretations; and even when the distinctive behaviour-pattern observed is acted out in the same way by every member of the population, the package of memes inside one native's head may, as I have emphasized already, be quite different from that inside another's. But the right just-so story will always be a story of how certain critical memes have succeeded in surviving translation from one to another language or medium or mode of transmission with sufficiently little modification that they find expression in phenotypic behaviour whose constitutive intentions are recognizably the same. The individual differences between carrier and carrier recede as always from view to disclose the bundles of information which have been favoured over their competitors at population level.

The relative reproductive fitness of a complex of co-adapted memes can be influenced both by where it is encoded and by how it is transmitted. Memes encoded verbally are not necessarily more adaptive on that account. Nor are written or spoken words, however widely diffused, necessarily the repositories of the memes of which the behaviour observed in the phenotype is the expression. There is no doubt that the printing press, and after it radio, television, tape-recording, and email, have enhanced the range as well as the speed of memetic transmission. But they have also enhanced the volume of redundancy. The Protestant Reformation is a familiar example where the printed word is agreed among its historians to have had a significant influence in replacing one set of 'religious' memes with another in the heads of the population of much of Northern Europe. But the voluminous output of anti-papal pamphlets from Calvin's Geneva was less effective in transmitting the Protestant message than the metrical psalms, which Calvin borrowed from the Huguenots of Strasburg and became, in the words of the historian Diarmid MacCulloch (2003: 307–8), 'the secret weapon of the Reformation not merely in France but wherever the Reformed brought new vitality to the Protestant cause'. They could be easily memorized, they could be sung by women and men alike in streets or market-places as well as churches, and they were accessible to those whose level of literacy fell well short of what was needed to master Calvin's *Institutes* (which, in any case, not many of them could afford to buy). What is more, singing the metrical psalms in unison could evoke in a Protestant crowd what MacCulloch calls 'ecstatic companionship' of the kind known, thanks to recent research, to be a psycho-pharmacological effect of the endorphins produced in the brain by singing in unison. Not any words sung to the same tunes would have had the same effect, any more than any rallying-cry will do as well as any other. Indeed, one of the features of the psalms which a reverse engineer would not fail to notice is that they gave the singers a choice which included, for example, those of Psalm 115 which MacCulloch cites as 'the perfect accompaniment for smashing up church interiors'. But the words would not have had the same effect without the tunes.

On the other hand, the printing of newspapers could promote the diffusion of memes with a significant effect on phenotypic behaviour even where the greater part of their contents was information of a different kind included for a different purpose. An example of this is the creation by that means of 'imagined communities' (Anderson 1983: Ch. 4) among the population of Hispanic America in the years between the restriction of the printing press to Mexico and Lima, which lasted until the end of the seventeenth century, and the achievement of independence from Spain. Much of the information transmitted will have entered the readers' heads as little more than noise – reports of changing commodity prices, of the movement of ships, of marriages or social events or political appointments which would be rapidly forgotten. But some of what stayed behind inside their heads generated a sense of shared cultural identity between people who, although aware of one another's existence, had no personal knowledge of, or contact with, them. The 'imagined community' was the sub-culture of locally born *creoles* whose beliefs and attitudes and consequential behaviour came to differentiate them increasingly from the Spanish-born *peninsulares* who might be indistinguishable from them in appearance, language, and religious denomination alike. As so often, the longer-term consequences were not perceived at the time. But when the institutional environment changed, *creoles* in separate regions of Hispanic America responded to the changes in ways which they would not otherwise have done, even to the point of putting their property and sometimes their lives at risk in what they now perceived as a common cause.

Before information could be transmitted from mind to mind by the technical means which are now taken for granted, the diffusion of memes from one population to another was normally effected by the physical movement of their carriers. Traders, soldiers, preachers, performers, craftsmen, colonists, exiles, pilgrims, and explorers could all bring with them into the territories into which they moved memes from their culture of origin which could be copied, with varying degrees of distortion or reinterpretation, and then reproduced down successive generations of the receiving population (or, usually, some sub-culture within it). Buddhist memes originating in the Ganges Valley were carried from one newly-founded hill-top monastery to another, Dualist memes originating in the Balkans were carried along the trade routes to North Italy and from there across the Alps; and Christian memes were carried from Europe to China by Father Ricci and Father von Bell, who brought with them as 'salesmen of a special kind' (Landes 1998: 337) their mechanical clocks and astronomical observations. But later, too, affiliation to the nascent Social Democratic Party in Sweden was diffused along 'mesolevel networks' which emerged from the routes travelled by itinerant agitators (Hedström *et al.* 2000). In the course of these peregrinations there is always scope for distortion of the carriers' messages along the way. But the distortion observed is much less than the scope for ongoing reinterpretation of memes might suggest. Some members of the receiving population reject the message outright. But those who accept it tend to accept the package as an integrated whole. Or at any rate, they do so sufficiently for its phenotypic effects to be easily visible: the converts conform to a new behaviour-pattern which immediately distinguishes them, irrespective of personal differences, from the hold-outs who continue as before. It is Gellner's Paradox from Section 1 of Chapter 2: distinctive cultures and sub-cultures are much more coherent and durable than the mutability of memes and the volatility of their individual carriers would appear to allow for.

7

The transmission of memes differs from the transmission not only of genes but of practices in the speed with which it can take place. Natural selection, even at its fastest, works too slowly in human populations to explain cultural and social changes which can, after all, take place within a single generation. But social selection, when contrasted with cultural selection, is as a rule relatively lethargic: in the metaphor of Fernand Braudel (1966: II, 62), societies 'seldom march with the steps of giants'. Information affecting phenotype transmitted by imitation and learning can spread like the proverbial wildfire. Rumours and fashions can be transmitted not only within but across whole populations in a matter of days. In social selection, by contrast, even if a radical change is imposed by the incumbents of roles to which there attaches a monopoly of the means of production, persuasion, and coercion, it may take years before the novel pattern of interacting roles is firmly in place and the practices defining them consistently reproduced in the relevant dimensions of social space. Rome wasn't built in a day, either physically or institutionally. But Wesley's preaching could (we are told) convert as large an audience as his voice could reach in the course of an afternoon.

This aspect of acquired behaviour serves also to re-emphasize the relative unimportance of formal instruction in much of cultural selection. Almost before (as the saying goes) you can turn round, all the kids on the block have turned their baseball caps back to front and switched allegiances from one rock group to another. This may not be the stuff of which major cultural changes are made. But time and again, when a population-level cultural change is examined in detail, it turns out to involve almost immediate imitation of behaviour observed and almost immediate acceptance of information verbally transmitted from a source that the recipients are willing to trust. In this, horizontal transmission of memes is very different from vertical, where the socialization of children involves much more transmission of memes by formal instruction over a longer period. In many of the smaller and simpler societies documented in the ethnographic record, the transmission of memes, and particularly techno-memes, is more likely to be vertical or oblique than horizontal, and to be relatively slower on that account. But in large and complex societies, memes inherited from parents account for less of the behaviour observed in the adult phenotype relative to parental genes on the one hand and horizontal transmission from the non-shared environment on the other than used to be widely supposed (Harris 1998). Moreover, children are more immediately receptive to novel memes than their elders are. This raises the theoretical possibility, which I touched on in Section 5 of Chapter 1, that among populations where the choice of life-styles is sufficiently wide and novelty as such is sufficiently highly valued, the rate of memetic mutation will rise to the point that cumulative selection becomes virtually impossible. But as long as the rate of variation does not rise to the point that it swamps the rate of reproduction, the extinction rate of emergent sub-cultures will not be so rapid that the ever-branching Darwinian tree grows no more solid branches but only (to remain with the arboreal metaphor) short-lived cultural twigs.

Meanwhile, in any case, there are always the hold-outs. No matter how fast a mutant meme may be galloping up the slope of the S-shaped logistic curve, there will be some natives into whose heads it fails to penetrate. The hold-outs' motives may well be of different kinds, and behaviour genetics may well have a contribution to make to the explanation of why, within a given population, some are more resistant than others. But where the cultural and social environment strongly sustains the continuing reproduction of long-established 'traditional' memes, neither frequency-dependence nor biased transmission in favour of prestigious role-models can accelerate the rate of conversion. For all the dedication and skill of the Jesuits who set up their missions along the route which Father Ricci had followed from Macao to Beijing, the Chinese literati were unlikely to conclude from what the Jesuits had to tell them about European astronomy, cartography, and music that they should take seriously a view of the cosmic order and the place of humanity within it which seemed to many of them 'only a bastard form of Buddhism sometimes mixed with borrowings from Islam' (Gernet 1982: 455). From a selectionist viewpoint, however, the story of the Jesuits in the Far East has a twofold interest. On the one hand, it illustrates the obstacles in the way of any attempt to displace a set of established beliefs and attitudes by imitation and learning alone without imposition of the political, ideological, and economic practices which have supported Christian missionary endeavours in other parts of the world. But on the other hand, the continuing reproduction of the novel memes within the few Christian communities where they achieved fixation illustrates the strength of the pressure to conform which is brought to bear within close-knit communities of adherents to teachings culturally defined by the majority population as unorthodox and institutionally persecuted as heretical. When the Jesuits were readmitted into Japan after their protracted expulsion under the Tokugawa regime, those who arrived in Nagasaki were astonished to be greeted by descendants of the original converts who came down from the hills clutching in their hands the crucifixes symbolic of their prohibited faith.

8

Taken together, the speed with which memes can invade a hitherto unaffected population and the resistance by which they can nevertheless be met within it constitute one of the reasons for which it can be claimed that memetic transmission is 'very similar to the transmission of infectious diseases' (Hewlett and Cavalli-Sforza 1986: 23). But this analogy, like the gene-meme analogy itself, is not to be taken too far. The implication of pathology may be appropriate to outbreaks of mob violence or medieval dancing manias. It may also be of rhetorical value to polemicists who regard 'religious' beliefs and attitudes as not only erroneous in conception but pernicious in effect, or to heresy-hunters, xenophobes, and counter-revolutionary propagandists eager to stigmatize their cultural enemies as carriers of plague. To think of a meme as if it were a 'virus of the mind' which copies itself wherever the opportunity offers (Brodie 1996) may help to bring out both that memes' reproductive success can be at the expense of their carriers and that some prospective carriers will be resistant to it. But an infection requires only a single carrier, whereas the displacement of one meme by another may require confirmation or reinforcement from multiple sources (Centola and Macy 2007). Whatever exactly memes are, they aren't bacilli, and the 'changes of mind', as we describe them to ourselves, which alter cultural behaviour-patterns do not leave us, like diseases, either dead or crippled or cured.

One possible rejoinder is that the notion of 'thought contagion' (Lynch 1996) need not exclude by definition the possibility that, whatever the information being passed from one person's mind to another's, it can be benign rather than pathogenic.[10] There is a whole psychological literature on 'disinhibiting', 'echo', and 'hysterical' contagion as distinguishable forms of interpersonal influence (Levy and Nail 1993), and such influence can be – according to your point of view – either for good or for ill. But the routes of memetic transmission which sociologists find themselves tracing in their comparisons between one culture or sub-culture

---

[10] There is an intriguing precedent in a letter to Rousseau of 6 June 1761 written by a Genevan correspondent in the aftermath of a civic festival, which is more often cited for its early invocation of the triad of *égalité*, *liberté*, and *fraternité*: 'si le mot Contagion *pouvoit être pris en bonne part, je vous dirois: la Contagion de l'amitié publique, avoit gagné tous les individus de la Société*' (*Correspondance complète*, ed. R. A. Leigh, IX: 12).

and another are far more diverse than the direct interpersonal transfers to which a literal reading of the term 'contagion' is appropriate. Memes can be encoded in so many different places, and pass through so many successive mutations before they find outward expression in phenotypic behaviour, that the search for the right just-so story of their local adaptedness may be as much hindered as helped by the parallels which the term 'contagion' suggests even if the implication of pathology has been disavowed.

Two examples drawn from the sociology of twentieth-century Britain illustrate this in different ways.

The first, which has the advantage of well-attested quantitative evidence, is the extent to which ' "social contagion" effects' (Ermisch 2005: 23) may explain the rapid rise in child-bearing outside marriage in Britain in the last quarter of the twentieth century. The percentage rose from 9 per cent in 1975 to 40 per cent in 2000. There is no evidence for a decline in marital fertility rates during that time, and the statistics for aborted conceptions show no increase. The researchers did not get far enough inside the natives' heads to assess the reciprocal adaptedness of their beliefs and attitudes about cohabitation, contraception, marriage, and childbearing. But it is apparent that what was going on was imitation of a chosen reference group, and that the probability of cohabitation was a function of the expected probability of cohabitation in the group being imitated. A mathematical model of the relation between actual and expected proportions cohabiting can be constructed which is consistent with the data and shows two stable equilibria between which temporary changes in the environment that alter parenting behaviour can cause a dramatic move. The increase in childbearing outside marriage fits the familiar S-shaped logistic curve. But it does not follow that anything is gained by reporting it in epidemiological terms. It is a straightforward just-so story of frequency-dependence. After a slow start, the transmission of memes which encode attitudes and beliefs about cohabitation outside of marriage generates a rapidly increasing rate of imitation which then starts to decline towards a new equilibrium where the hold-outs are no longer influenced by the expected probability of cohabitation in the reference group. It is a story more of symbolic detoxification than of quasi-epidemic contagion. Imitation of a reference group is not the same as catching an infectious disease.

The second example is one which furnishes another of those quasi-experimental contrasts of which comparative sociologists are always in quest. A mid-twentieth-century observer studying British industrial relations during the inter-war depression could well have wished to be able to engineer the insertion, as if by introducing a bacillus, of the beliefs and attitudes of militant trade-unionism into the working-class population of a region where unemployment was relatively low and the workforce relatively unorganized in order to see whether militancy proved to be contagious or not (Whiting 1983). On a 'contagion' hypothesis, the expectation would be that the militant memes would start to be transmitted from the newcomers to those of the local workforce with whom they came into contact and that these would in turn infect their fellow locals until the point was reached where individual attributes of the hold-outs were such as to keep them immune. But that is not what happened when the experiment was, in effect, realized by mineworkers with a strong cultural tradition of militancy who migrated from regions of high unemployment to where the expanding motor-vehicle industry was recruiting workers for its assembly-lines. The locals did not, in the event, 'catch' the newcomers' memes. Instead, they adopted a strategy of free-riding on the increasingly intransigent negotiations with the employers which the newcomers conducted in their institutional roles as trade-union convenors empowered to organize collective withdrawals of labour.

9

I remarked in Section 3 of Chapter 1 that sociologists are often confronted with a problem of overdetermination. There are so many selective pressures favouring the reproduction and diffusion of a practice such as wage-labour, or formal education, or military conscription which has invaded a hitherto unexposed population that the increase in the number of wage-workers (and their employers), students (and their professors), and soldiers (and the officers commanding them) invites more explanations than it needs. But there are cultures, too, in which so many memes which appear to be altering phenotypic behaviour are encoded in so many media of transmission and transmitted along so many pathways that the reverse engineer, who cannot conduct the experiments by which the problem could in principle be resolved, is at a loss to distinguish the critical mutations from the noise.

A familiar topic on which this difficulty is particularly acute is the complex of memes and practices subsumed under the concept of 'nationalism' – another word which sociologists, anthropologists, and historians are quite unable to do without but which makes it more difficult, not less, to identify the particular memes which in different local contexts find expression in 'nationalistic' behaviour.[11] Is it 'modern', or also 'ancient', 'secular' or 'religious', 'progressive' or 'reactionary'? Does it apply equally to appeals by 'medieval' monarchs to their subjects to think of themselves as 'English' or 'French', to the Anglo-Saxon representation of *Engla Lond*, and to the sentiments which Thucydides attributes to Pericles in his commemoration of the Athenian war-dead? There is obviously a difference between the memes in the heads of Pericles' audience and those in the heads of nineteenth-century European or twentieth-century African and Asian nationalists aware of living in an environment of industrialization, secularization, and the control of the means of persuasion by the incumbents of increasingly powerful institutional roles. But from the perspective of selectionist sociology, the explanandum is the emergence, whether by convergent evolution, lateral diffusion, or homologous descent, of cultures in which the universal, innate disposition to stigmatize out-groups defined as 'other' takes a local form in which self-identification as members of a distinctive in-group involves more than language, religion, territory, and kinship by themselves. Not any trait can, as one sociologist has put it, be 'packaged into a nation' (Bruce 1998: 89), any more than any words could have been set to the metrical psalms which were the 'secret weapon' of the Protestant Reformation or any battle-cry could be substituted for 'St George for England!' But the problem is to account for the collective behaviour-patterns of populations whose members would not act as they do if they did not think of themselves as belonging to a 'nation' (or a word in their vernacular language which corresponds to it, which may simply be a word designating the 'such-and-such' people). It is, moreover, an exercise not only in meme-tracing but in practice-tracing. The reverse engineer who has identified the memes whose combination and reproduction has enabled them to outcompete memes encoding loyalty to clan, or locality, or systact, or creed has also to identify the practices which enhance the probability of continuing reproduction of those memes by attaching institutional sanctions to the roles of rulers and their agents who by controlling the means of persuasion can impose on the population a formally nationalist ideology.

This, however, can sometimes be done. Consider the just-so story told by the historian Linda Colley of the emergence in eighteenth-century Britain of a distinctive form of nationalism which can be traced to an identifiable combination of critical memes. The phenotypic effect to which Colley

---

[11] This is brought out in the revealing admission by an author who has written extensively on 'nationalism' that 'we can really only hope to demonstrate an 'elective affinity', in terms of subjective meaning between certain features of national identity and ideology, and particular beliefs and practices of one or more ethnic communities and kingdoms over a period of time' (Smith 2003: 5).

draws particular attention is the readiness of young and even middle-aged males to volunteer for military service during the Napoleonic wars and the 'speed and unanimity with which militia and volunteer corps in different parts of Great Britain unfailingly assembled during the various false alarms of a French landing' (1992: 310). The 100,000 militiamen who had volunteered for service by the time that the Supplementary Militia Act of 1796 was in full effect will have done so from a variety of individual motives: fear of unemployment, deference to landlords or clergy, susceptibility to persuasion by family or friends, or simply the prospect of a legitimate outlet for innate pugnacity. Nor does Colley neglect to mention the evoked behaviour observable when recruiting parties arrived in small villages and exploited to the full the impact of their wind instruments, drums, and cymbals. But the turnout of such a significant proportion of the age-cohort at population level reflects the reproduction and diffusion of distinctively Protestant memes when they were combined with stereotypical representations of French 'Papists' and encoded in tracts, homilies, newspapers, almanacs, Foxe's *Book of Martyrs*, sermons, folktales, songs, plays, ceramics (Brewer 1982: 328), and bonfire nights. Inevitably, there are no means of reconstructing the evidence which would make possible a conclusive test of Colley's hypothesis. But if the data could cover in full the provenance, upbringing, and peer-group relationships of both volunteers and non-volunteers, the standard techniques of multivariate analysis would generate the quasi-experimental contrasts from which it could be inferred not only how much a greater or lesser exposure to separately identifiable memes increased or diminished the likelihood of volunteering but by how much more a combination of them did so. If Colley is right, the probability of volunteering would be found to increase exponentially to the extent that patriotic and Protestant memes were identified side by side inside the heads of British males socialized into the distinctive culture of 'Britishness' which evolved in the aftermath of the 'Glorious Revolution' of 1688 and the Act of Settlement of 1701.

COLLECTIVE MINDS AND WHAT MOVES THEM

10

Although selectionist theory admits no such entity as a group mind or *Zeitgeist* or *conscience collective*, and unanimity is not to be assumed even in the most 'traditional' cultures, that does not require all talk of the 'Greek', or 'Protestant', or 'Victorian', or even 'Asian' as opposed to 'Western' mind (Nisbett 2003) to be expunged from the literature of comparative sociology,[12] any more than talk of the 'Amerindian' as opposed to the 'Cartesian' conception of the relation between nature and culture (Viveiros de Castro 1998) or Hindu, Buddhist, and Confucian as opposed to Christian conceptions of 'evil' (Parkin 1985). Nor does it imply any disagreement with the cultural anthropologists' insistence that meaning is always a function of social context and individual behaviour inseparable from social relationships. What it does, however, require is for such talk to be validated by accurate reports of the distribution and ongoing reproduction of identifiable memes which significantly influence the course of cultural and social evolution. Herbert Spencer's bulky two-volume *Descriptive Sociology, or Groups of Sociological Facts*, with its peculiar list of such headings as 'watchmen on every public building' and 'smoke tobacco till senseless', still serves as an awful warning of what to avoid in this respect. Memes which have significant influence on changes in large-scale cultural behaviour-patterns have to be sifted out from the noise, and they have to be shown to reproduce with sufficient fidelity, despite the conscious reinterpretations and unconscious distortions, for assertions of the form of 'the Greeks now believed ...' or 'the Victorians' attitude became ...' to stand up to detailed scrutiny.

It should need no re-emphasis that such assertions must be advanced with care. Think how foolhardy it would be to generalize about, say, the 'Christian mind' or 'the Buddhist mind'. Any such attempt would immediately disclose the wide diversity of memes carried in the heads of self-proclaimed Christians or Buddhists, even if all of them can be traced back by homologous descent to their origins in doctrines attributed respectively to Jesus, son of a carpenter of Nazareth, and Siddartha Gautama, son of a Kshatria of the Sakya clan. Only in local sub-cultures such as (perhaps) Anglican Christianity in mid-sixteenth-century Southern England, or twentieth-century Theravada Buddhism in rural Thailand, might it be possible to identify packages of memes with consistent phenotypic effects which approached fixation at population level. In even the most restricted environment, the search is likely to lead to the discovery not of a core tradition but only of family resemblances between related clusters of memes. The problem is the same as that familiar to sociologists

---

[12] That is not to say that Nisbett's conclusions about the different memes which he claims to find in 'Western' as opposed to 'Asian' heads are correct or that the criteria which he applies in distinguishing 'Western' from 'Asian' are not open to criticism: Lloyd (2007: 169) points out the irony that a characteristic insight of Aristotle's 'looks distinctly "Eastern" and conflicts with what Nisbett takes to be characteristically "Western"'.

studying the systactic structures of capitalist industrial societies who find that survey respondents mean very different things when they say in interviews that they regard themselves as belonging to the 'middle class' or the 'working class', even if their self-attributions turn out to correlate significantly at population level with their life-styles and voting habits. Conversely, similarities between different local environments can explain the convergent evolution of, for example, representations of intermediate supernatural beings to whom there is attributed the power to influence human affairs – the saints and devils of Christianity on the one side and the *devas* and Nat spirits of Buddhism on the other.

Construction of the right just-so stories of cultural evolution is often made more difficult still by the fact that just as the same individuals can occupy roles within several different institutions, so can they carry in their heads the memes of several different sub-cultures, like Bede's Anglo-Saxon king cited in Section 1. To go back to the elusive concept of 'nationalism': what did 'Englishness' mean to the population of England, as opposed to 'Britain', at the beginning of the twentieth century? That it did have a meaning shared by the overwhelming majority of the population of England can hardly be doubted. Both domestic and foreign observers were well aware of an English sense not only of nationhood but of national superiority – which Engels characteristically denounced as a sense of 'imaginary' national superiority – extending across all systacts and milieux. But bellicose patriotism co-existed both with a marked sub-cultural differentiation of working-class from middle-class attitudes and beliefs[13] and with what one historian calls the 'culture of local xenophobia' which on occasion gave loyalty to 'parish, township, hamlet, or estate' (Snell 2003: 4) precedence over loyalty to either nation or class. The volunteers from all sections of their local communities who took part in the pageants celebrating the Alfred Millenary in 1901 (Readman 2005: 171) were giving expression to an unforced interest in commemorating an explicitly 'English' past. But that could be quite consistent with a repudiation of the beliefs and attitudes of the English elite and a refusal to accord approval to what many saw as England's exploitative mode of production, inegalitarian mode of persuasion, and undemocratic mode of coercion. If there were some memes affecting phenotypic behaviour which virtually all English men and women had acquired by imitation or learning from parents or teachers during the course of their upbringing, there were

---

[13] Gender and ethnicity can be relevant also, as illustrated by Byrne (2007) in a study based on interviews with white mothers of young children living in South London.

others which they had acquired from competing English sub-cultures, including those which generated collective behaviour-patterns directly in conflict with 'English' beliefs and attitudes as defined by England's ideological elite.

II

The best prospect for identifying the critical memes is where there is a diversity of sub-cultures within a larger common culture and the environment changes in such a way as to reveal those whose mutation or, as it may be, extinction has had a detectable effect on phenotypic behaviour across the population of the common culture. Of this, there is an instructive example in one well-documented part of the culture of 'ancient' Greece. The 'Greek mind' included a unanimous awareness of a shared cultural identity which distinguished the 'Hellenes', as they saw themselves, from the Egyptians to the south, the Persians to the east, and the Thracians and other 'barbarians' to the north (Macedon being a socially as well as culturally troublesome borderline case). But the hundreds of separate *poleis* (and the tribal *ethnē* which survived alongside them) transmitted down successive generations their own distinctive cults, coins, calendars, dialects, and artefacts whose accurate reproduction was sustained by strict in-group conformity and sustained out-group hostility. Their sense of shared Hellenism did not inhibit them in the least from fighting one another. On the contrary: peace was, as Plato said (*Laws* 626a), merely a state of undeclared war between *poleis*; 'neighbourtown' (*astygeitones*) wars, as Aristotle called them (*Politics* 1330a), were regarded as a normal part of the experience of the adult male citizen; and Herodotus (I.30.4–5) has Solon say that an otherwise unknown Athenian called Tellus was the happiest of men because he died in a victorious battle in precisely such a war and was accorded a public burial at the spot where he fell. The Hellenic culture, in other words, of which all Greeks saw themselves as members, was among other things a warrior culture which not merely sanctioned but encouraged organized lethal violence against fellow Greeks whose sub-cultural differences it thereby helped to preserve and even exaggerate. But this warrior culture was being radically modified under an unanticipated selective pressure at the very time that Plato and Aristotle were taking it for granted.

At that time, intra-Hellenic wars were being fought by citizen armies of heavy-armed infantry drawn up in close order (and instinctively edging, as I mentioned in Section 6 of Chapter 1, to the right) who engaged in hand-to-hand fighting with stabbing weapons which was brutal, strenuous, and frightening to a degree unparalleled among other societies of peasant agriculturalists (Dawson 1996: 50). It cannot be explained in terms of either a behavioural-ecological hypothesis about maximization of inclusive reproductive fitness or an evolutionary-psychological hypothesis about a supposedly universal 'territorial imperative'. Although sexual exploitation of foreign or servile women was a matter of course (Dover 1974: 210) and concubines were apportioned among victorious Greeks after the defeat of the Persians at Plataea (Herodotus IX.81.1–2), women were not normally part of the spoils of victory. The enslavement of the women and children of a defeated *polis*, where it occurred, was motivated by the wish to inflict exemplary punishment, not to augment the victor's population. Nor was the objective the annexation of territory. The enemy's crops might be destroyed and vines deliberately damaged, but without occupation and subsequent exploitation of their productive land. The citizen-soldiers of the hoplite phalanx fought to hold their own against potential threats to their independence, or to take or retain control of a strategic location that might be used against them, or to support an ally who called for help, or to exact revenge, or to prevent a threatening accretion in the power of a rival *polis*. The true significance of hoplite warfare, in the words of one historian, is to be found 'in its close links to almost every major feature of the culture' (Connor 2004: 35), or in the words of another, in its being 'more than a tactical formation. It represented a way of life, a code of manliness and morality' (Ferrill 1985: 145).

Young Greek males acquired from parents, mentors, and role-models a criterion of prestige whereby it was accorded not to heroic warriors of the type of Hector and Achilles but to those who could be relied on not to break ranks. Commanders fought alongside their men and shared with them a local social life in which they knew each other by name and ate (and more importantly drank) together in clubs or messes (Murray 1991). Cowardice was not merely stigmatized individually but ideologically sanctioned by strong reciprocity. Victories were celebrated, but never by Roman-style triumphs. Battles were fought in accordance with a sequence of prescribed rituals in which invocation of chosen gods was combined with symbolic reaffirmation of civic solidarity: omens, oaths, prayers, libations, divinations, sacrifices, trophies, dedications, funerals, and commemorations constantly reminded performers and their audiences of the collaboration incumbent on them as fellow Athenians, fellow Spartans, and the rest. Whatever the proportion in the various armies of reluctant conscripts and cowardly hoplites (Christ 2006: Chs. 2 and 3), the solidarity reaffirmed and strengthened by wars between *poleis* was both a collective self-differentiation against the 'other' and a cultural celebration of the social role of the self-governing, arms-bearing, adult male citizen.

The obligation to fight when called on to do so was supplemented in the package of mutually adaptive memes by specific injunctions both to commemorate the fallen and to dedicate the spoils of war to the appropriate god. The tradition of paying homage to the fallen pervades not only the literary sources, including the speeches put by the historians into the mouths of generals or political leaders, but also the many inscriptions recorded by Pausanias in the first century of the Christian era and confirmed by subsequent archaeology. At Athens, an empty bier was garlanded and carried in procession for any whose bodies had not been recovered (Thucydides II.34.3–4), and Plato has Socrates emphasize (*Menexenus* 234a) that the poorest citizen who dies in battle will have no less splendid a funeral than the richest one. At the same time, the helmets and shields of the enemy dead were used to 'crown the pure dwelling-places of the gods' (Aeschylus, *Seven Against Thebes*, line 278) on a remarkable scale, both at local temples and at pan-Hellenic sanctuary-sites such as Delphi and Olympia. It has been calculated by applying a multiplier taken from the surviving Panathenaic amphorae that an average of 1,000 helmets per year were dedicated by Olympia alone between 700 and 500 BCE (Snodgrass 1980: 131). At this distance, and without the benefit of evidence from participant-observation or questionnaires, it is difficult to tell how far the guiding motive was conspicuous display of superior status rather than expression of gratitude to a quasi-personal supra-human agency presumed to have favoured the winning side. But bronze was expensive, and the hoplite panoply required many hours of skilled labour. Economic rationality had nothing to do with it.

The subsequent demilitarization of the collective Greek mind is a classic just-so story of meme-practice co-evolution. The change which brought it about was the rapid expansion in and after the Peloponnesian war in the number of mercenaries who fought in intra-Hellenic wars on Hellenic territory. The role of mercenary warriors is attested from the earliest period of hoplite equipment and tactics, and surplus males, particularly from the more mountainous and infertile regions of Greece, were always available for hire in the service of the rulers of Egypt or Lydia. But as campaigns became longer, tactics more diversified, sieges and ambushes increasingly supplemented pitched battles between opposing phalanzes, the *ville-foyer* (Garlan 1974: 277) from which citizen-soldiers sallied out to defend their farmsteads became a *ville-bastion* protected by elaborate fortifications, and commanders became managerial strategists rather than fighting tacticians. Richer societies recruited increasing numbers of mercenaries from poorer ones and the ratio of mercenaries to citizen soldiers steadily rose. Mercenaries presented themselves at known centres of recruitment, and would appear 'even unbidden' (McKechnie 1989: 87) at places from which rumours had spread about forthcoming military operations. The mercenaries formed cooperative groups with their own internal sub-cultures. The memes which had found phenotypic expression in the campaigns fought by citizen-hoplites were steadily driven to extinction. Young Greek males no longer assumed, as their fathers and grandfathers had done, that they would at some time in their lives have to be ready to prove themselves in combat. Rituals commemorating the fallen were no longer performed when these were 'strangers' (*xenoi*), as Xenophon and Demosthenes called them. Panoplies taken from the enemy dead were no longer dedicated in local temples or at pan-Hellenic sanctuary-sites. And the stigma attaching to cowardice steadily weakened as the *miles gloriosus* became a stock figure on the comic stage (Humphreys 1978: 174, citing Webster 1953: 39).

12

So far, it might be said, so good. But selectionist theory has also to account for what doesn't go on – that is, for the absence of change where it might be expected as well as its occurrence where it might not. In cultural evolution, where both frequent mutation and rapid diffusion of memes are commonplace, there are at the same time cultures where it needs to be explained why the collective mind remains unmoved even though the population is open to invasion by a variety of competing beliefs and attitudes expounded by active and eloquent innovators. Of this, the culture of 'ancient' Rome is a particularly revealing case because of its unique combination of 'religious', 'scientific', and 'magical' memes transmitted down successive generations of the Roman population from the early monarchy until the adoption of Christianity as the official religion of the Roman state. Despite widespread and sometimes drastic changes in its social institutions, the culture of Rome passed down from generation to generation with no effective challenge whatever to ancestral tradition. Why not?

Nowhere in Roman culture did there ever emerge the idea that the wisdom of the ancestors (*maiores*) ought to be discarded and replaced, or that a 'Mandate of Heaven' might be withdrawn from an unjust ruler, or that entitlement to occupancy of a political role might depend on conformity to a standard of morality laid down from on high, or that rulers might be under a binding obligation to meet the needs or further the interests of the ruled. There is no reason to doubt the authenticity of Cicero's disapproval of the abuse of power by a provincial governor like Verres, or his admiration for Brutus and Cassius as tyrannicides, or his willingness to regard Roman laws of inheritance as framed for the benefit of men and therefore unjust to women (*de Republica* III.x). But it is symptomatic that when, in his forced retirement from politics, he set himself to write two dialogues based on Plato's *Republic* and *Laws*, his ideal republic turns out to be the Roman state and his ideal laws those of the state already agreed to be best, i.e. Rome. Neither the *pontifices* nor any other of the priesthood saw themselves as carriers of a transcendental ideal by which the holders of economic, ideological, or political power might be judged and found wanting. Nor, for all the interest shown by literate Romans in the doctrines of the Stoics, did that interest extend beyond acknowledgement of the ideals of moderation, clemency, detachment, and self-discipline in the exercise of power. There is nothing in the writings of Posidonius (so far as they can be reconstructed), who appears to have been the philosopher most admired by members of the Roman elite, which suggests other than that the triumphs of Roman imperialism were comfortably in accordance with divine providence. However many Romans dabbled in philosophical speculation, or combined together in the name of a chosen divinity for ceremonial purposes, this never amounted to a self-identification with a creed and associated injunctions about the right governance of the good society. At most, it was felt that, as one authority puts it, 'the gods could not be asked positively to maintain the state, while the Romans were behaving in ways that must undermine it' (Liebeschutz 1979: 100).

Yet this lack of what Weber called a 'salvation ethic' has to be reconciled with the abundant evidence that Romans at all systactic levels, and not merely those whom their social superiors regarded as 'stupid' (Ovid, *Fasti* II.531), shared with Marcus Aurelius, as quoted in Section 3, a belief in the capacity of unseen quasi-personal agents to influence the course of both natural events and human affairs. It is unlikely that any of them seriously expected to see gods appear on earth in seemingly human form.[14]

---

[14] Pausanias says he believed that gods at one time used to appear among men but then ceased to do so (VII.2.4), as does Catullus in a poem (LXIV.386) where the gods are alleged to have appeared in the time 'when piety was not yet held in contempt (*nondum spreta pietate*)'. Compare Sir Thomas Browne in *Religio Medici*: 'that Miracles are ceased I can neither prove nor absolutely deny'.

But not only prayers and sacrifices but the reading of omens, the casting of spells, mystery cults, haruspications, incantations, dedications, and incubations were facts of everyday Roman life. There were the predictable sceptics, scoffers, and cynics, and the politicians who manipulated customary rituals for their own self-serving purposes. But the consultation of the Sibylline Books was not merely play-acting, and the despatch of Fabius Pictor to consult the Delphic Oracle after the Carthaginian victory at Cannae was not merely a hypocritical exercise in public relations. The Romans regularly celebrated seasonal festivals, displayed votive terracottas at sanctuary sites, erected statues of guardian spirits in houses or at crossroads, credited practitioners of the occult with suspect 'magical' powers, and treated certain places, spaces, and features of the natural world as sacred. Due dates were studiously adhered to, traditional formulae repeated, and gods correctly addressed.[15] Conformity to established procedures and formulae did not rule out reinterpretation of inherited memes: an example for which there is good epigraphic as well as literary evidence is the cult of the 'Arval Brethren', whose rituals, after being initially concerned with ensuring the fertility of the soil, were modified to include vows and sacrifices directed to the well-being of successive emperors. Foreign deities were admitted into the Roman pantheon, and foreign cults tolerated as long as they posed no threat to the Roman state. But nowhere in all this can there be found any serious challenge to ancestral tradition.

The answer to the conundrum is to be found not in Roman religion (however 'religion' is defined) but in the memes and practices constitutive of Roman law. From its shadowy beginnings in and before the Twelve Tables of the mid-fifth-century BCE, historians and sociologists of all theoretical persuasions have acknowledged its uniqueness. The early *leges regiae* seem to have been as much *ius divinum* as *ius civile*. But even if some trace of supra-human authority survives in the Twelve Tables, it disappears in the simplified *legis actio* (Jolowicz and Nicholas 1972: 79). The selectionist just-so story can be summarized by saying that the politicization of Roman religion evolved in co-adaptive relation to the secularization of Roman law. It is a story of meme-practice co-evolution in which the practices defining the roles of the Roman priesthood clearly reveal just what was going on. The *pontifices* were for a long time responsible

---

[15] Not that this was peculiar to paganism: Christian *reverentia* towards the saints involved a homologous 'etiquette towards the supernatural, whose every gesture was carefully delineated' (Brown 1981: 119).

for control of the Roman calendar as well as for the rules which ordinary citizens were required to follow in such matters as the burial of the dead. But they never claimed theocratic legitimacy, and they never challenged the presuppositions on which the *ius civile* rested. The conflicts which periodically broke out among the incumbents of priestly roles were social conflicts over who was to occupy the roles to which there attached control of the priestly colleges, not cultural conflicts over doctrine. Roman priests were no more disposed than Roman jurists to question the entitlement of the rulers to rule, and the jurists were explicit about the impropriety of challenging the *rationes* for things ancestrally established (*a maioribus constituta*). Although the jurists recognized an implicit distinction between the spirit and the letter of the law – *aequitas* versus *ius* – they concerned themselves in their opinions (*responsa*) only with the application of traditional legal concepts and procedures to the particular needs and circumstances of those to whom their advice was being given: nowhere did any of them expound a doctrine of rights or a philosophy of law which could be construed as seriously critical of the system with whose interpretation they were charged. Anachronistic laws were not abolished but simply allowed to lapse. In the absence of an earlier law which could be taken as a precedent, the appropriate guide was custom (*consuetudo*). When the eminent Gaius Cassius Longinus, as reported by Tacitus (*Annals* XIV.42–3), said that he had never doubted that what had been laid down in former times was always right, and change always for the worse, he was voicing conventional senatorial opinion at its most uncompromisingly reactionary. But he was not arguing against would-be reformers for whom respectful allegiance to the wisdom of the ancestral *maiores* as inherited by the senatorial *patres* was inherently misconceived. There were no heterdox reformist memes against whose carriers argument needed to be made.

In the Roman mode of persuasion, the practices which defined the role of priest made its incumbents agents of the Roman state no less than did those which defined the roles of the magistrates in the mode of coercion. Not every magistrate was a priest. But priests and magistrates shared a common systactic origin as well as inheriting the same traditional set of memes. (They also, in many cases, shared their genes, although high mortality rates among the senatorial elite entailed frequent recourse to adoption.) Rome was not a 'traditional' society in the sense that its political and ideological institutions were embedded in each other to the degree that no distinction could be drawn between them. But it evolved in such a way that the law became disembedded from religion without religion becoming disembedded from politics. Ambitious individuals had no scope for upward social mobility within a Roman church institutionally distinct from the Roman state. When Augustus as emperor arrogated to himself the role of *pontifex maximus*, his behaviour was consistent with a trend going back two centuries earlier when a *pontifex maximus* had been at the same time a consul. Not until after the conversion of Constantine was there an area of social space in which mutant practices could form roles whose incumbents might have been carriers of memes expressive of a tension between some transcendental moral standard and the performance of their traditional economic, ideological, and political roles by the acknowledged members of the Roman elite. Cultural inertia, in this instance, was due neither to memetic isolation nor to the costs of imitation or learning, but to the effect of the practices defining the roles constitutive of Rome's ideological and political institutions on the ongoing course of meme-practice co-evolution.

WINNING ORTHODOXIES AND LOSING HERESIES

13

In cultural evolution, heresies are losers by definition, since if they succeed they become orthodoxies in their turn. But the outcome of the competition between orthodoxy and heresy is, for the reasons outlined in Chapter 1, seldom decided by dispassionate assessment of intellectual merit: even in the history of mathematics, there are innovators who to their successors are pillars of orthodoxy but were initially stigmatized as heretics. We have seen that where the carriers of memes culturally defined as unorthodox are subjected to social sanctions as heretical and therefore subversive, the 'mere adherents' can be expected to fall away at the same time as the zealots are strengthened in their commitment. But the prospect of imposition of institutional sanctions only arises after the heretical memes have been sufficiently widely diffused by imitation and learning for the need to counter them to be perceived by the incumbents of the roles to which there attaches the power to impose the sanctions.

In any culture, the growing child inherits an initial set of memes from parents or other guardians and mentors. Where both parents share the same memes with institutional mentors such as schoolteachers and priests, the probability of their ongoing reproduction in relatively unmodified form is high. As they grow towards adulthood, some will be more receptive to the alternatives than others for reasons which behaviour genetics may be able to explain.[16] But in comparative sociology, the problem for the reverse engineer is to identify what it is in the memetic design of a heresy which enables it to mount a successful challenge to the established orthodoxy at population level. Designed adaptedness may be involved, but it may be involved on both sides in a cultural arms race. The memetic engineers of the Roman Catholic Church who transferred the doctrine of purgatory from the fourth book of Gregory's *Dialogues* across into the appendix to the Second Lateran Council's constitution *cum sacrosancta* (Le Goff 1984: 285) could fairly congratulate themselves on having promoted a heightened consciousness of sin among the faithful at the same time as encouraging bequests for masses to be said on behalf of the dead. Conversely, sectarian competition at a time of religious revival can significantly enhance the adaptedness of rival memes (Froese 2001). Chance can be expected to play its usual part. The great Byzantine controversy between Iconophiles and Iconoclasts which the Iconophiles finally won in the year 843 was only settled after a succession of wholly unpredictable twists and turns in dynastic inheritance, ecclesiastical policy-making, and the fortunes of war. The leading protagonists may have had strong and well-argued views about whether images are symbols through which worshippers can be brought closer to the unseen reality which exists beyond the range of human vision or whether to treat them as objects of worship is a blasphemous repudiation of God's own commandments to the people of Israel. But how many of the worshippers put it to themselves in those terms? Reproduction of Iconophile memes was favoured by the appeal of their extended phenotypic effects among carriers for whom pictures of Christ, his mother, his apostles, and his saints in churches and private houses answered a felt need for visible representations of unseen powers thought capable of giving or withholding comfort and protection in times of misfortune and danger. But the existence of such a need is no guarantee that it will be met. The right just-so story has to identify both the critical memes whose probability of diffusion and reproduction was enhanced as the environment changed and the critical events, which might as well have been random, which changed the environment as they did.

Not all orthodox memes are expelled from a cultural population through direct confrontation with their heretical competitors. They may simply cease to be transmitted down successive generations as they previously were. According to the so-called 'secularization thesis', which was itself something of an orthodoxy among late twentieth-century

---

[16] Relevant also may be association of rebelliousness with birth order (Sulloway 1996).

sociologists of religion, this is just what was going on in the many cultures whose members no longer shared their parents' or grandparents' beliefs in gods, demons, witches, ancestral spirits, miracles, portents, prophecies, and ghosts. That in the course of cultural evolution many such beliefs have gone extinct in populations among which they had once seemed close to fixation is not in doubt. But a decline in the rate of reproduction of 'religious' practices and a narrowing of the scope of 'religious' institutions are perfectly compatible with an increasing intensity of individual 'religious' experiences (Gorski 2000: 162). The 'secularization thesis' is as mistaken if it is interpreted as positing an extinction of beliefs in quasi-personal supra-human agents as if it is interpreted as positing an extinction of sacralizing attitudes. Adaptive mutations within long-established traditions such as Judaism, Christianity, and Islam have taken the form not only of heretical variants of the orthodox core but of explicit reaffirmations of orthodoxy of the kind conventionally labelled 'fundamentalism'. The problem for selectionist sociology, here as elsewhere, is to separate cases of meme-practice co-evolution from cases where the universal, innate psychological receptivity to memes constitutive of metaphysical beliefs and sacralizing attitudes generates a new 'religion' by cultural selection alone. The selective pressures in the institutional environment are as obviously relevant to the probability of reproduction and diffusion of the memes which originated in the heads of Confucius or Marx as to that of the memes which originated in the heads of Muhammad or Luther. Commitment to any set of shared metaphysical beliefs and sacralizing attitudes will be biologically adaptive to the extent that it enhances the probability of within-group cooperation and therefore, as Darwin envisaged, a higher probability of reproduction of the genes of the members of the group relative to the groups with which they are competing. But what will explain the cultural adaptedness of the particular memes which have this effect, and where will the reverse engineer find cultural group selection at work in its purest form?

Of all the heresies which have become orthodoxies, early Christianity affords the most promising example on record for addressing that question. This is not because Christianity's eventual success would have been as astonishing as it assuredly would to any contemporary observer. The same could be said of Islam and the extraordinary sequence of chance events which guided its early history. It is because, unlike Islam's, Chistianity's just-so story comes in two distinct parts, first of cultural and then of social selection. Without Constantine's victory at the Milvian Bridge and his attribution to it of the support of the Christian God,

Christianity would have remained one among many rival creeds competing for adherents within the Roman world. Only after the institutional innovations which followed, including not least the immunities granted by Constantine to the clergy 'in the first ardour of his conversion' (Jones 1964: 92), did the economic, ideological, and political sanctions attaching to the roles of the emperors and their subordinate officials guarantee its success. But Constantine's choice would not have arisen at all had not such a small group become such a big problem (Brown 1971: 65) – so big that the emperor Diocletian was prodded by his Caesar Galerius into publishing the edict of February 203 which initiated what the Christians called the 'Great Persecution'. The early Christians had been members of a small, obscure, and studiously apolitical Jewish sect. As it grew, the roles of elder or preacher evolved into the role of bishop, and bishops became local grandees with whom Roman officials dealt as such. But the diffusion of Christian memes prior to Constantine's conversion is a just-so story of cultural selection to which social selection is almost totally irrelevant.

14

During that early period, there was none of the organized missionary activity of the kind later undertaken across Europe and beyond. Christian memes were acquired by informal transmission at workplaces or on street-corners or among friends or by the personal influences of an estate-owner or household head whose dependents followed his (or sometimes her) lead. The younger Pliny's celebrated testimony, in a letter to the Emperor Trajan from Bithynia, to the universality of Christianity's appeal has to be qualified by its rarity in the Roman army, among the senatorial elite, or in the barracks of the rural gang-slaves. But it was neither (as Nietzsche maintained) a 'slave uprising' of the oppressed nor (as Weber maintained) a religion of urban artisans who had bought, or were buying, their freedom. Christians were, as Pliny told Trajan, drawn from all ages, all ranks of society ('*omnis ordinis*'), and women as well as men. Yet it is not as if Christianity was unique in holding out to its adherents the hope of a life after death or the comforts of ceremonial, mystery, and companionship in this one. Nor was it unique in its monotheism, since even apart from Judaism an increasing number of philosophers and intellectuals were ready to postulate a single, supreme deity. Nor was it unique in its offer of supernatural help in sickness: numerous competitors offered the same, with the same attestations by eye-witnesses to support them (including, on one occasion, a cure allegedly affected by the Emperor

Vespasian). Nor is it as if the traditional religion of Rome had lost its erst-while support, as evidenced not least by the time it took for 'paganism', so called, to be driven to the cultural margin which the carriers of Christian memes had once occupied and non-Christians to become, as one histor-ian puts it, 'outlaws at last' (MacMullan 1984: 101). The explanation of Christianity's diffusion has to be located somewhere in the sub-culture of the local communities which were 'exclusive and totalistic in a way that no club nor even any pagan cultic association was' (Meeks 1993: 78).

Christians were initiated through the ritual of baptism (which they might be permitted to defer, if they so chose, until nearer to death) into a worldwide community whose members were thereby symbolically cleansed of sin and offered the prospect of salvation. The overwhelming majority of them remained in their same social roles after their conver-sion, and doctrinal disputes, acrimonious as they might be, were of as little concern to the generality of ordinary men and women in the streets of Rome or Antioch or Ephesus or Edessa as to those landowning gen-try and local politicians who chose adherence to Christianity for prag-matic reasons of their own. But they met with fellow Christians at regular intervals to reaffirm their commitment, participated in common meals, assisted one another during life, and cared for one another at death. They were not expected to take literally the injunctions of the Sermon on the Mount. They were expected only to be willing to offer some part, at least, of their time, attention, and money to their churches. Rival Christian communities often quarrelled with one another, and with their bishops, thereby giving obvious pleasure to pagan commentators like Ammianus Marcellinus. But among the injunctions which they were expected to take seriously was a duty of benevolence towards out-group members as well as fellow Christians.

Almsgiving as such was not a phenotypic effect of uniquely Christian memes. But in the Jewish cultural tradition from which Christian almsgiving descended, distributions from the synagogues were much more closely restricted to fellow members than were distributions from the churches. There was in the Roman cultural tradition also the idea of disinterested *benevolentia*. But benefactions were made *ob honorem* to enhance the prestige of the benefactor on the model of the relationship between patron and client, not out of Pauline *agapē*: recall from Section 5 of the Prologue the disdain of the *urbis moderator* Lampadius for the beneficiaries of his largesse. In Stoic philosophy, it is proper to offer help to the suffering, but out of mercy (*clementia*), not pity (*misericordia*). Distributions of goods or money were periodically made by the state, but by the criterion of rank, not need. 'Alimentary' schemes like Trajan's, which provided for the maintenance of children up to the age of fifteen or sixteen, 'did not constitute the one exception to the rule that the Roman world had little compassion for the poor and that no ancient government ever regarded them as their responsibility' (Woolf 1990: 227). No other agency provided orphanages or almshouses or homes for widows or hospitals in the way that the Christian churches did.[17] Convincing evidence for the uniqueness of Christian charity comes not only from Christians like Lactantius (in Book 6 of his *Divine Institutes*) but from Christianity's opponents, most notably from the letters of the 'apostate' emperor Julian in which he points to the need for the priests and high priests whom he created to match their Christian counterparts in benevolence to those in need, including prisoners as well as the poor.

Whoever the recipients, however, Christian almsgiving takes us directly back to Section 6 of the Prologue and Darwin's contrast between the 'low' motives of those who expect something in return and the motives of the genuine altruists who exemplify the 'noblest attribute of man'. Christians who were generous towards non-Christians, although they did not look to them for anything in return, might still have been motivated by the anticipation of reward in the world to come. If they seriously believed that by giving away their earthly possessions they would secure posthumous bliss, rational self-interest would presumably dictate that they did so. This is the cost-benefit calculation explicitly presented by Clement of Alexandria in *The Rich Man's Salvation*, where he offers as a 'beautiful deal' (*ō kalēs emporias*) the purchase of eternal incorruption with perishable cash. But there is no evidence that this is what was in fact going on inside the converts' heads. The expanding Christian communities were guided neither by the primitive communism depicted in the *Acts of the Apostles* nor by the asceticism of the later monastic movement. Renunciation on the model of the advice of Jesus to the rich young man in the gospel story to give up all he had and 'follow me' was as rare as self-chosen martyrdom. Cyprian of Carthage appears to have been one of the few who gave away his personal fortune, but there are hints in the sources that he either kept some of it back or later acquired other property of his own. In any case, to buy favour from God on the model of a market purchase or of the *do ut des* of pagan sacrifice would be the antithesis

---

[17] There were infirmaries (*valetudinaria*). But they were not for the poor. Initially, they were for soldiers, and then by extension for members of the imperial court or the households of the rich (Hands 1968: 141).

of Christian *agapē*. The 'prime almsgivers' were the rich (Countryman 1980: 114). But regular donations on a scale compatible with the normal conduct of daily life were the staple of Christian almsgiving. Much of what each local community received was applied to the support of the churches themselves, the maintenance of their own officials, and help to Christians in need including the ransoming of captives. In Rome, according to Eusebius (*Ecclesiastical History* 6.43.11), the Christian community looked after 1,500 needy persons in addition to its own officials. But the difference was that they combined the sanction of disapproval which sustained conformity to the injunction to give with a norm of benevolence to people to whom they had no other ties of any kind.

This, therefore, produced a textbook example of the free-rider problem. Whatever the individual motives of more and less generous Christian almsgivers, the Christian communities were bound to be vulnerable, as the satirist Lucian remarked at the time (*The Passing of Peregrinus* 13), to any clever charlatan (Lucian's word is *goēs*) who took money off gullible Christians and then moved on. Internally, the Christian communities were so constituted that selective pressure favoured strong reciprocity. The congregations of the house-churches were small enough for their members to know one another personally, to monitor one another's behaviour directly, to preserve recollections of non-cooperation, and to pool information about the trustworthiness of different individuals. No doubt they were exploited from time to time in the way that Lucian suggests. But it was, as always, the trade-off that counted. If, for every stranger who turned out to be a cheat, there was on average more than one who joined the community of unconditionally benevolent almsgivers and abided by its norms, the strategy would be, however slowly, diffused; and if Christian parents brought up their children to be unconditionally benevolent likewise, it would be reproduced in proportion to their fertility (which some historians believe to have been consistently higher on average than that of pagans).

There is, moreover, an aspect to the unconditional benevolence of the Christians to which the American sociologist of religion Rodney Stark has drawn particular attention (1996: Ch. 4) and which must to some degree have increased the number of converts: their willingness to nurse non-Christians as well as Christians during the plagues by which the population of the Roman Empire was periodically afflicted. Stark draws on the estimate of present-day epidemiologists that in epidemics of the kind that, so far as we can tell, these were, rudimentary care – water, a little food, a blanket, and an attentive nurse – can reduce what would otherwise be the mortality rate by as much as two-thirds. The rhetorical account given by Eusebius (*Ecclesiastical History* 7.22.7, 10) of pagans abandoning their nearest and dearest to die in the streets while Christians nursed the sick without regard to the risk to themselves cannot be taken at face value. But it needs only to have been the case that Christians were more likely than non-Christians to nurse the sick, and that they nursed at least some non-Christians even if they gave preference to Christians, for it to follow that significant numbers of non-Christians will have seen for themselves that a significant number of non-Christians nursed by Christians were cured. The epidemic of the year 165 was succeeded by another in 189, which according to Dio Cassius (LXII.14.3–4) killed 2,000 people in Rome in a single day, and then by another in 250. Successive generations of pagans will therefore have included a proportion, however small, of survivors nursed by Christians of whom some may have remained attached to the traditional religion in which they had been brought up but some will have been converted to Christianity by the experience and transmitted their accounts of that experience and their conversion to their subsequent families and friends.

Given the irremediable lack of quantitive evidence, this is yet another topic where the mathematical models available to present-day theorists of cultural selection cannot be put to effective use. Twenty-first-century historians of Christianity are no better placed than was Gibbon himself to revise either upwards or downwards his guess that 5 per cent of the population of the Roman Empire were Christians by the time of Constantine's conversion. But the just-so story outlined above does fit the evidence that we have. At any level approaching Gibbon's 5 per cent, the rate of growth of a diminutive Jewish sect which barely survived the execution of its founder can only, in the absence of imposed conversions, be explained by the adaptedness of some distinctive package of mutant or recombinant memes of its own; and of these, the most plausible candidate is the peculiar norm of unconditional benevolence which was extended to strangers in a way that no competing cult or sect attempted to do.

15

The subsequent success of Christian memes in an increasing number of mutant forms is still, in part, a story of cultural transmission by phylogenetic descent and lateral diffusion which could in principle be modelled in the same way as that of languages or artefact types. But it turns also into a social-evolutionary story of geopolitical differentiation, forcible conversion, and colonial or imperial imposition in which institutional sanctions are as important as interpersonal imitation and learning. By the time that Protestantism was approaching fixation among the populations of Northwest Europe and North America, the beliefs and attitudes passed down from parents and mentors to children in its name were, as in the example cited in Section 9, as much to do with nationalism as with theology, and the relation of conduct in this world to the hope of salvation in the next was such as to lead Weber to link the teachings of Luther and Calvin to the emergence of a distinctive behaviour-pattern among Protestant capitalist entrepreneurs.

The 'Weber thesis' is, as I already remarked in Section 3, untenable in its original formulation. But if we turn from Weber's depiction of the Protestant capitalists of seventeenth-century Europe to his depiction of those he encountered in person on his visit to the United States in the early twentieth century, there emerges a selectionist just-so story in which there is a striking similarity between the memes in the heads of the latter and those in the heads of the members of the early Christian communities. The selectionist hypothesis is that in small-town Protestant American communities where memes constitutive of the norms of fair-dealing with outsiders and restrained personal consumption had been transmitted both vertically and laterally to successive incumbents of entrepreneurial roles, the commercial practices of those entrepreneurs who adhered to them enjoyed a competitive advantage within their local economic environment. There is no suggestion in this that Protestants were in general more likely to be capitalists in consequence of their religious beliefs or that in other environments, in North America as elsewhere, these norms might not be disadvantageous in competition with the 'Pierpoint Morgans, Rockefellers, Jay Goulds, etc.' whom Weber characteristically described in Nietzschean terms as 'beyond Good and Evil' (1922: 214). The just-so story is one of meme-practice co-evolution in which a locally optimal equilibrium was uninvadable by alternative strategies for as long as certain distinctive environmental conditions obtained.

This story begins in the Puritan communities of seventeenth-century New England. Their founder populations were very obviously not a representative sample of the population from which they were drawn. As MacCulloch puts it (2003: 538), 'not all who had crowded the Atlantic migration boats were pure in heart or sought godliness'. But the adult males were predominantly small manufacturers, farmers, artisans, merchants, and traders who knew each other personally, engaged in repeated transactions with one another, and remembered each other's strategies in past interactions. Like the early Christian communities in the towns of the Roman Empire, they were vulnerable to free-riders and cheats who could exploit them in one-off encounters and then move on. But the costs imposed by the defectors could be off-set by the gains perceived by new entrants who, if they conformed to the community's norms, would receive payoffs underwritten by strong reciprocators ready to deploy the sanctions of ridicule, censure, and ostracism against fake-signalling hypocrites who exploited the gullible while paying lip-service to the principle of 'Honesty is the best policy' as conduct pleasing to God.

At the same time, vigilant monitoring by neighbours and fellow churchgoers reinforced the norms of frugality, diligence, and unostentatious personal consumption. In the words of the historian on whom Weber principally relied, the New England Puritan, having 'lost the capacity for luxurious expenditure', must, when he prospers, 'keep his money in a strongbox or else employ it in trade' (Doyle 1887: 35). In this, the New England capitalists were, as Weber was well aware, different not only from the slave-owning gentry of the Southern States but from the big Anglican merchants of New Hampshire and Maine. But their attitudes and life-styles are recognizable to this day in those parts of the United States where small-town Protestant businessmen are regular churchgoers, are totally committed to the businesses they manage, have comfortable but not ostentatious life-styles, and practice both honesty and thrift. It is not that ascetic lifestyles are unique to Protestant Christianity. But, as Weber emphasized, it tends elsewhere to take the form of withdrawal from, and repudiation of, the economic institutions of the society within which ascetic sub-cultures are formed and sustained. Whatever reservations are necessary about Weber's thesis in its original formulation, he was not mistaken in identifying what he called 'inner-worldly asceticism' as a distinctive variant of what he called 'religious rejections of the world'.

Unconditional cooperation was not, and never can be, an adaptive strategy in large and fluid populations where fair-dealers 'lost in a sea of anonymous others' (Macy 1991: 2, quoting James S. Coleman) will never be able to build up networks of mutual trust and the payoffs to free-riders and cheats are multiplied by the opportunities available to them in one-off encounters and the difficulty for strong reciprocators to form stable coalitions. Over large parts of North America during the nineteenth century, as the frontier moved westwards, the economy expanded at an accelerating rate, and the population was steadily augmented by successive waves of incomers, the 'anonymous others' came to include not only the Pierpoint Morgans, Rockefellers, and Jay Goulds but the whole army of fast-talking, get-rich-quick promoters, landboomers, carpet-baggers, pedlars, quacks, guns-for-hire, cardsharpers, and showmen who feature in the pages of Melville's novel *The Confidence Man* (Tanner 2000: Ch. 5). But what Weber observed at first hand during his visit to the United States in 1904 was the survival and ongoing reproduction, in the communities which he visited, of memes and practices still recognizable from Puritan New England. The small and medium-sized towns where much of the growth in domestic output was generated during the nineteenth century were not replicas of those of the seventeenth century. But they were sufficiently small, and their populations sufficiently stable, for local manufacturers, traders, and bankers to integrate new entrants into their existing networks of churches and other voluntary associations, to monitor their commercial conduct, and to bring the sanction of public opinion to bear on them if they failed to conform. The cost of punishment to the punishers was cheap, but the cost to a fake-signalling manufacturer, trader, or financier offering a reputation for trustworthiness[18] was severe. No doubt the occasional deviants cheated their customers, reneged on their agreements, and absconded with other people's money. But as long as the community remained small and stable, such episodes would be more likely to reinforce the vigilant monitoring of new entrants than to encourage a runaway effect of frequency-dependent defection.

How far Puritan capitalists were more successful than their competitors, and how far the practices of which they were the carriers were more adaptive in consequence, cannot be measured with anything approaching the requisite accuracy. But in a fast-growing market, a readiness to deal fairly with outsiders even without the guarantee of reciprocity, if coupled with retention of investible surpluses which had not been dissipated in personal consumption, created opportunities for increasing market share less readily available to competitors of whom neither was true. Some such competitors no doubt prospered, and some honest and frugal entrepreneurs failed. But on average, over time, and until economies of scale gave decisive advantage to the large corporations with their multiple shareholders, salaried bureaucracies, and impersonal social relationships, the gains to the carriers of still recognizably Puritan memes outweighed the losses. There is, moreover, a similar just-so story which has been told for Scotland. Calvinist Protestantism did nothing initially

---

[18] In a revealing anecdotal example, Weber witnessed in North Carolina the baptism of a newcomer who wanted (as a relation of Weber's explained to him) to open a bank in a nearby town (1922: 210).

to accelerate the diffusion and reproduction of capitalist practices. But later, when the opportunities became available in a different economic environment, the carriers of Puritan memes were those best fitted to exploit them (Marshall 1981).

The example is an apposite one with which to conclude this Chapter for three reasons. First, it illustrates the continuity which persists between the insights of the founding fathers of twentieth-century sociology and their reformulation within selectionist theory. Second, it illustrates how homologous descent and convergent evolution can both be involved, as well as lateral diffusion, in just-so stories of cultural selection which extend across large distances in both time and space. But third, it illustrates the benefit to be gained from the reformulation in terms of meme-practice co-evolution of the perennial question of the relation between 'ideal' and 'material' interests as the drivers of change. In Weber's well-known metaphor, ideas function like switchmen directing the course of institutional change down one rather than another railway-line. But the metaphor is misleading twice over. There are no tracks laid down for evolution to follow, and there are no termini at the end of the different lines. The interaction between mutant or recombinant memes and mutant or recombinant practices is continuous and open-ended, and its outcomes are explicable only by reference to selective pressures whose effects cannot be identified except in hindsight. In any human population where the transition from culture to society has been made, 'meme-practice co-evolution' is the right answer to the question 'just what is going on here?' as it bears on the fundamental questions of comparative sociology as formulated in other terms by Spencer, Marx, Weber, and Durkheim.

CHAPTER 4

Social selection and imposed behaviour

ROLES, SYSTACTS, SOCIETIES, EMPIRES

I

It should by now be abundantly clear just how different are the mechanisms of heritable variation and competitive selection of information affecting phenotypic behaviour when social rather than natural or cultural selection is the driving evolutionary force. If the archetypal just-so story of cultural selection is the visionary preacher from whom an expanding group of disciples acquires by imitation and learning a novel set of memes and a consequential life-style whose ongoing reproduction the environment turns out to favour, the archetypal just-so story of social selection is the innovative entrepreneur who in the environment of a putting-out economy – with or without the memes of a 'Protestant Ethic' inside his head – imposes the novel but highly adaptive practice of wage-labour on an expanding workforce and thereby forces his competitors either to exit the market or to employ wage-workers themselves. There is of course no single practice 'for' a distinctive mode of production (or persuasion, or coercion) any more than there is a single meme 'for' a distinctive cultural behaviour-pattern or a single gene 'for' a distinctive personality trait. But at the social, as at the cultural and biological, level there are somewhere in all the noise and clutter the critical mutations and combinations in the information affecting behaviour at population level which have to be identified and traced.

Like cultural selection, social selection is neutral between intentional and unintentional design. The most unequivocal examples of designed adaptedness are to be found at times of constitutional choice when the makers of the institutions into whose constitutive roles future incumbents are to enter lay down the practices which will define them: elections to political office on a specified franchise, trials for offences defined as criminal before a judge and jury, compulsory recruitment of adult males into military service in time of war, and so on. But even there, the constant renegotiation of practices, like the constant reinterpretation of memes in the ongoing process of cultural selection, introduces an element of evolutionary adaptedness and of scope for the diffusion and reproduction of mutations of which the original designers had neither knowledge nor foresight. In the primordial transition from culture to society, random drift and individual trial-and-error may on occasion have been as significant as social learning. But once the practices are there defining the natives' institutional roles, the interacting role-dyads have formed, and the terms for the complementary roles have entered the natives' vocabulary, it is the selective pressure of the environment on their phenotypic effects which determines which practices win and which lose at population level down the subsequent generations of carriers.

It is easiest to see just what is going on when a role is deliberately designed by a person to whose own role there attaches the power to impose directly a mutation of existing practices, as in Peter the Great's 'Table of Ranks' of 1722, which laid down that merit rather than birth was to be the basis of appointment to Russian governmental offices, or Solon's division of the citizens of Athens into four property classes in 594 BCE. But proclamations, as I have remarked already, are seldom to be taken at face value, and rules are often flouted or ignored. There are also many borderline cases, not only during periods of transition but when the economic, ideological, or political power attaching to a recognized role is so tenuous as to be hardly discernible at all. The Christian bishops of Section 15 of Chapter 3 are as clear an example of an evolutionary transition from interpersonal influence to institutional power as are the emergent roles cited from the ethnographic record in Section 8 of Chapter 1. But sometimes the transition is impossible to make, even where the incumbent of the role is a person of exceptional ability and determination. Weber's classic analysis of 'charismatic' legitimacy and its inherent impermanence shows how the leader whose command of a following rests on personal prowess which fuses the source of authority with its agency generates the expectation of a continuous run of quasi-miraculous successes: 'routinization' (*Veralltäglichung*) can be achieved only if the 'gift of grace' is somehow transmitted from the person to a role which others can subsequently occupy (*Amtscharisma*). An almost ideal-typical example from the ethnographic record of a role which, without a change in the environment, cannot become fully institutionalized is that of a sheikh among the Rwala Beduin: since he can bring the means of coercion to bear only by the deployment of his personal wealth and his personal standing as a 'good man' (*rajul tayyib*), it can be said that this is a society in which 'political power does not exist' (Lankaster 1981: 96). Indeed, something of the same is true where, as over much of pre-colonial Africa, land is not a scarce commodity and leaders have to 'attract as well as restrain' (Goody 1971: 30). The difference is that African chiefs, although their roles did not (except in Ethiopia, which had the plough) evolve into lordship over a peasantry tied to the soil, could nevertheless keep close coercive control over their subordinate soldiers, women, and slaves and were maintained in their roles by the render of food and other material goods produced by the labour of subordinates outside of their own families and personal followings.

The textbook example of a borderline role is that of the 'big-men' who briefly appeared in Section 9 of Chapter 1. Big-men are particularly well documented for Western Melanesia, where the standard comparison is with the Polynesian chiefs at the head of their conical clans who command permanent bodies of professional soldiers, ceremonial attendants, and supervisors of stored resources. But analogous practices defining similar roles are found not only among nomadic pastoralists but, for example, in Iceland where the *godi* (who is literally a 'priest') depends for his position on retaining personal popularity among followers willing to fight for him (Foote and Wilson 1970: 135), or in early medieval Brittany where the power of local 'machtierns' to tax, hold courts, and take fines depends on the goodwill of their local *plebs* (Davies 1987: 139). There are numerous examples in the ethnographic record of leaders of factions whose positions derive from their personal qualities of intelligence, fighting ability, generosity, craft skill, and knowledge of local customs. The essence of all such roles is that, as the anthropologist Marshall Sahlins has put it, their incumbents must 'personally construct their power over others' in contrast to roles whose incumbents 'come *to* power' (1974: 139).[1] Although Melanesian big-men are quite often succeeded by their sons, and are occasionally able to designate a preferred successor, the successors have then to prove themselves in their turn – which is made still more difficult in areas of the New Guinea Highlands where there is a high rate of migration. (In Brittany, by contrast, there were machtiern families extending across several *plebes*.)

An archetypal just-so story of how a self-aggrandizing big-man can bring off the transition is the story which Herodotus (I.96–100) tells of

---

[1] A revealing symptom of the difference is that whereas a 'big-man' feasts his followers, an Anglo-Saxon 'king' is feasted by them (Wickham 2005: 344).

Deioces, who, having acquired his reputation as a successful mediator of disputes, refused to continue until granted armed retainers and a palace, after which he was able to impose himself on a now subject population as the first king of the Medes. But that is by no means the only way in which the transition can be achieved. A monitor's role can be the outcome of a voluntary agreement without the sanctions attaching to it enabling a self-aggrandizing incumbent to convert it into kingship. As I remarked in Section 6 of Chapter 2, social contracts can be freely negotiated between independent persons who decide among themselves to bring an institutional role into being, whether to be occupied by a designated outsider or by one of themselves, to which there attaches the capacity to observe and report on defectors without application of the means of coercion. There are on record examples from places as far apart as Switzerland and the Philippines where institutions for the management of common-pool resources conform to a game-theoretic model of self-financed contract enforcement. Not all of them are successfully reproduced, and those that are may remain stable only through further renegotiation of the practices defining their constitutive roles. But, as one early contributor to this literature put it, 'Stable primitive cultures appear to have discovered the dangers of common-property tenure and to have developed measures to protect their resources. Or, if a more Darwinian explanation be preferred, we may say that only those primitive cultures have evolved which succeeded in developing such institutions' (Gordon 1954: 134–5).

2

Institutional roles are, however, not only parts to be acted out – of which the same individual can play several – but vectors within a bounded three-dimensional social space. The inherent inequality of power within such familiar dyads as capitalist and wage-worker, bishop and parishioner, or warlord and conscript joins the dominant and subordinate roles respectively into systacts which rise and fall in relation to one another at the same time that individuals move up or down between the roles themselves. Just-so stories of, for example, the 'decline of the aristocracy' and 'rise of the bourgeoisie' are group-selectionist stories to the extent that the diminished cohesion of the one systact and the enhanced cohesion of the other affects the reproductive success of the associated mutations in the practices defining 'aristocratic' and 'bourgeois' roles. In the case of English society in its 'early modern' period, what was going on was a displacement of lord/retainer role-dyads by capitalist/tenant (and therewith tenant/wage-worker) role-dyads – an evolution to which Adam Smith attached particular importance in the contrast which he drew between England and Scotland. And later, when wage-workers combined to form trade unions, the most successful were those which contained the highest proportion of strong reciprocators ready to punish not only free-riders but fellow workers unwilling to punish them. (The employers on their side faced the same problem when members of trade associations reneged on an agreement to hold out against a strike called by a trade union.)

But inter-systactic struggles resulting from institutional inequalities of power are not always drivers of social evolution. A society can be riddled with endemic economic, ideological, and political conflict without its modes of production, persuasion, or coercion being changed on that account. Mamluk Egypt is one example, and nineteenth-century Haiti another. The prerequisite for change is that mutant practices must appear, no matter from where, which either modify existing roles or create new ones. Thereafter, their reproduction and diffusion can be a matter of either individual or group selection. If trade unions competing for members at the same time as they negotiate with their employers for better terms are a textbook example of group selection, a textbook example of individual selection is given by Marc Bloch when in his discussion of vassalage he speaks of 'the process of evolution which transformed what was formerly a personal grant into a patrimonial property and an article of commerce' (1961: 212). The mutation of a practice which had originally bound a single vassal to a single lord into one which permitted a plurality of potentially conflicting ties created by homage to different lords in exchange for different fiefs was not, as Bloch pointed out, logically necessary. In Japan, although vassal fiefs were both hereditary and alienable, multiple fealty was known only as an occasional abuse. But the politically fragmented environment of post-Carolingian Europe favoured its spread from individual to individual to the point that the jurists were soon dealing as a matter of course with the dilemmas and contradictions which resulted from it.

When there does emerge a novel role defined by mutant or recombinant practices, it can sometimes amount to a modal change by itself, as when Augustus turned Rome from an oligarchic republic into an autocratic monarchy. But more often, the practices defining the novel role have to be diffused across the relevant population: a single wage-paying entrepreneur doesn't create a capitalist mode of production any more than a single consecrated priest creates an ecclesiastical mode of persuasion or a single elected office-holder a democratic mode of coercion. Sometimes, the practices are laterally transmitted by imitation or learning: a land-lord switches from demesne cultivation to money rent because of seeing that other successful landlords have done so, or a congregation decides to institutionalize the hierarchy of a rival church, or a parliamentary govern-ment models its electoral procedures on those of another. In thirteenth-century Italy, the diffusion of the role of professional *podestà* is a textbook example of 'institutional imitation' (Epstein 1999: 18). But sometimes, it is not so much imitation as convergent evolution in response to inescap-able selective pressure: if outdated military practices are not replaced in time, the army will go down to defeat and the country be conquered. New systacts can also be formed simply by a sufficient increase in the rate of individual social mobility. Although a handful of manumissions leaves the structure of the society unchanged, a steady flow out of slavery cre-ates a systact of freedmen and freedwomen, who, even if they never act jointly in pursuit of a perceived common interest, continue to be collect-ively ranked in social space below those born free.

3

After the transition from culture to society, societies of increasingly diver-gent kinds evolve out of the heritable variation and competitive selection of practices in the same way that after the transition from nature to cul-ture, cultures of increasingly divergent kinds evolve out of the heritable variation and competitive selection of memes. But at the same time, these societies – unless, like Tasmania, they have for many centuries no contacts of any kind with any other – are likely to be in competition with other societies for territory and economic, ideological, and political power. The imposition of the practices of a stronger society on the population of a weaker one does not have to be by force, although it often is. But once the rulers of a central, metropolitan society are able to exercise effect-ive domination over one or more peripheral societies, we are in a world not only of societies but of empires. Empires are at the same time more than big societies and less than leagues of allied societies of which one is more powerful than the rest. Sometimes, forcible annexation results in the absorption of the members of the weaker, peripheral society as addi-tions to the central population of the stronger. The English absorption of the Scots enabled an ambitious Scot to occupy one of the topmost roles in what was by then the 'British' state, just as the Roman absorption of the Latins enabled an ambitious *inquilinus* to become a Roman consul. But in the comparative sociology of empire, the interesting cases are those where the initial annexation is neither so complete that the distinction between big society and empire is eliminated nor so short-lived, as in the cases of Lugal-zagesi or Charlemagne or Asoka,[2] that there is no time for what might have been adaptive mutations of imperial memes and practices to be reproduced. Empires call for explanation as such where the central society dominates the peripheral societies for an extended period without either wholly absorbing them or wholly disengaging from them. The peripheries may be as remote as the Philippines from Spain or as close as Tibet to China. The centre may be represented in the peripheries by a handful of soldiers, traders, and missionaries, or by permanent garrisons, large commercial enterprises, and an implanted network of temples or churches or schools. The peripheries may be colonies or vassals or tributaries or satellites or clients of the centre. But the most apt single word is 'protectorate' as defined by Lord Halsbury in 1890 (Burroughs 1999: 194): 'a convenient state between annexation and mere alliance'. The question then is: can the relationship between the central and peripheral roles reach a local fitness peak where it is uninvadable by practices which will make it impossible to sustain?

The answer is no. Societies can survive revolutionary class conflict, subversion of traditional hierarchies of status, and military defeat or civil war. But empires can't. No empire lasts forever, or anything like it. The difficulties which they face are well recognized by their rulers: the costs are so high, the frontiers so exposed, the revenues so hard to collect, the resentments so entrenched, the administrators so inefficient, the monopoly of military technology so impermanent, the trading routes so riddled with extortion, bribery,[3] contraband, and piracy, the rebellions so frequent, and

---

[2] There is, however, a distinction to be drawn between the collapse of an empire on the death of its founder and the defeat of the founder in war by a rival imperialist: in Lugal-zagesi's case, no sooner has he emerged out of the Sumerian transition from culture to society and the world of assemblies and temples and landowners and kings to claim rule 'from the Lower Sea along the Tigris and Euphrates rivers to the Upper Sea' (Oates 1979: 28) than he finds himself put on display in a neck-stock at the gates of Ekur by Sargon of Agade. In Asoka's case, although 'fragmentation, local reassertion of independence, and interregional rivalries and invasions swiftly followed the demise of the God-King-Father', 'the first great dynasty of Indian history continued to rule over Magadha at least until 184 B.C.' (Wolpert 1977: 69).

[3] Some imperial rulers, and some historians, are tempted to blame 'corruption' for the difficulty of maintaining central domination over the peripheries. But practices and roles whereby favours are exchanged in apparent contravention of official rules can be stable in the precise sense in which stability is defined in evolutionary game theory, and the pay-offs are such that the 'corrupt' system is uninvadable by any mutant strategy. As Elliott says of Spanish America (2006: 229), 'In practice, the spread of systematized corruption endowed the imperial structure with a flexibility that its rigid framework appeared to belie.' Cf. Veyne (1981) on corruption '*au service de l'état*' in the later Roman Empire.

so on. In view of them, it may seem remarkable that any empire should manage to last as long as some of them do.[4] The imperial engineer who is the notional colleague of the religious engineer of Chapter 3 can be asked to design the roles whose defining practices will have the best prospect of continuing reproduction, but they will be adaptive only in an environment where there is little or no selective pressure driving the centre and the peripheries in the direction of either absorption or disengagement; and such pressure is always there. In the heyday of the most famous empires, the prospect of disengagement may have seemed as remote as the prospect of absorption. A contemporary observer of the British Empire at the time of Victoria's Jubilee in 1895 would have been as unlikely as an observer of the Roman Empire at the time of Diocletian's abdication in 305 to question its success. But the history of the British Empire under Victoria is a history of crises and improvisations which followed one after another and repeatedly failed to produce a lasting solution to the problems which had given rise to them, just as Diocletian's reforms were a response to a period of breakdown and disorder during which the Roman Empire had virtually ceased to exist. After Victoria, it turned out to be a short step from Halsbury's 'convenient state' to colonial self-government and then to imperial disengagement, and after Diocletian, it turned out to be a short step from the defeat and death of the emperor Valens at Adrianople to the settlement of barbarians within the frontiers, the sackings of Rome, the seizure of Carthage, and the by then irrelevant deposition of Romulus Augustulus in 476. For a time, the domination of the centre over the peripheries may look not only politically but economically and ideologically secure: the practices defining the roles of viceroys, proconsuls, corregidors, harmosts, and commissioners are co-adaptive both with those defining the roles of contractors, traders, entrepreneurs, financiers, and planters and with those defining the roles of missionaries, schoolteachers, propagandists, and priests. But they do not do away with the selective pressures driving the system in the direction of either absorption or disengagement.

---

[4] Chance, as always, plays its part, including what might be called 'mineral luck'. How could the Athenian Empire have been sustained if the silver mines of Attica had not, by geological accident, been spared the need for advanced pumping technology to combat the risk of flooding (Finley 1965: 30), or the British Empire without abundant cheap coal located near consumer demand and artisan skill (Pomeranz 2000: 66)? It is true that the 'Industrial Revolution', which was not, sociologically speaking, a revolution and only partly industrial, depended on the technological innovations which allowed Britain's mineral wealth to be exploited; but escape from the Malthusian constraint imposed, as Ricardo believed, by the laws of nature (Wrigley 2003: 166) was only possible because of the quantity and accessibility of a mineral-based, as opposed to organic, energy source.

Every empire, from those of the Egyptians and Hittites onwards, has its own evolutionary trajectory. But if there is one common problem which confronts all imperialists unable or unwilling either to absorb or to disengage from the populations of the peripheral societies subordinated to them, it is the problem posed by the practices which define *intermediary* roles. Whether the intermediaries are agents of and from the imperial government or local elites exercising power over the peripheries on terms which the imperial government has laid down, the imperial government is faced with the same dilemma: the less the power that attaches to the intermediaries' roles the greater the risk that the peripheries will escape from the centre's control, while the greater the power that attaches to the intermediaries' roles the greater the risk that they will themselves escape from the centre's control and take the population of the peripheral society with them. The intermediate roles may constitute a distinctive systact located in one or more of the three dimensions of social space. Tax-farmers are a straightforward example of an economic class, but scribal gentries can equally constitute a distinctive systact within the mode of persuasion and local warlords a distinctive systact within the mode of coercion. Sometimes, as in the Ottoman and Mughal empires, landholding by dispensation from the centre was combined with delegated local control of the means of coercion. Sometimes, as in Spanish America, churches or monastic orders were substantial landowners, or lenders to local landowners who might find it as difficult to clear those debts as subordinate peons to clear their debts to the landowners. But in no combination of practices and the roles defined by them was the problem of the intermediaries ever permanently solved. Time and again, practices which were adaptive in the short term turned out to be maladaptive in the long. In the mode of production, tax-farming can seem a promising device for extracting resources from the periphery only for it to aggravate both the excesses of the collectors and the resistance of the payers. In the mode of persuasion, the founding of mission-stations and schools can seem a promising device for educating the children of the population of the periphery as the imperial government requires only for the children to use their education to foment ideological opposition to the centre. In the mode of coercion, recruitment of young adult males from the periphery to serve in the imperial army can seem a promising device for reducing the likelihood of local rebellions and enhancing the capacity to put them down only for the native troops to mutiny. Although no lawlike generalization can be framed about such outcomes, it is more than a truism to say that empires are harder to keep under long-term control without absorption or disengagement than they were to acquire in the first place.

Cultural selection of beliefs and attitudes can sometimes enhance both the acquiescence of the populations of the peripheries in their subordination to the rulers of the centre and the effort made by rulers and their advisers to design for the purpose monumental architecture and the rituals and ceremonies to be enacted at or within it. But the cultural selection of memes which cause their carriers to behave as they do through genuine imitation or learning has as always to be clearly distinguished from the social selection of practices which impose on the incumbents of subordinate roles, whatever the memes inside their heads, behaviour which conforms to the imperial rulers' ideology. The impression made on the emissaries from the peripheries of the Assyrian empire who were led through the courtyards and colonnades of Assurbanipal's enormous palace into his presence may have been as effective as that made on the dignitaries ushered into the presence of Louis XIV at Versailles. But rulers of empires who are conscious of the institutional prestige which attaches to their roles are sometimes too ready to assume that there are therefore memes in the heads of the natives at the periphery which may not be there at all.[5] Among the peripheral elites, the attraction of the culture of the imperial centre is as evident among the belted and bejewelled chiefs of the barbarian tribes along the Rhine and Danube in the time of Diocletian as it is among the billiards- and polo-playing rulers of the Indian princely states in the time of Victoria. But the resentments of the liturgists of Roman Egypt which are eloquently documented in the surviving papyri are as readily explicable as those of the representatives from every province in British India who attended the first meeting of the Indian National Congress in Bombay in December of 1885. How can a discourse be engineered which will implant in the heads of people whose labour has been 'connected, subjugated, and made tributary' (Bayly 2004: 64) memes which will permanently reconcile them to their subjected and tributary roles? Some forms of acquired behaviour may be diffused from the centre by lateral transmission throughout the entire population of the

---

[5] The parallels between the rhetoric of imperial Britain and imperial Rome are almost too easy to draw: 'land of hope and glory' matches '*rerum pulcherrima Roma*'; 'the empire on which the sun never sets' matches '*quae caret ora cruore nostro?*'; the proconsular paternalism of Cromer in Egypt matches that of Cicero in Cilicia; and the effusions of the late-Victorian propagandists for *pax Britannica* are, if anything, outdone by those of Aelius Aristides for the *pax Romana*. But the victims of the British soldiery's dum-dum bullets could endorse as readily as the victims of the Roman soldiery's broadswords the much-quoted dictum that 'where the Romans create a desert (*solitudinem*) they call it peace' (Tacitus, *Agricola* 39).

peripheries. Indigenous traditions can be displaced through frequency dependence and imitation of prestigious role-models to the point that, for example, the children of poor Jamaicans take up the game of cricket and their parents give them 'Christian' names borrowed from those of the British aristocracy. But that is no solution to the dilemma which the imperial rulers face when they seek to persuade the population of the peripheries of their benevolent paternalism. Paternalism implies that the docile child will grow up to be the equal of the putative parent. But in that event, the children become entitled to be treated as adults, whether as fellow members of a common culture or as independents who learn or imitate from the imperial culture as much or as little as they choose. No more in cultural relationships where behaviour is acquired rather than imposed than in social relationships of economic, ideological, and political domination and subordination is it possible to preserve a stable intermediate state between absorption and disengagement for more than a limited period.

There is, moreover, a further reason for the inherent impermanence of empires. Natural, as opposed to either cultural or social, selection may seem relevant to the study of empires only to the extent that it has endowed the human species with the innate disposition for in-group collaboration and out-group hostility which gives rise to them in the first place. Recall, however, the general problem posed by populations larger than can be held together by the combination of Hamilton's Rule with reciprocal altruism. Cultural selection helps to resolve it by altruistic punishment, strong reciprocity, and information networks through which a reputation for trustworthiness can be monitored and assessed. Social selection helps to resolve it by economic, ideological, and political practices which extend the reach of the power attaching to dominant roles: regulated markets link progressively larger numbers of buyers and sellers in more extensive economic relationships; churches and schools draw progressively larger groups of disciples into relationships of ideological subordination; and the negative allometry of elites monopolizing the means of coercion enables 10,000 soldiers to control ten million people more easily than one soldier can control a hundred. But they will not hold the members of a subordinated peripheral society under the indefinite control of a dominant central one unless absorption, whether forced or voluntary, turns the empire into a big society; and even big societies, like both Russia and China at certain times in their respective histories and the United States of America in the mid-nineteenth century, may be at risk of fragmentation in much the same way that empires are.

MODES OF PRODUCTION, PERSUASION, AND COERCION

4

One consequence of adopting a selectionist approach to the comparison of different societies and their constitutive economic, ideological, and political roles is that the inadequacy of the standard sociological vocabulary – feudalism, capitalism, absolutism, totalitarianism, socialism, democracy, oligarchy, theocracy, plutocracy, and so on – becomes very quickly apparent. (Worst of all is the entrenched metaphorical dichotomy of 'Left' and 'Right', which has done as much to retard sociological explanation as to encourage tendentious political rhetoric.) Consider 'feudalism'. Historians have long inveighed against the 'tyranny' (Brown 1974) of the concept and the contradictions and confusions which surround it. Yet they have been consistently reluctant to discard it. Although they can, as Bloch himself did (1961: 446), put together a list of 'fundamental features' common to European and also Japanese 'feudalism', it is equally easy to put together a list of 'fundamental' differences, including for a start the difference that in Japan the practice of vassalage defined a chain of relationships between dominant and subordinate roles which culminated in the role of the shogun, not the emperor (*tennō*). If 'feudal' is defined in terms not of a fusion of benefice and vassalage or conditional military tenure or the tying of peasants to the land but simply of decentralization of the economic, ideological, and political power attaching to the society's dominant roles, then societies as far apart as Japan, China, Iran, Ethiopia, Poland, and Mexico at certain periods of their histories can all be classified as 'feudal'. But this explains nothing about how their decentralized economic, ideological, and political institutions evolved as they did until the different practices defining the different decentralized roles have been identified and their adaptedness linked to the critical features of their local environments. In the mode of production, do the local power-holders extract economic surpluses through rent, tribute, labour services, or taxation? In the mode of persuasion, does their status derive from birth, life-style, or access to sacred symbols and rituals? In the mode of coercion, are their soldiers and administrators conscripts, or clients, or salary-earners, or arms-bearing landholders? Does a society cease to be 'feudal' if the local power-holders are integrated into an international mercantile and monetary system, or if they form a closed endogamous caste, or if they are liable to serve by royal command in a national army? Are societies of nomadic pastoralists 'feudal'?

These rhetorical questions do not lead directly to the right just-so story with which to explain the part-similar, part-different evolutionary trajectories of the 'feudal' societies of post-Roman Europe. But notice what that much-told story is *not* a just-so story of. The researches of the historians of the post-Roman world who have exploited to the full the documentary, archaeological, numismatic, epigraphic, and papyrological evidence have left standing little or nothing of either Marx's just-so story of a progression into a feudal out of a slave mode of production or Weber's just-so story of a regression from a nascent capitalism stifled by bureaucracy to a decommercialized feudal economy.[6] It is a story to which the practices defining control of land and the relations between its controllers and the incumbents of the subordinate roles who worked it is critical, as it was in theirs. But it is only in part a story of the evolution of 'serfdom' out of slavery. It is more a story of a diverse renegotiation in shifting local environments of practices defining relative degrees of institutional inequality in the three dimensions of social space. Slavery, moreover, continues to be part of it for many centuries longer, and the concept of slavery, unlike the concept of 'feudalism', remains central to it as the limiting case of total subordination. It provides both the historical and the analytical contrast by reference to which the powerlessness of the *coloni, villani, colliberti, prebendarii, aldi,* and *originarii* of the documentary sources for 'feudal' Europe (or their counterparts elsewhere) can be measured, and the difference made by the mutations in the practices defining their roles assessed.

5

There is always scope for argument about how exactly 'slavery' is to be distinguished from all other forms of what anthropologists sometimes call 'rights-in-persons' (Kopytoff and Miers 1977: 7) such as pawnship or purchase of adoptive kin. But where there is a set of practices defining a role to which there attaches no institutionally sanctioned countervailing power in any of the three dimensions of social space, any word for it in the vernacular terminology can be translated *salva veritate* into the English word 'slave'. Comparative sociology then reveals a complex of

---

[6] A striking example is the way in which the papyrological evidence has transformed historians' understanding of the sociology of Roman and Byzantine Egypt by revealing the diversity and flexibility of the practices which defined the relationships between landowners on the one side and slaves, tied tenants, sharecroppers, casual wage-labourers, lessees and sub-lessees, and full-time resident employees on the other (Banaji 2007).

variable gradations between the total subordination of the slaves and the practices which define the roles of those above them. The relatively freer are not necessarily better off in their own terms than some slaves. But slaves cannot negotiate the practices defining their role except in purely personal terms (foot-dragging, insubordination, malingering, or alternatively ingratiation, manipulation, and seemingly willing compliance). If the institutional subordination is total, it does not become less so if it is represented in a language of fictive kinship or lawful punishment, or if slaves are as kindly treated as Cicero treated his Tiro, or if they are granted privileges or perquisites by their masters,[7] or even if they exercise delegated powers as extensive as those which astonished Western observers of the Ottoman empire. Slavery is found in the societies of pre-colonial sub-Saharan Africa no less than in Pharaonic Egypt, Rome, Anglo-Saxon England, Muscovy, China, Korea, Zanzibar, Hispanic and Portuguese America, the Northwest Pacific Coast, India, the Caribbean islands, the Southern United States, Nazi Germany, and the Soviet Union.[8] So widespread is it in the historical and ethnographic record that its emergence, or re-emergence, might be said to pose less of a problem for the theory of social selection than its extinction. Its convergent evolution is – or should be – no more surprising to comparative sociologists than that of the feud.

Slavery is not by any means a social universal, and where found it always exists alongside other economic, ideological, and political relationships of domination and subordination. But there are many different environments in which reverse engineering can show it to have been a locally optimal design. The origin of the initial mutation is, as always, of limited relevance to the explanation of its adaptedness. Somebody, somewhere, must have

---

[7] Including slaves of their own: in one inscription well known to historians of Rome (*Corpus Inscriptionum Latinorum* 6.5197), the tomb of a servile cashier in a provincial treasury in the reign of Tiberius carries a dedication by no less than sixteen under-slaves who were with him when he died. But slaves are no less slaves when they have slaves of their own than tenants are tenants when they have sub-tenants and wage-earners are wage-earners when they also pay other wage-earners for their labour.

[8] In the Soviet Union, the inmates of the gulag incarcerated under indefinitely renewable sentences were not traded as commodities, since in a socialist mode of production they were state not private property, and they were freed by discharge rather than manumission. But as well as being deprived of any share in the product of their labour and subject to physical coercion at the hands of their guards they were deprived of their ideological status as Soviet citizens even if they were members of the Communist Party, and their families could be deliberately broken up (Sawyer 1986: 199). Similarly, the forcibly indentured peasant labourers of Kampuchea under the regime of 'Pol Pot' (Kiernan 1996: Chs. 5 and 6) were not only under the total coercive control of the Communist Party 'centre' but ideologically stigmatized by a mode of persuasion which categorically excluded any member of the population defined as 'not true Khmer'.

been the first person to enslave enemies captured in battle rather than either killing or ransoming them; somebody, somewhere, must have been the first person to sell a child into slavery to avoid starvation in a time of famine;[9] somebody, somewhere, must have been the first person to organize a raiding party for the express purpose of kidnapping prospective slaves from among the members of a neighbouring population; somebody, somewhere, must have been the first person to fall into slavery by losing a wager staked against their own person – an unusual route of downward social mobility, but one which is documented for Thailand (Feeny 1993: 97) as well as the Kwakiutl (Macleod 1925). But where slaves are a desired commodity, whether for their productive capacity or because of their value as items of conspicuous consumption, and where in addition they are drawn from an ideologically disprivileged status-group and held under close coercive control, the combination of practices by which the role is defined has a high probability of continuing reproduction for as long as the servile population can be replenished by purchase, capture, or breeding. Nor, given replenishment, is that probability diminished in societies where the possibility of manumission is as far from neglible as in Rome or, later, Brazil.[10]

At the same time – and again, as always – chance has much to do with whether these conditions are met. In the evolution of large-scale plantation slavery in the Caribbean and the Southern United States, the cultivation of not only sugar but cotton and tobacco might seem overwhelmingly favourable to the exploitation of the labour of slaves working

---

[9] Not that children might not be sold into slavery for other motives than allowing their 'heads', as an entry in the Durham *Liber Vitae* puts it, to be 'taken for food in the evil days' (Whitelock 1979: 610). In the Mamluk system, where 'there is ample evidence for the cooperation of the rulers and the chiefs of the nomads in the slave trade and also for the readiness of the nomads themselves to sell their relatives' (Ayalon 1975: 56 n.3), parents could see opportunities of a better life for their children who might rise to positions of secondary power even though remaining at the ruler's disposal and at risk of summary punishment or death.

[10] Despite the occasional availability of numerical evidence (e.g. Libby and Paria 2000, where the rate in one Brazilian parish is around 1% per annum), manumission rates are notoriously difficult to calculate. Some reported grounds for it can only have applied to an insignificant number of cases. How often was a Visigothic slave ever freed for informing on a counterfeiter (Claude 1980: 164), or a Roman *ancilla* freed because she was sold with a condition against prostitution which the buyer subsequently broke (Buckland 1908: 550)? But there are obvious advantages to owners of slaves with marketable skills or attributes (including suitability for prostitution) in the practice of allowing them to buy their freedom in instalments, particularly if, as 'almost universally' (Patterson 1982: 240), a condition of manumission is continued performance of services to the former owner (or his or her heirs). Cicero, in one of his speeches (*Philippics* VIII.x.32), implies in passing that hard-working (*frugi et diligentes*) slaves could anticipate freedom within six years. But they had to be in a position to show that they *were* worth freeing: contrast the fate of Seneca's doorkeeper left behind in the country (*Epistles* 12) with that of Lucilius Voltacilius Pilutus, a city doorkeeper freed for his display of intelligence and interest in literature (Suetonius, *Grammarians* 27).

in gangs under the coercive supervision of overseers. But the right just-so story is a different one. Far from being the first stage in an evolution out of a domestic mode of production in the direction of a tributary and then a capitalist mode, Caribbean and North American slavery was an unforeseen consequence of the maladaptiveness of a practice which had initially appeared to be spreading towards fixation: indenture. Indenture, moreover, was a mutation not, as might be supposed, of the practice of apprenticeship, but of the practice of service in husbandry (Galenson 1981: 6), the difference being that the indenture was negotiable and the creditor free to sell at any time before the servant's debt had been extinguished by the amount of work performed. Able-bodied young men dissatisfied with their prospects in their society of origin could negotiate their passage to a society which offered more attractive opportunities by mortgaging their labour for a limited period, and employers chronically in need of labour could hire it from a distance with the option of onward sale if the worker failed to perform. Initially, both black and white labourers on the tobacco plantations had laboured according to 'customary English practices' (Berlin 1998: 32) which descended from the Elizabethan Statute of Artificers. But indenture was a maladaptive practice to the extent that employers had a strong incentive to exploit the indentured servants and the indentured servants a strong incentive to break free in an environment where land was plentiful and labour scarce. It then so happened that the supply of recruits ran low at a time when the supply of Africans seized inland by local rulers for sale to slave-traders on the coast was enough to keep down their price, and an increase in the ratio of slave to indentured labour did not increase the marginal cost of labour in the way that attracting more indentured servants would do. When, in due course, slaves were no longer as readily available for purchase by the owners of the means of production, the practice of indenture became adaptive once again where the demand for labour in expanding economies could be met from other parts of the world where population growth had outstripped the capacity of the local economy to absorb it. Meanwhile, in the mid-seventeenth century, an apposite quasi-experiment is to hand in the history of the short-lived Puritan colony established on Providence Island in 1630, where, when imported black slaves turned out to be significantly cheaper than white indentured servants, 'considerations of godliness therefore lost out to harsh financial realities' (Elliott 2006: 103).

Such is the moral repugnance for slavery felt by the overwhelming majority of those who write about it, and such is the appeal of the teleology implicit in both Marxist and Whiggish stories of emancipation, that it is tempting to underemphasize just how mutually adaptive slavery's defining practices have often been under local environmental conditions. In the case of the United States, it was an institution which had been explicitly accepted by the signatories to the Declaration of Independence, even though repudiated in the different environment of the North. The abolition of the Atlantic slave trade had no effect on a society in which the slave population had become self-sustaining.[11] Fugitives were distinguishable on sight from the free population, since black/white interaction was categorically forbidden and the manumission rate was virtually nil. Slaves had no realistic prospect of amassing a *peculium* sufficient to enable them to purchase their freedom, since the local petty economy was the preserve of the poorer whites. Nor did they have the opportunity of escaping to long-established and well-defended maroon communities as opposed to short-lived bands of runaway outlaws surviving as best they could on robbery and brigandage. Large-scale rebellion was impossible to organize, and small-scale uprisings easy to suppress. Before the war, as one historian has put it (Hahn 1990: 78), the Southern planters 'stood as one of the most – if not the most – imposing of landed elites in the Western world'. The outbreak of the war was not inevitable. Chance played its usual part. The government was initially willing to accept the continuation of slavery if the rebels would rejoin the Union. Even after hostilities had broken out, there might have been a negotiated peace. Even if the trade-off was a slower rate of growth in gross domestic product per head than that of the North, that did not preclude the continuing reproduction of slavery.

Although slaves have often been physically indistinguishable – to the annoyance of, among others, Athenian gentlemen in the time of Plato who found themselves jostled in the street – and fellow members of the same long-established society can nevertheless be condemned to out-caste status by birth,[12] the association of slavery with skin colour in the

---

[11] Slave-breeding was not unknown in Rome (Appian, *Bellum Civile* 1.1.7): slave overseers, in particular, were permitted wives and children, and there was a vernacular term for the roles of home-bred domestic slaves (*vernae*). But there is no evidence, whether literary, epigraphic, or archaeological, which would license an inference to demographic reproduction of the slave population on anything approaching the American scale. *Vernae* 'seem to have had a privileged position and not infrequently to have become their masters' heirs' (Rawson 1989: 18).

[12] As, notably, in the case of Japan's 'invisible race' (De Vos and Wagatsuma 1966) – the *Burakumin* descended from the members of residential communities attached to regional lords who were assigned the performance of occupational tasks which the mode of persuasion stigmatized as polluting. The American and Japanese anthropologists who studied them in the aftermath of the Second World War found that ordinary Japanese believed them to be dirty, dangerous, and diseased although (or precisely because) they never associated with them (Donoghue 1957).

American South was an additionally adaptive aspect of its design.[13] So too was the combination of a few deliberate concessions on the masters' terms with the twin sanctions of unrestrained physical coercion[14] and the ever-present threat of being 'sold down river'. Asked to design a set of practices which would give the institution of slavery the highest probability of ongoing reproduction in a favourable ecological and demographic environment, a reverse engineer would be likely to suggest that the slaves should be allowed to rear their own families, but not necessarily to keep them together; be given plots ostensibly of their own to tend for occasional days or hours, but remain dependent on their masters for rations; be conceded a 'freedom of the soul' (Morgan 1988: 688) which could find expression in forms of worship, speech, and dance, but be denied any opportunity of formal education; and be rewarded by modest privileges, including oversight of other slaves, for loyal service at the same time as being severely punished for disobedience. Northern denunciations of the brutality of Southern slaveowners impervious to injunctions to 'use their people well' were no more going to drive slavery to extinction than Southern denunciations of the rapacity of Northern employers exploiting their wage-labourers to the limit were going to drive to extinction the practices defining the roles constitutive of industrial capitalism. The practices which denied the slaves any countervailing power against their masters were mutually co-adaptive in all three dimensions of social space. Viewed comparatively, it was not quite the 'peculiar institution' which contemporaries frequently called it; and in the event, it was driven extinct only when the society whose peculiar institution it was had been defeated in war.

6

Yet if slavery was as adaptive as it was in the environment of the Southern United States, how did it come to be driven extinct in the Caribbean without a war despite similar selective pressures in its favour? This story has been told many times and from many different viewpoints. There are

---

[13] Contrast the situation in Peru, where freed non-whites passed where they could as dark-skinned Spaniards (Bowser 1974: 333).

[14] Masters were not free to kill their slaves at will, but the courts seldom returned a verdict of unlawful killing: the constraint was only the sanction of public opinion in local communities conscious of the risk of 'cheapening the deterrent itself' (Wyatt-Brown 1982: 372). As the ex-slave Frederick Douglass deliberately understated it in his autobiography (1855: 53), public opinion is 'not likely to be very efficient in protecting the slave from cruelty' in a rural community of slaveholding neighbours.

stories of inexorable progress towards emancipation, stories of rival inter-est-groups in pursuit of perceived short-term advantage, stories of saints and heroes routing the forces of evil, stories of an inescapable contradic-tion between slavery and capitalism, stories of emancipation 'from above', and stories of emancipation 'from below'. But when viewed from within selectionist theory, the sequence of unpredicted events through which it came about offers as striking a contrast to the story of the decline of slavery in post-Roman Europe as it does to the story of its extinc-tion in the Southern United States. Chance once again played its usual part. Abolition was favoured by unforeseen events which ranged from the American and French Revolutions and the slave uprisings in Haiti and Jamaica to the changed distribution of seats in the British House of Commons which followed the passage of the First Reform Bill by a single vote. But whatever the disagreements between rival historians over the might-have-beens, the abolitionists' success at the culmination of a protracted series of arguments and compromises depended among other things on a diffusion and reproduction of two independent cultural muta-tions which had happened to coincide.

No observer present at the Peace of Paris would have been other than surprised to be told that slavery would be condemned by the Congress of Vienna. Until the middle of the eighteenth century, abolitionist memes barely existed outside the heads of a handful of jurists or philosophers. The occasional criticisms voiced by Christian priests were no more suc-cessfully diffused and reproduced than those of their Islamic counterparts (Clarence-Smith 2006). But then there occurred a memetic mutation centred in one particular Christian sub-culture: that of the Quakers. As one historian reports two of the significant incidents in the story, 'In 1758, Philadelphia Yearly Meeting cautiously resolved to exclude from business meetings any members who subsequently bought or sold black slaves; the meeting also authorized a committee to visit Quaker slaveholders, begin-ning a quiet, charitable, and ultimately effective campaign to persuade all Friends to manumit their slaves. In 1761 London Yearly Meeting ruled that henceforth Quaker slave dealers should be disowned' (Davis 1984: 107). The speed with which this attitude was diffused among the mem-bers of other Christian denominations during the following decades is remarkable not only because it is an instance of an unexpected runaway effect but because the Quakers were not, sociologically speaking, located any higher within their society's mode of persuasion than their denomina-tional competitors. They might be admired for their piety and respected for their quietism, but they did not command the ideological resources of either the Methodists or the established Anglican church. There was no obvious reason to expect their opposition to slavery to be any more widely endorsed by other Christians than their opposition to war. But the abolitionist memes in Quaker heads were so successfully diffused among other dissenting and evangelical congregations that their phenotypic effects extended to 'recurrent bursts of petitioning on an ever larger scale' to Parliament, culminating in over 5,000 at the climax of the campaign in 1833 (Turley 1991: 65). At the same time, those same memes were carried to Jamaica, in particular by Baptist and Wesleyan missionaries from whom they spread first by direct transmission from missionary to convert and then, after a further mutation, to the expanding population of 'Native Baptists' – 'a generic term for a proliferation of sects in which the slaves developed religious forms, more or less Christian in content, that reflected their needs more closely than the orthodox churches, black or white' (Turner 1982: 58).[15] When the missionaries sent back to the readers of the Baptist and Wesleyan church magazines and the *Anti-Slavery Monthly Reporter* reports of the ill-treatment of slaves, they combined to adaptive effect both with Protestant doctrines of atonement and with anti-Catholic beliefs and attitudes of the kind whose phenotypic effects in an earlier context were discussed in Section 11 of Chapter 3.

At the same time, but for quite other reasons, slavery was coming under increasing attack from political economists in whose eyes it was short-sighted, retrograde, and wasteful. It is true that Adam Smith's objection to it was moral as well as political: he thought that it corrupted the slave-owners by gratifying their 'love to domineer'. But he and others like him believed that slaves, because they were denied any opportunity of bettering their own condition by their exertions, were bound to be less productive than wage-workers recruited in an open competitive labour market. The puzzle in this, as Smith's commentators have frequently pointed out, is that his claim in Book III of *The Wealth of Nations* that 'the experience of all ages and nations' has shown slaves to be less productive than wage-workers is supported by nothing more than three references to Pliny, Columella, and Aristotle respectively. In any case, once the slaves were freed they preferred the role of smallholder to the role of wage-worker. In Antigua and Barbados, where there was much less land available on which they could settle, the selective pressure in favour of proletarianization was

---

[15] Here, the instructive contrast is with the 'Folk Catholicism' of Spanish America (Palmer 1976: 152), which was similarly diffused among the slave population but without any equivalent condemnation of slavery as such.

for that reason stronger. But in Jamaica, the production of sugar was halved once the former slaves were fully free and not indentured (as they were for an initial four-year period following emancipation). The planters' arguments against the economists turned out to be better-founded than the abolitionists had been prepared to concede. But from a selectionist viewpoint, it is a just-so story of meme-practice co-evolution driven by indirect bias. The economists were believed not because their arguments had been tested, but because they were the people who were putting them forward and the evangelizing abolitionists were the beneficiaries of their prestige.

The comparison which the extinction of slavery in the British Caribbean then invites is its abolition in Brazil, where abolitionists were increasingly successful in the years up to the formal legislation enacted in 1880 in encouraging local slaveowners to manumit. The memes in the Brazilian abolitionists' heads were, however, not at all the same as those in the heads of their British and North American predecessors. After the Brazilian government's belated decision, under British pressure, to suppress the Atlantic slave trade on which replacement of Brazil's 2½ million slaves depended, members of the Brazilian elite 'imbibed [in the authors' chosen metaphor for memetic transmission] liberal values with undiluted enthusiasm' (Cain and Hopkins 1993: 300). But their motive was to preserve their standing and therewith their creditworthiness in the eyes of the British government and the City of London and to be perceived as 'modernizers'. The Brazilian planters had no choice but to acquiesce in emancipation when faced not only with the cutting-off of the supply of slaves but with 'decentralized direct action' (Drescher 1988: 45) by slaves migrating en masse from the plantations to 'free zones'. Compared to the planters of the American South, they were at a double disadvantage: the much more widespread practice of manumission had narrowed the ideological distance between dark-skinned slaves and free whites, and the planters lacked the means of coercion available to their counterparts in the American South (or Rome in the time of Spartacus) which would have enabled them to hunt down and kill or re-enslave the fugitives. The evolution of the Brazilian mode of production out of near-total reliance on slavery in regions where it was based on sugar or coffee to one based on wage-labour (including immigrants from Europe as well as native-born Brazilians) was, when it occurred, as rapid as its occurrence had been unforeseen by the members of the first post-colonial governments. There had not, as in Mexico and Peru, been a history of extensive recruitment of the surviving indigenous Indian population into wage-labour through the practices and roles which created the institutions of *repartimiento* and *mita*. The practices by which Brazilian slavery was defined were doomed to extinction in a way that had applied neither to the Caribbean nor to the Southern United States. The selective pressures which doomed them are easily discernible in hindsight: the story I have briefly summarized is not, so far as I am aware, controversial among present-day historians of Brazil. But it demonstrates once again just how differently the common underlying process of heritable variation and competitive selection of information affecting phenotype can work to produce the same evolutionary outcome in different local environments.

7

It is, accordingly, because of the diversity of practices which fall between slavery and other forms of domination, not because slavery is a predetermined stage in a teleological progression out of 'ancient' through 'feudal' to 'modern' society, that the just-so story of the evolution of the modes of production, persuasion, and coercion of the societies of post-Roman Europe is as instructive for comparative sociology as it is. The starting-point is an environment in which plantation-type chattel slavery like that of the Caribbean or the Southern United States was confined to a relatively few areas in certain parts of Italy, Southern Gaul, and Sicily: as one historian has put it, the system expounded by Cato, Columella, and Varro, rather than driving to extinction the practices of smallholding and tenancy, 'filled a gap' in Italian agriculture (Rathbone 1983: 162). It is not in dispute among historians of Rome that there was a large-scale importation of slaves in the period following the Punic Wars. But the slaves were distributed across the whole civilian labour force. They included the unproductive retinues of domestic servants in the households of the rich, the possessors of marketable skills buying their freedom in instalments, the servile government functionaries of the emperors' households, and the incumbents of quasi-professional roles such as supervisor, secretary, architect, and doctor. Numbers of successful escapees[16] are even less possible to calculate than manumissions. But there were always some of both. Weber's arresting simile of the Roman economy devouring human beings as a blast furnace devours coal is misleading twice over: slaves were not

---

[16] Including those who made collusive bargains with a slave-catcher by using either their *peculium* or stolen goods (Daube 1952).

to that degree the fuel on which its per capita output depended, and they were not to that degree systematically worked to death.[17] But the proportion of slaves in the population as a whole may well have been comparable to that in the Caribbean and the Southern United States, and its decline has to be explained as a part, although only a part, of the just-so story of the evolution of the modes of production, persuasion, and coercion of the societies of post-Roman Europe.

After the fall (if that metaphor is the right one) of the Roman Empire in the West, there was nowhere a Quaker-like cultural mutation which substituted abolitionist memes for the long-held acceptance that one person could legitimately be held at the total disposal of another. Men and women still designated as *servi*, *ancillae*, or *mancipia* were still bought and sold, listed alongside livestock and tools in testamentary dispositions, denied freedom of movement, forbidden to marry whom they pleased, and subjected to punishments of a degrading kind. The change was that the practices defining their roles became increasingly negotiable as the roles constitutive of the institutions of the Roman state lost the control of the means of coercion which had previously attached to them. The 'slaves' began to have goods whose use they fully controlled, homes which they could call their own, and wives who were recognized as such.[18] Their entitlement to days off work began to be publicly recognized. They began to receive perquisites which acquired the sanction of local custom. Their roles were still located close to the apex of the inverted pyramid of economic, ideological, and political power. But a 'slave' who is institutionally accorded a customary right is no longer wholly unfree.

When the different evolutionary trajectories of the different societies which emerged in the territories of Italy, France, Germany, England, and Spain are contrasted with one another, the underlying theme which emerges is the simultaneous decline in the numbers of the wholly unfree and increase in the rate of mutation of the practices defining the roles of the relatively freer. This emphasis may result in part from the nature

---

[17] Ironically, Weber's simile could more aptly be applied in his own country a generation after his death to the roles of the slave labourers in the underground 'Central Works' of Nazi Germany during World War II (Speer 1970: 500). Death rates may, however, have been as high (that is, in the German case, up to 4 per cent per month) in the slave-worked mines of Roman Spain (Diodorus Siculus V.38), as also in the gold and silver mines of Hispanic America and Brazil.

[18] This last was true also – or appeared to be true – of Brazilian slavery, where the *Constituições primeiras* published in Lisbon in 1719 required slaveowners to allow slaves to marry 'without hindrance or threat' (Schwartz 1985: 385). But slave unions could be broken at any time by separate sale at the owner's whim.

of the documentary sources, particularly the records of disputes between landholders and their tenants preserved by the landholders for self-interested reasons of their own. But the general impression which they leave is of societies in which roles are being renegotiated all the time in all three dimensions of social space, with the courts being 'used within strategies of social negotiation' (Fouracre 2005: 49; cf. e.g. Goetz 1993: 42) which are themselves competitively selected as the environment changes. The practices defining the roles of the minimally free, the half free, the tacitly free, and the formally freed are subject to constant mutation despite the social distance between lords and their inferiors in economic, ideological, and political power alike. In the mode of production, not only the rent-payers but the dependents rendering services on the demesnes of bipartite estates are doing their day's work according to customary formulae: corvée labour is compulsory, but corvée labourers are not slaves whose obligations are limited only by the amount of work that can be extracted from them by force. In the mode of persuasion, even *mancipia* 'subject to total economic and legal subjection', are, as a historian of the middle Rhine valley has put it, 'also seen as moral actors in their own right' (Innes 2000: 79). In the mode of coercion, although rebellion would be met outright with military repression, *concilia* or *coniurationes* might secure concessions by which open resistance would be averted. The 'speaking tools' (*instrumenta vocalia*) of the Roman jurists, for whom the law was nothing other than their master's will, can now act in defence of their status as persons, however limited the countervailing power attaching to their modified roles remains.[19]

The mutations of practices which generated the new institutional relationships between the members of the dominant systacts and their vassals, clients, soldiers, tenants, retainers, administrators, bailiffs, tenurial serfs, personal serfs, landless labourers, domestic workers, and the town-dwelling merchants and artisans with whom they also dealt were little influenced by the memetic mutations which were taking place alongside them. There were many of these which can be as readily identified and traced as mutations of practices. Beliefs and attitudes about the creation and application of wealth, about the criteria of social prestige, and about the use and misuse of the means of coercion were being actively reinterpreted all the time. The ongoing story of European

---

[19] A critical difference was that 'being sold along with landed property, however the conveyancing was formulated, had nothing like the personal consequences of being sold and transported. The one kept family and humanity; the other did not' (W. Davies 1996: 246).

Christianity is full of passionate doctrinal controversies. But it was not the Church which designed the role-maps of the societies within which its own institutional structures evolved. On the contrary, the Church reflected them. Acceptance of equality before God and expectation of a life to come were quite consistent with acquiescence in economic, ideological, and political inequality in this one. Slaves might be manumitted as acts of personal piety, but slavery as such was never condemned as unacceptable to God and ecclesiastical foundations were as jealous as any lay lord of the powers which they sought to retain over their dependants both servile and free. For the abbots and bishops, the trade-off was between total control of the labour of the servile and extraction of tithes and scot from the freed. Monasteries and nunneries mirrored in their internal organization the hierarchies of the outside world. In contrast to the just-so story told in Section 5, the selective pressures which determined the relations between topmost and lowermost roles in post-Roman Europe were overwhelmingly social, not cultural. In this environment, the drivers of meme-practice co-evolution were the practices, not the memes.

Sociological comparisons between post-Roman Italy, France, Germany, England, and Spain (Wickham 2005) are complicated by the difficulty that the best-documented regional just-so stories are often constructed from within national historiographical traditions which presuppose that one must be the model of which the others are variants. Thus, the controversies surrounding the paradigm of *seigneurie banale* and *mauvaises coutumes* imposed by castellated lords after the *mutation de l'an mil* – if such there really was (Barthélemy 1997) – are in part a function of a longstanding disagreement between French and other historians about whether what happened in the territory ruled, or at any rate claimed, by Charles the Bold can be generalized as a pan-European evolution. But the sociology of the Ile de France is not at all the same as that of the West or South, to say nothing of the sociology of Catalonia or Latium. The institutional vacuum left by the collapse of Roman power offers an exceptionally favourable opportunity to observe the process of social selection in operation in different ways as different populations moved into the social as well as geographical spaces now open to them. One society, in particular, offers what Bloch himself (1961: 181) called 'the most precious of examples – that of a society of Germanic structure which, till the end of the eleventh century, preserved an almost completely spontaneous course of evolution': Anglo-Saxon England.

8

The social space that the Romans left behind them after their evacuation of Britain was more nearly empty than anywhere except Iceland, where people similar to those who raided and sometimes settled in England moved into a totally unpopulated territory and created a feud-riven society of independent slave-owning farmers loosely united under the ideological leadership of their priests. Although the archaeological record reveals some continuity of occupation of Roman villa-sites, it is a long time before there is evidence of elaborate artefacts, large buildings, or extensive trade; and although the indigenous British population was neither exterminated nor expelled by the incomers, institutional survivals other than a few churches and burial-grounds are hard to find. The roles and institutions of 'late' Anglo-Saxon society evolved out of centuries of near-continuous raids, invasions, conquests, and reconquests within a mode of production in which 'the plough is king' (J. H. Round, quoted by Lennard 1959: 350), a mode of persuasion controlled (despite some obstinate pagan survivals) by a Roman rather than a Celtic Church, and a mode of coercion in which armies of high-ranking leaders and their subordinate foot-soldiers, supported by unarmed auxiliaries, fought each other with swords, axes, lances, daggers, javelins, and spears. England was not impervious to the lateral transfer of both memes and practices from the societies of continental Europe: the imitation of Frankish styles in female dress and jewelry is as well attested as the adoption of Frankish-style consecration by anointment of a royal heir, and in areas of Danish occupation and settlement manorial practices are much less in evidence than further West. But social selection can be observed at work across half a millennium in a society whose just-so story, for all the resemblances between its constituent roles and those of the other post-Roman European societies, was very much its own.

The starting-point is an environment of small tribal kingdoms – 'kingdoms', since they are headed by acknowledged leaders who, as I remarked in Section 1, are not 'big-men' but rulers who, in Sahlins' phrase, have come *to* power; and 'tribal', since relations of kindred are critical both to the acknowledgement of common social identity and to the maintenance of order. Out of these there evolved through a combination of aggregation and aggrandizement (Bassett 1989) a society which, as I remarked in Section 5 of Chapter 1, was in many ways similar, despite the obvious differences in ecology and climate, to Hammurabi's Babylonia. It had in broad terms the kind of four-tiered systactic structure which convergent evolution has brought into being at countless times and places. At the top was an elite of kings, nobles, and both secular and ecclesiastical landholders to whose roles there attached a near-monopoly of economic, ideological, and political power. At the bottom were the mendicants, outlaws, prisoners, and slaves: an estimated ten to twelve per cent of the population of England were slaves at the time of the Norman Conquest (Moore 1998), not in the houses of the rich or the administrative offices of the king, but on the rural properties of non-noble *ceorls* as well as of bishops, abbots, and *thegns*. Above these were the dependent agricultural tenants, the smallholders, the craftsmen, the servants, the men-at-arms, the shepherds and swineherds, the fowlers, the bakers, the salters, the blacksmiths, the millers, and the occasional wage-workers (*hyrmen* or *hyringmanna*). But above these, and below the elite, there evolved out of the roles of the warrior companions of the early tribal kings the roles of the adjutant administrators and officials on whom the incumbents of the topmost roles came increasingly to depend. Alongside the burgesses, merchants, lesser clergy, and country gentlemen (Gillingham 1995) are the 'riding-men', the *drengs*, *geneats*, and *radcnihts* whose roles involve the performance of services for their lords which are not, in the ideological dimension of power, degrading. The role of reeve (*gerefa*) becomes increasingly ubiquitous: there are king's reeves and high-reeves and village-reeves and port-reeves and toll-reeves and wapentake-reeves and reeves charged with the collection of tithes and scot and reeves paying *hyrmen* their wages, and reeves responsible for the execution of convicted criminals. It is a story in which the careers of the leading protagonists, dramatic as they often are, are incidental to the selective pressures which, as the society's total resources continued to expand, brought into being a growing systact of roles empowered to oversee their use. But there are, at the same time, three things which it is *not* a just-so story of.

To a comparative sociologist who comes to the historiography of Anglo-Saxon England from outside, the long debate between the partisans of a 'manorial' model on one side and a 'peasant proprietor' model on the other is puzzling. A story of rapid and wide-ranging exploitation by seigneurial lords of unarmed and impecunious villeins is as implausible as a story of a rapid and wide-ranging entrenchment of democratically organized bands of free warriors holding their acreages (or 'hides') under no superior other than their elected kings. The *ceorls* of the sources for the early kingdoms were clearly men of some substance with rights in ploughland, meadows, and woods and dependents of their own.[20] But what went on thereafter

---

[20] The laws of Ine, from whose text generations of historians have sought to squeeze every possible semi- or quasi-deductive inference, are unequivocal both about the possession by lords of estates on which they have tenants who owe them rent or labour (in marked contrast to contemporary

varied in accordance with the different selective pressures which came to bear in the different environments of different regions. By the time of the Norman Conquest, there are numerous manors of the kind depicted in the memorandum on estate management known as *Rectitudines Singularum Personarum*. But that document comes from Bath (Harvey 1993) – a by no means typical area where there had long been opportunities for building up large estates divided between a directly exploited 'inland', which 'was recognized as privileged, in the sense of being exempt from a wide range of public service and eventually from the payment of geld', and an outer 'warland' liable to *geld* from whose inhabitants public rather than private obligations were due (Faith 1997: 16).[21] Manorial inlands are characteristic particularly of ecclesiastical estates worked by substantial numbers of monks or 'semi-monastic personnel' (Blair 2005: 255) whose roles are not easily distinguishable from those of other unfree tenants whose labour generates the surpluses on which the minster depends for the support of its unproductive members and its expenditure on new land and new buildings, and the acquisition of prestige goods. There is little doubt that extraction of surpluses and imposition of services intensified under both lay and ecclesiastical ownership. But there are large areas of England, both within and outside of the Danelaw, where manorial practices had hardly penetrated by the time of the Conquest – remote uplands with scattered farmsteads and hamlets, settlements newly carved out of woodland and waste, regions of partible inheritance and jointly held family farms, regions where rent-paying *censarii* perform minimal labour services, villages subordinated to no single lord, regions where *agrarii milites* are needed for the purpose of defence, and regions where sheepfarming by prosperous sokemen supplements the produce of ploughlands. Behind the variegated pattern of landholding in different local environments and the histories (to the extent that they can be reconstructed) of different individual estates, there is a general trend away from the tributary mode of production of the early tribal kingdoms in the direction of rent (*gafol*) and tax (*geld*). But it is a trend within which some large estates were built up while others fragmented, some *ceorls* acquired enough land to rank

---

Ireland, where the adaptive practice was clientship rather than tenancy) and about the relations with one another of independent *ceorls* with their own households, cattle, ploughs, and shares in common woods and meadows. In the laws of Aethelbert, King of Kent, it is explicitly envisaged that a *ceorl* may have his own 'loaf-eater' (*hlafaeta*), and the payment due to him if someone kills his loaf-eater is the same as that due to him from the first of several intruders who force their way into his homestead (Liebermann 1903: 4).

21 Roffe (1990: 317) draws attention to the 'elaborate calligraphic conventions' adopted to distinguish tributary from demesne land in *Domesday Book*.

as *thegns* while some lesser *thegns* were left with manors barely deserving of the name, and some dependent cultivators were confined to smaller and smaller holdings while others were able to purchase their freedom of movement in land or cash. Land was constantly changing hands not only by inheritance, usurpation, or bequest but in an active sale and leasing market (in which the surviving wills show women as well as men participating directly), and new territories were being settled or resettled at the same time that established holdings were being more systematically organized and exploited to better effect.

Surprising also to a comparative sociologist is the popularity among Anglo-Saxon historians of a third just-so story: that of the progressive evolution of a strong central state. 'State', like 'institution', has generated unhelpfully many definitional disagreements in the literature of sociology, and there is always scope under any definition for alternative views about how the strength of a state is to be assessed. In selectionist theory, a society is a 'state' if and only if institutional control of the means of coercion attaches to specialized extra-familial roles in which rulers and their associated deputies and officials succeed one another on a regular basis: a state is not a state, any more than an empire is an empire, if it does not outlast the death of its founder and the charismatic legitimacy attaching to the founder's person. The practices which defined the roles of the late Anglo-Saxon kings made them significantly more powerful than their itinerant predecessors dependent, along with their retinues, on the food-rents drawn from the different parts of their shires. They had 'the first regular and permanent land-tax known to the West in the Middle Ages' (Loyn 1962: 305) which they could on occasion use their troops to collect (Campbell 2000: 227); they controlled a coinage which was both sophisticated and flexible and enabled them to benefit directly from new issues (Lawson 1993: 197); they could call up fighting-men for *expeditiones regum* on something approaching a national scale; and their administration of justice extended down through the holders of sake and soke to the hundreds and wapentakes. But they failed the standard sociological test: they did not sufficiently control the means of coercion across the territory occupied by those who acknowledged their titular roles. Theirs was, in Weberian terminology, a 'patrimonial' state in which the assessment and collection of tax, the recruitment of soldiers and auxiliaries, and the apprehension and punishment of malefactors were in the hands of ealdormen, abbots, bishops, and *thegns* whose roles were no more those of a service nobility than they were those of a salaried bureaucracy. The kings are careful to consult them as *seniores* or *sapientes* whenever royal initiatives are in prospect. Although the justice which they administer is the king's justice, they can draw profit from doing so directly. A king can be deposed, and the witan can choose one aspirant over another. The kings have no corps of informants and spies reporting to them. They cannot be certain that their subordinates will fulfil their obligations to keep bridges and fortifications in repair or discipline the lawless men of their districts as they are supposed to do. Their law-codes are statements of aspiration as much as of fact.[22] They have not abolished the feud and they cannot enforce payment of compensation in place of killings in revenge. There are no royal burghs north of York. There are *villani* too rich to be punished.[23] The kings are acknowledged as rulers of all England, but the unity of the kingdom is more ideological than either economic or political. Maitland was right to remark as he did that it was their splendour which had grown more than their power.

There is no way of knowing how English society would have evolved without the Norman Conquest, any more than there is of knowing how the American South would have evolved without its defeat by the North. But to a selectionist sociologist trying to detect just what was going on up until 1066, the two distinctive features of Anglo-Saxon England's modes of production, persuasion, and coercion are, first, the diversity of the roles constitutive of them, and second, the extent of both inter- and intra-generational social mobility between those roles. Mobility rates do not in themselves constitute a modal difference between one society and another: individuals can rise and fall in all three dimensions of social space without their movement having any effect on the practices which define the roles between which they move. But institutional sanctions against any possibility of mobility do constitute a modal difference: if in the mode of production sons are compelled to follow their father's occupations, or in the mode of persuasion members of a stigmatized status-group can escape from their origins only by 'passing', or in the mode of coercion participation in political decision-making is forbidden to any member of the population who is not a citizen by birth or formal decree, their relationship with the incumbents of the other roles by which their society is constituted will be qualitatively different as a result. In Anglo-Saxon

---

[22] Of them all, the one whose sanctions are least convincing is King Edgar's, promulgated some time between 959 and 963 (Liebermann 1903: 194–207). How often are we to believe that a late payer of 'St Peter's pence' took it to Rome in person and paid 120 shillings to the king on his return, or a judge who made an unjust judgement paid the king 120 shillings, or a willing buyer and willing seller of wool at other than the prescribed price paid the king 60 shillings each?

[23] As explicitly admitted in a letter from the bishops and 'wise men' of Kent to King Athelstan (Liebermann 1903: 170).

England, the social distance between economic, ideological, and political roles steadily widened as the ongoing mutation and renegotiation of practices brought into being the systactic structure outlined above. But the gradations between roles were close and the possibility of movement from one to another was always open. However it is to be classified, it was emphatically not a society of castes.

Sociologists calculating mobility rates for present-day industrial societies from survey and census data are familiar with the combination of an increase in the proportion of high-ranking roles occupied by entrants from below with the absence of a corresponding increase in the chances of individuals born to lower-ranking parents rising into higher-ranking roles. 'Structural' mobility increases because of the expanding number of higher-ranking roles needing to be filled, but there is little 'exchange' mobility in which downwardly mobile individuals born to higher-ranking parents are directly replaced from below. But in Anglo-Saxon England there is plentiful evidence for both in all three dimensions of social space. Not only did large landowners need skilled assistants, but an expanding Church needed literate priests and local lords needed experienced warriors who would – however unreliably – pledge fealty (Abels 1988: 153). At the same time, downwardly mobile *thegns* were being replaced by upwardly mobile sokemen, 'unhappy ex-clerks' (John 1977: 180) were being replaced by better-educated (*gelaeredum*) novices, and slaves (according to Archbishop Wulfstan) were running away to the Vikings and enslaving the *thegns* who had been their masters. If, at the time of the Conquest, some three-quarters of the English population were in the roles of *villani*, *cottarii*, or *bordarii* (with almost all women taking 'secondary rank', in the technical sociological sense, from men), only a very small proportion of them could hope to rise above their systact of birth. But the roles above theirs were not all being filled by individuals born at that level. Moreover, of those who remained *villani* some were becoming significantly richer than others in land or plough-teams, some enjoyed higher prestige than others as witnesses and compurgators, and some were better able than others to defend themselves against predators or, as it might be, the agents of royal justice. These differences evolved out of the different practices negotiated by subordinates with their superiors[24] in an environment of endemic violence, intense competition for control of land, and a decline

---

[24] The way in which *gesith*, as the vernacular term for a companion rather than servant, 'fights a losing battle against *thegn*' from the beginning of the tenth century (Loyn 1955: 530) is directly symptomatic of the mutation of practices defining the relationship of nobles to kings.

in wergild as the criterion of status in favour of the nature of services performed and the life-style that went with them. To say that it was a society in constant flux is to restate the obvious. What is remarkable about what was going on is that it was a society in which the roles constitutive of its changing economic, ideological, and political institutions could be occupied by individuals moving into them from other systactic origins without the constraints which might have been expected to keep them within their systact of origin – *gesithcund* children of nobles as nobles, *ceorls* as children of *ceorls*, and children of slaves as slaves.

Once again, therefore, as so often in just-so stories of social selection, it is what wasn't going on which is as instructive as what was. To look behind the rhetoric of the law-codes, the questionable reliability of the narrative sources (Bede's *Ecclesiastical History* included), the terminology of the haphazardly surviving wills, charters, letters, and writs, the hints embedded in contemporary literature (Aelfric's *Colloquy* or the homilies of Wulfstan no less than *Beowulf* or *The Battle of Maldon*), and the tantalizing ambiguities and inconsistencies of *Domesday Book* to the practices which defined the society's roles is to be struck by the absence of inter-systactic conflict, whether between economic classes, ideological status-groups, or political factions. There are no peasant revolts or collective withdrawals of labour, no heretical churches or millenarian sects, no revolutionary uprisings or breakaway states. England, as its historians have often observed, was by 1066 an old society, and by then a very different one from what it had been half a millennium before. But its evolution had been gradual, for all the relentless competition within it for economic, ideological, and political power. What, therefore, is the wider implication to be drawn for comparative sociology? Does that make it an exception, or a rule?

INCREMENTAL MUTATIONS
AND PUNCTUATED EQUILIBRIA

9

Biologists have disagreed ever since Darwin about whether natural selection proceeds more, as Darwin thought, by a protracted sequence of gradual changes or by long stretches of stability punctuated by occasional abrupt leaps. To comparative sociologists for whom examples of both gradual and sudden change come easily to mind, it may be surprising that the disagreement among biologists should be as vehement as it has been.

Don't natural, cultural, and social selection all proceed at different speeds under different environmental conditions? But there is a larger question at issue. It may be that there can be listed specific antecedents of crises, breakdowns, and upheavals which make major transformations of social institutions more likely. But practices have a capacity to reproduce themselves for longer periods, and with fewer and smaller mutations, than contemporary observers expect. Contemporary observers, however well informed, are as capable of convincing themselves either that nothing has changed, institutionally speaking, when in fact it has as that a revolutionary social transformation has taken place when in fact it hasn't. As always, it is the practices, not the people, on which the attention of sociologists as opposed to historians needs to be fixed.

'Revolution' is yet another word which neither sociologists nor historians are able to do without but which, like 'nationalism' and 'feudalism', means too many different things to different people. Defined as the sudden replacement of one set of practices and therefore roles by another which is sufficiently pervasive and sufficiently lasting for all observers to agree that the society has evolved out of one mode of production, persuasion, or coercion into another, 'revolutionary' change can be driven either from below or from above, and imposed either from without or from within. But it is more than a phase in a recurring cycle of practices, and more than the replacement of one set of incumbents of existing roles by another. The mutant practices have to be identified, their transmission traced, and their adaptedness accounted for. That the makers of revolutions can set in train events whose consequences are not merely different from, but contrary to, their stated aims is a historical commonplace. But the phrase 'punctuated equilibrium' captures the distinction between qualitative change which results from a steady, ongoing renegotiation of practices and qualitative change which results from near-instantaneous jumps within a three-dimensional institutional design-space. Some mutations in heritable information affecting phenotype are more revolutionary than others, and selectionist sociologists need to find out just what is going on when they are.

Of all the revolutions in the historical record, the one which at first sight looks closest to the ideal type of a rapid, comprehensive, and prospectively lasting institutional transformation is the Bolivian Revolution of April 1952. After three days of fighting, a textbook alliance of middle-class radicals, mineworkers, and peasants under the leadership of an avowedly revolutionary party defeated the government in power and the army supporting it. Thereafter, control of the means of coercion was handed over to civilian militias; the Indian population was accorded the ideological equality of status it had long been denied; and hacienda land was handed over to peasant syndicates at the same time that control of the mines was handed over to the government-controlled *Corporacíon Minera de Bolivia*. But there were no mutations or recombinations of practices sufficient to transform the roles constitutive of the modes of production, persuasion, or coercion of Bolivian society. The army was reconstituted. The peasants were concerned above all with holding title to the land they had taken, and the supply of food to the cities was so far reduced that the government became dependent on large-scale imports funded by the United States. The *hacendados* were replaced by syndicate bosses, but if they remained (as many did) they continued to perform the functions necessary for commercial agricultural production and marketing. The mineworkers continued to sell their labour for wages under similar conditions of employment. The members of the urban middle class suffered a drastic reduction in the value of their property as a consequence of devaluation of the currency, but they were not dispossessed. The ex-*hacendados* no longer enjoyed the personal services which the practice of *pongueaje* had imposed on the Indians on their estates,[25] but patronage roles, and associated expectations of services from clients and their families, passed to the bosses of the local *sindicados*. To sociologists whose interest is in the roles rather than their incumbents, the interesting question is why the practices which revolutionaries are determined to drive extinct are, as in this case, so often capable of survival and ongoing reproduction nevertheless. And that applies not least to what is, to many historians, 'the' revolution – the one which in 1789 dismantled the institutions of what thereby became, almost literally overnight, France's *'ancien régime'*. As a topic in selectionist sociology, the French Revolution offers an almost ideal-typical case-study of a punctuated equilibrium whose evolutionary outcome was as paradoxical as its occurrence had been unforeseen.

10

Not even those historians of France who believe that the *ancien régime* was doomed to inevitable extinction will dispute the conclusion of Georges Lefebvre that the Revolution required a 'truly extraordinary

---

[25] *Pongueaje* had, ironically, been formally abolished in 1945 by Gualberto Villaroel, who was to be hanged by the mob from a lamp post outside the presidential palace in the following year. But the decree was never put into force (Klein 1982: 219).

and unforeseeable (*vraiment extraordinaire et imprévisible*) combination of immediate causes' (1954: 247). The many might-have-beens in the sequence of events which culminated in the measures passed by the Constituent Assembly on the night of 4 August 1789 extend all the way from the decisions which led to the defeat of the French by the Prussian army at Rossbach on 5 November 1757 to the decisions which led to the withdrawal of the troops from the streets of Paris on the evening of 12 July 1789.[26] All historians of the period agree that the conduct of Louis XVI introduced a random disturbance into a sequence which would have been very different without him. Lefebvre was as ready as any other to concede that matters would have turned out otherwise if the throne had been occupied by '*un Henri IV, ou même un Louis XIV*' (1939: 29). Had Louis XVI been willing in 1787 to allow a commission of auditors to oversee the government's management of its finances, or had he allowed a vote on the registration of new loans at the royal session of the *Parlement* of Paris held on 19 November of that year, or had he agreed to announce at the royal session of the Estates-General on 23 June 1789 that the three orders could deliberate and vote in common, or had he not timed his dismissal of Necker so that the news of it broke on a Sunday (which meant that, although the Assembly wasn't sitting, the working population was free to riot), there would have been no fall of the Bastille on the 14th.[27] But the king would not have been faced with the choices which it fell to him to take if there had not been the chance conjunction of the worst harvest in living memory with the collapse of the government's ability to borrow money. It is true that bad harvests, and a consequential rise in the price of bread to the point of provoking public disorder, were a perennial risk which every eighteenth-century government faced. It is also true that the parlous state of the government's finances had been known since at least the summer of 1786. But on no theory can it plausibly be hypothesized that there was a predetermined connection between the two. Both were the outcome of sequences of cause and effect which historians of the period have analysed in detail. But to a sociologist, their conjunction was

---

[26] We shall never know what might have happened if, at a council of war held by the King on the morning of 16 July, Marshal de Broglie had not repeated his view of the previous day that the attitude of the troops precluded any hope of military operations against Paris. But we do know that at Rennes on the following day, the troops of the Artois and Lorraine Infantry and Orléans Dragoons refused to obey the order of the military commander of the city to fire on the crowd (Scott 1978: 60, 70).

[27] Nor, in any case, need the Bastille have fallen then. Even in the orthodox Marxist account given by Godechot (1965: 271), it is conceded that 'a determined commander (*un chef résolu*)' could have held out against the attackers.

as much a random intrusion into the course of social evolution as is, to a biologist, a sudden climate change which alters what would otherwise have been the evolution of an animal species.

Once, accordingly, the equilibrium of the *ancien régime* had been punctuated, the three-dimensional institutional design space open to invasion by mutant practices expanded on an accelerating scale. But the scope which it offered for liberty, equality, and fraternity was much less than that slogan implies. The royal exchequer was bankrupt and tax-collection had been brought to a standstill, but the economy continued to function and to favour the propertied over the propertyless. The ideological domination of the monarchy had been fatally undermined, but ascriptive distinctions of social status survived. The means of coercion were no longer in the monopoly control of the king and his ministers, but they were still deployed by the incumbents of roles to which there attached effective command over bureaucrats, soldiers, and police.[28] Although there was, despite violent opposition in some parts of France, no successful counter-revolution, it turned out that for all the ambition of its leaders and the fervour of their followers, the Revolution changed far less in the economic, ideological, or political institutions of French society than its supporters had expected and its opponents had feared.

If a comparison is drawn in terms of the institutional differences still visible a decade after the equilibrium was punctuated, France in 1799 was more different from France in 1789 than Bolivia in 1962 from Bolivia in 1952, although less different than either Russia in 1927 from Russia in 1917 or China in 1959 from China in 1949. Detailed regional studies have shown that what went on in those years and thereafter was far from the same across the whole of France. Indeed, by the time that the electoral geography of twentieth-century France could be plotted by political sociologists, the pattern of voting was found to reflect many of the same regional differences that had been discernible in and after 1789. But no historian goes so far as to claim that the systactic location of the nobility as it had been in 1789 was ever again the same. Seigneurial rights and revenues were never restored; the same degree of deference was never accorded to status derived solely from birth; and political careers remained open to aspirants who laid no claim to nobility. The change was not merely cyclical, and it did not merely involve the upward and downward mobility

---

[28] It is symptomatic that, for example, the Convention should have re-established coercive control over the itinerant book-selling *colporteurs* as soon as they were suspected of peddling counter-revolutionary material (Hemmings 1987: 97).

of individual incumbents between roles. There is no need for either historians or sociologists to start disputing among themselves whether the French Revolution was 'really' a revolution. But what makes it of particular interest for selectionist sociology is that many of the mutant practices which emerged from it turned out to be maladaptive, and many of those which turned out to be adaptive would have been favoured by changes in their environment which were happening in any event.

In the mode of production, although substantial amounts of previously noble- or church-owned land changed hands, it did not pass to the members of what would thereby have constituted a new class of independent peasant proprietors. Many nobles recovered at least some of the hectares they had lost, even if they might have to borrow extensively in order to do so. The practices defining the familiar roles of cultivators, proprietors, tenants, sharecroppers, smallholders, and landless agricultural labourers and servants continued to be reproduced in the countryside as before. So, in the towns and cities, did those defining the roles of the industrial and commercial employers, the financiers, the independent professionals, and the wage-earning employees (including the numerous domestic servants). Industrial workers were still required to carry their pass-books (*livrets*),[29] and their attempts at collective organization in pursuit of improved wages and conditions were still denied legitimacy. Taxes continued to be levied in much the same way as under the *ancien régime*: in the words of one historian, 'the Revolution had done little more than give them new names. The *taille* became the *impôt foncier*, the *capitation* became the *personnelle-mobilière*, the *droits de jurande* were transformed into the *patente*' (Zeldin 1973: I, 710). Successive generations of young men and women continued to succeed each other as before in roles constitutive of a formally free market in commodities and labour.

In the mode of persuasion, the immediate impact of the Revolution was observable in the disappearance of deferential forms of address, the ostentatious wearing of revolutionary clothes, the decapitation of statues, the pulling-down of churches or their conversion to stables or workshops, and the pillaging of libraries and archives. The phenotypic effects of the new ideology included marriages of priests and nuns and abjuration of clerical offices, as well as the imposed substitution of Revolutionary for Catholic rituals, reform of the calendar, and the replacement of the priest by the schoolmaster as the moral preceptor of the young. Yet the extent

---

[29] Although employers were frequently ready, as might be expected, to take on workers *sans papiers* (Kaplan 1979: 54).

and depth of popular hostility to dechristianization, even in the absence of organized clerical leadership, is as striking as the furious iconoclasm of the *armées révolutionnaires*.[30] It is, as remarked by one historian, a 'remarkable expression of the enduring force of popular religiosity' that 'hundreds of communities which had lost their priests replaced them with laymen, sometimes humble artisans or peasants, often former parochial schoolmasters and other church assistants, who could perform the ceremonies that tradition required' (Andress 2004: 253). Not only were priests who refused to take the loyalty oath sheltered and protected from arrest, but priests who did take it were ostracized and sometimes assaulted. Although the clergy, like the nobility, never reoccupied its systactic location of 1789, on no theory does the sociology of nineteenth-century France reflect a fulfilment of the Revolutionaries' proclaimed objectives in the ideological dimension of social space. Quite apart from the continuing hold of the Catholic Church over the means of persuasion, the standard sociological indicators – commensalism and endogamy – reveal a pattern of relationships between higher- and lower-ranking status-groups which would have been immediately familiar to any survivor from the *ancien régime*. The roles of financier, landlord, trader, manufacturer, and salaried professional constituted not only a capitalist class but a bourgeois status-group which excluded not only women but 'petty' bourgeois (Harrison 1999: 224) and was firmly located above the general body of workers and peasants whom the Revolutionary pamphleteers had initially included with them in the Third Estate.

In the mode of coercion, the practices which proved adaptive were those which attached increasing power to the roles of the agents of central government. Whatever the expectations of those revolutionaries who believed, or claimed to believe, in direct democracy, a minimal state, and open access to elective office, the selective pressures arising out of domestic unrest and war against foreign enemies favoured bureaucratic practices over those which had defined the roles of *officiers* and *commissionaires* under the *ancien régime*. But at both the higher and the lower levels of the new civil service 'administrative stratification' was 'closely connected to social distinctions' (Church 1981: 203), just as it was for military careers. Selection by merit as assessed in the competitive examinations set up in the course of the Revolution was perfunctory. Personal patronage and

---

[30] As is the *'rapidité incroyable'* of the runaway diffusion of dechristianizing memes, and therewith desacralizing festivals and masquerades, all over France within the same fortnight in 1792 (Bianchi 1987: 231).

family connections remained as useful as they always had been. The fitful extension of the suffrage, which at first included only a miniscule proportion of the total adult male population of France, did not transfer political power to *le peuple*, as opposed to giving rhetorical legitimacy to those who acted in its name. Despite the importance of women in the events of the Revolution, they were not enfranchised until 1945.

None of this is, so far as I am aware, controversial. But the conclusion to which it points is that from a sociological, as opposed to a historical, perspective the Revolution was in a double sense unnecessary. It would not have occurred at all without an extraordinary conjunction of chance events and of decisions, or failures to take decisions, on the part of individual agents whose characters and temperaments would in other circumstances have had no impact on the evolution of France's modes of production, persuasion, or coercion. At the same time, the changes in these which did take place over the course of the nineteenth century were the outcome of mutations and combinations of practices which would have been selected in any case. It is not, therefore, a question of choosing between a just-so story of gradual change and a just-so story of sudden transformation. The story of the evolution of French society after 1789 is a story of both.

But there is more to it than that. The events of 1789 created not only a vacant social design-space enabling mutant practices to be diffused across the modes of production, persuasion, and coercion but a vacant cultural design-space enabling mutant memes to be transmitted from mind to mind across as well as within systactic boundaries. The outcome was that revolutionary memes turned out to have a much higher probability of ongoing reproduction than did revolutionary practices.

II

Beliefs and attitudes hostile to both the monarchy and the Church had been widespread during the 1770s and 1780s, and all historians of the period agree that the conduct of Louis XVI and Marie Antoinette did nothing to moderate them.[31] But on no theory is it plausible to suppose that the memes in the heads of the *philosophes* and Jansenists and

---

[31] That is not to say that the attacks on the hapless Marie Antoinette were all founded on fact. She cannot fairly be held responsible for the affair of the diamond necklace in 1783 and the flood of *libelles* which it provoked if 'the whole scheme was a swindle organized by a gang of confidence tricksters' (Blanning 2002: 413). But the *libelles* are in themselves symptomatic of the disesteem in which she was held.

Freemasons and *parlementaires* and scurrilous journalists and disaffected army officers were going to overturn the institution of monarchy. Neither the *philosophes* nor the Freemasons were preachers of revolution or regicide, and the grievances articulated in the *cahiers* of the Third Estate cannot be construed as anticipating the program of the Constituent Assembly. Only after the initiative for devising a solution to the problems confronting France had passed to the Estates-General, and the power to legislate had then passed to the National Assembly, was there a runaway selection of memes in the heads of the deputies and their public which turned reformist beliefs and attitudes into revolutionary ones. In the months which followed, the phenotypic effects of novel symbols and discourses were everywhere visible, and whatever was culturally defined as 'privilege' was denounced in all its forms. Although the impervious die-hards were not confined to the First and Second Estates, and not all nobles and clergy were among them, the scale and speed of transmission of information by imitation and learning was such that memes which had been nowhere inside the heads of even the most vehement of the government's critics in 1788 had reached the populations of all regions and systacts by 1790.

From a selectionist viewpoint, the most intriguing aspect of what went on between then and Napoleon's *coup d'état* of 1799 is the fate of the deliberately designed and sedulously propagated rituals through which the ideal of republican virtue was intended to inspire and uplift the entire population of France. Some of the behaviour to be observed was as much evoked as acquired or imposed. Clothes, caps, cockades,[32] and even plateware and playing-cards became objects the sight of which could evoke not merely verbal insult but physical assault.[33] Many of the tens of thousands of 'liberty trees'[34] planted across the country by the Revolution's supporters were dug up again with equal enthusiasm by its opponents and then replanted by the municipal authorities. But the 'elaborate

---

[32] As with the symbolic markers which differentiated one human group from another in the very earliest stages of cultural evolution, the origin of the symbolism is, or might as well be, random. The tricolor itself was a substitute, in the contemporary observation of the Duke of Dorset, for an initial choice of green for the patriotic cockades (Hunt 1984: 57 n.12) – green being associated with the followers of the radical Duc d'Orléans.

[33] The *bonnet rouge*, which in 1792 was still being worn by Parisian men (but not women) as a marker of revolutionary enthusiasm, was by 1795 exposing those still wearing it to being attacked in the street by 'young dandies' (Harris 1981: 310).

[34] The trees have been interpreted as a recycling of the 'archetypal image of the tree' which 'drew from the remote symbolism of genealogical trees, as if the liberty tree made visible the will to root out the ancient hierarchical power structures' (Malaussena 2004: 162). But perhaps they should be decoded simply as 'symbols of a revolution taking root' (Hébert 1995: 141).

ceremonies which centred on oaths of brotherhood and loyalty', like that enacted by 10,000 national Guards from Eastern France on the Plaine de l'Etoile in November 1789 (Maza 2003: 92), were intended to influence the subsequent behaviour of those who took part at the same time as enabling them to act out sentiments of patriotic allegiance. They were explicitly religious,[35] and they deployed a complex iconography of their own. But again, for the purpose of comparative sociology the sources of the symbols deployed are irrelevant. Many of them vanished as quickly as they had arisen, while others – notably the tricolor and the commemoration of the fall of the Bastille – did not. But whichever were or weren't reproduced over the longer term, there had been set in train a sequence of heritable variation and competitive selection of memes of which some continued to be reproduced long after the extinction of the practices with which they had at first appeared to have a selective, and not merely an elective, affinity.

The history of recognizably socialist – and alongside them of anarchist and Communist – doctrines and programmes in the culture of nineteenth- and twentieth-century France can be told as a sequence of sectarian disputes, personal rivalries, shifting alliances, short-lived polemical publications, and evanescent groupings which failed to outlast their charismatic founders. But there is clearly discernible within it all a reproduction and diffusion of both beliefs and attitudes in which opposition to monarchy and nobility was selectively combined with opposition to large-scale ownership of private property. As so often, the combinations were as important as the mutations. The critical memes were those by which there was linked hostility to the inheritors of aristocratic privilege and hostility to the 'bourgeois' possessors, as Louis Blanc defined them, of the 'instruments of labour'. It was before, and independently of, Marx that the bourgeoisie came to be defined in France not as a *classe moyenne* but as a quasi-noble systact at once separate from, and hostile to, the *peuple*. The same opprobrium was never (so far as I can discover) directed by republican critics at the incumbents of either military or administrative roles. The bourgeoisie were, in their critics' eyes, those Frenchmen who had profited from the Revolution at the expense of those in whose name it had been achieved and by whose exertions it had been saved from its enemies. It was, therefore, the extinction of the mutant practices that the Revolutionaries had sought to introduce into the society of France which

---

[35] 'Religious', that is, in the sense of what the leading historian of the Revolutionary festivals calls a 'transfer of sacrality' (Ozouf 1988: 267). Cf. note 4 in Section 3 of Chapter 3.

created an environment favourable to the ongoing fitness of the mutant memes which they had introduced into its culture.

Of the many texts which have been excavated by historians of the culture of post-Revolutionary France, one which is particularly revealing in this context is the prospectus for the journal *L'Artisan*, which was founded at the outset of the July Monarchy of Louis-Philippe. This was a time when workers were still organized in *compagnonnages* and *societés de secours* rather than in trade unions, and socialism was what was being preached by Fourier and the Saint-Simonians rather than what would be preached by Proudhon and after (and against) Proudhon by Marx. But it offers a textbook example of memetic reinterpretation. Its significance, as pointed out by Sewell (1981: 656), is 'its "creative adaptation" (*adaptation créatice*)' of the standard revolutionary rhetoric. In particular, it singles out as targets for invective journalists shutting themselves up in their '*petite bourgeoisie aristocratique*' who persist in regarding the working class as nothing but machines of production for the satisfaction of their sole needs. The seemingly anomalous idea of a *petite bourgeoisie aristocratique* deliberately combines hostility to unjustified privilege with the assumption that the most important systactic dividing-line is that between the downtrodden makers of material goods and their ungrateful consumers. In the following decades, the evolution of France's capitalist mode of production becomes a story of increasingly intensive meme-practice co-evolution, as the ongoing reinterpretation of revolutionary memes acts on, and is acted on by, the ongoing renegotiation of practices defining the role-dyad of *patron* and *ouvrier*. In France as elsewhere, episodes of proletarian factionalism and rivalry alternated with episodes of solidarity and collaboration. But the sub-culture of the French working class now included a representation of proletarian fraternity whose homologous descent can be traced through successive mutations back to the memes in the heads of revolutionaries who had not themselves seen a fundamental class conflict between propertied bourgeois and propertyless proletarians.

The might-have-beens from 1789 onwards have a voluminous literature of their own in which the myths of the Right are no less tenacious than those of the Left. On the Right, a belief in what would have been the nobility's own capacity to effect reform combined with an attitude of revulsion at the violence unleashed by the Revolution to represent the *ancien régime* as a constitutional monarchy in the making which was driven off course by malevolent fanatics. On the Left, a belief in what would have been the creation of a nation of free and equal citizens combined with an attitude of hatred of the partisans of reaction to represent the Revolution as a democratic republic in the making which was driven off course by domestic treachery and foreign aggression. But the selectionist contrast is between the adaptedness of the memes which continued to influence the phenotypic behaviour of subsequent generations of would-be revolutionaries and the maladaptedness of the practices which those memes encouraged the would-be revolutionaries to try to impose on their fellow citizens. The institutional equilibrium was briefly punctuated again in 1848 and 1871, and the new revolutionaries who punctuated it carried in their heads recognizably 'Jacobin' memes. 'Jacobinism' both then and since has, like 'revolution', meant different things to different users of the term.[36] But there is no dispute that their cultural legacy, combined sometimes with that of 'Gracchus' Babeuf's ill-fated 'Conspiracy of the Equals' of 1796, motivated would-be successors to imitate and learn from them. In the event, and through a different sequence of equally extraordinary events, it was the Bolsheviks who, when the equilibrium of Russian society was punctuated in 1917, put the Jacobin conception of revolution into practice. But this time, the paradox is that it was mutant practices in the mode of coercion which enabled the Bolsheviks to carry through their revolution in the name of a theory which privileges modes of production over modes of either persuasion or coercion. The original Jacobins, by contrast, had been neither willing nor able to do anything to replace the capitalist practices by which existing property relations were defined.

DIRECTIONS OF SOCIAL EVOLUTION

12

Evolution never goes backwards. Successive generations of the carriers of the units of selection are never going to come increasingly to resemble their ancestors, biologically, culturally, or socially. When, in Section 13 of Chapter 3, I said that the so-called 'secularization thesis' is mistaken twice over, I didn't mean that European Christianity could ever become once again what it was in the days of Aquinas. But that doesn't rule out what biologists call 'atavisms': stick-insects, for example, have shown

---

[36] Differences over its meaning are reflected equally in the interpretations of each other's writings by rival historians: cf. the 'misunderstanding of French political sensibility' attributed to William Doyle, in a review of the French translation of Doyle's *Origins of the French Revolution* by François Gresle (1989: 646), on the grounds that Doyle's treatment of Lefebvre confounds Jacobinism and Marxism.

that they can re-evolve wings long after the genes of which wings are the phenotypic effect had been thought extinct, just as there can re-emerge phenotypic effects of memes long thought to have been forgotten and of practices long thought to have been abolished. Conversely, traits which were adaptive in an earlier environment can turn out to be maladaptive in a later one to the point that they are eliminated altogether from the population. Selectionist theory has to take account not only of sub-optimal design but of the frequent failure of locally optimal designs to sustain the ongoing probability of reproduction of the genes, memes, and practices from which they were initially put together. Maladaptions are as familiar in sociology (Friedman 1982; Tainter 1988; Edgerton 1992) as in biology. But in the study of social selection, a distinction needs to be drawn between the decline of a society and its collapse. A society can suffer a large-scale fall in its population, its productivity, its influence over others, and even its capacity to defend itself without its modes of production, persuasion, or coercion being modified. But in the sudden collapse of the Central Maya in the period conventionally designated 'Terminal Classic', a drastic fall in population was accompanied by the cessation of both monumental and residential building, the disappearance of other than essential manufactured goods, the near-total loss of writing, and the total extinction of the practices defining the roles of the hitherto dominant elite. The relative weight to be assigned to the several contingent causes of the collapse is the subject of continuing archaeological debate. But once a tipping-point is reached, as when the rulers of the Western Roman Empire could no longer raise sufficient taxes to pay for an army and bureaucracy adequate to defend the frontiers and ensure that the taxes were paid, long-established practices can be driven to extinction as quickly as they had once ascended the S-shaped logistic curve.

An equally well-known but smaller-scale example is what has been called 'the closest approximation we have to an ecological disaster unfolding in complete isolation' (Diamond 2005: 82) – Easter Island. Diamond's own just-so story has been challenged by Hunt (2007), who attributes the halted regeneration of the forest to predation by rats. But the enigma of the giant stone statues whose ruins have astonished visitors ever since the Dutch explorer Jacob Roggereen first sighted them on Easter Day 1722 has been solved by the combined researches of archaeologists, ecologists, petrologists, dendrologists, and climatologists. Thor Heyerdahl of *Kon-tiki* fame was wrong. The island was settled (although Hunt disagrees with Diamond also about the date) by Polynesians from the West who brought with them an existing cultural tradition of which statues representing high-ranking ancestors were an extended phenotypic effect. For several generations, food surpluses were adequate to support a grow-ing population and the workforce required for the quarrying of the stone and construction, transport, and erection of statues which could be as tall as 30 feet and as heavy as 75 tons. Then, whatever exactly the proximate causes may have been, accelerating deforestation and the over-exploita-tion or extinction of edible species of birds and fish resulted in starvation, demographic collapse, and internal war. Sociologically, the story is a story of rival clans of dominant chiefs and subordinate commoners who col-laborated sufficiently to make it possible for all of them to erect their sep-arate statues and compete with one another in their size. The result was a runaway effect reminiscent of the islanders of Ponapae, who continued to compete with one another in growing larger and larger yams long beyond the point of nutritional efficiency (Bascom 1948). In a closed environment, the memes and practices whose co-adaptation had initially enabled the statues to be constructed and erected became increasingly maladaptive for the natives' genes. The islanders encountered in 1774 by Captain Cook (as quoted by Diamond 2005: 109) struck him as 'small, lean, timid, and miserable'. After the collapse, there evolved a new mode of production based on much reduced crop yields and extensive chicken-rearing, a new mode of persuasion based on the cult of a single creator God, and a new mode of coercion based on dominance by military leaders whose role was designated by a new vernacular term (*matatoa*). But no inconsistency with selectionist theory is implied in characterizing the story which preceded those changes of mode as one of a decline which turned into a collapse.

13

A further possibility is that social evolution is prevented from follow-ing the path-dependent trajectory that it would otherwise have taken by a parasitical practice which reproduces itself at others' expense. The example I have chosen because it is directly relevant to the topics dis-cussed in Section 11 is the sale of offices in France between 1467, when offices were made tenable for life subject only to royal suppression, and 1789, when venality was abolished (subject to compensation) by the National Assembly. Sale of offices is one of those practices whose short-term adaptedness may all too easily conceal its maladaptive longer-term consequences. In Section 3, I cited the farming of taxes as a familiar example where the attraction to rulers seeking to extract resources from their imperial peripheries can lead to over-exploitation by the farmers and consequential default by the taxpayers. But in France, the range of offices sold, many of which had been created simply in order to be sold, extended so widely that it becomes the exceptions which call for comment – the navy, the law, and the collection of direct taxes by commissioners appointed specifically for the purpose. Nobody suggested at the time that the incumbents of venal roles were being individually selected for their ability to perform them well. On the contrary, one of Louis XIV's comptrollers-general is alleged to have quipped that no sooner did the king create offices than God created fools to buy them. Nor did anyone suggest that the practice furthered the country's trade or its level of productive investment or the efficiency of either its central or its local administration. Yet by 1789, there were some 70,000 venal roles occupied by what amounted to 1 per cent of the total adult male population of France. What was going on?

The answer is to be found in the society's mode of persuasion. The motive of the purchasers was to acquire social prestige as institutionally defined by an ideology of inherited rank, and therewith the deference imposed by it, which descended from the king through the *ducs et pairs*, the *nobles d'épée*, and the *nobles de robe* to the well-born rustics whose poverty was such that they had to have swords lent to them when they came forward as potential delegates to the Estates-General in 1789 (Cobban 1964: 29). But the nobility was not, although sometimes depicted as such by its critics, a caste. Of the 70,000 venal offices of 1789, over 4,000 ennobled either their incumbents or their incumbents' heirs, and this was a privilege for which a steady supply of bourgeois were happy to pay and, if necessary, to borrow from intermediaries in order to be able to do so. There were some pecuniary returns to be had from investment in offices, even if the topmost financial roles giving access to the revenue of the crown were the only ones whose purchasers would become seriously rich. Some offices carried entitlement to levy fees, some entitled their holders to interest on the capital sum they had paid, and many exempted them from taxes to which they would otherwise have been liable. But privileges 'were a far more important attribute of most advertised offices than any financial return', and 'privilege was as much about prestige as profit, and not merely prestige as obvious as ennoblement' (Doyle 1996: 155). Social standing in a local community, an occupation with duties disproportionately small in relation to the ostensible role, a red robe, a fine-sounding title, a seat on a *fleur-de-lys*-covered bench in a sovereign court, and association on equal terms with others similarly privileged – these were the institutional rewards which venality placed on offer and which

enabled the purchasers to rise above their systactic origins in the ideological dimension of social space.

Yet the practice of venality was constantly being criticized, and the critics always had the best of the argument – which may in part account for
the runaway willingness to abolish it in August 1789 on the part of deputies, many of whom held venal offices themselves. Its few defenders saw
it more as a necessary evil than as a positive good. The Estates-General of
1614 protested against it, but in vain. Colbert, Maupeou, and Necker in
turn attempted to suppress it, but despite their efforts the market became
more active than ever and tradeable offices continued to be created or
reinstated. In Doyle's chosen metaphor, the system 'spawned' lesser offices
(1996: 10) for which bidders could always be found. It was in the interests
of successive governments, whatever the personal opinions of individual
ministers, to maintain the system in being, not only because they could
not afford to buy out the existing holders but because the demand was
such that the market could bear periodic manipulation of the terms in
favour of the crown. The idea that social prestige could be bought and
sold was as offensive to those for whom patrilineal descent was the sole
legitimate criterion of noble status as it was to those for whom careers in
the service of the state should be open to talented aspirants drawn from
all systacts of origin. But the buyers got what they were paying for and
the sellers ensured that they did. The population of venal roles was uninvadable by mutant practices defining roles of the alternative kinds that
serviced the needs of the state in England or Germany or Russia.

The diversion of resources from what might otherwise have been productive investment no more condemned venality to extinction than slavery in the Southern United States was condemned to extinction by what
might have been the greater productivity of investment in manufacturing
industry and the employment of formally free wage-labour. But the parasitical nature of the practices defining venal roles becomes apparent as
soon as the 'just what is going on here?' question is focused on that part of
the system where the pecuniary rewards to the purchasers of offices were
highest. France had no central bank, and the amounts which could be
raised on the government's behalf by the municipality of Paris or the provincial estates were limited. So was the scope for a reduction in expenditure sufficient to eliminate annual deficits. Subsequent historians have
been no more able than contemporaries were to calculate just how serious
was the state of the royal finances throughout the 1780s. But whatever
the sums involved, the government could not solve its financial problems
without fiscal reform but could not afford fiscal reform until its financial

problems had been solved. Whoever they were, the incumbents of ministerial roles had no choice but to go on borrowing on terms sufficiently attractive to compensate investors for the risk of default, with the consequence that existing borrowings could be serviced only from cash raised through new ones. Control of the government's finances was in the hands of the Farmers-General and the purchasers of the lesser offices of treasurer or receiver who lent the king's own money back to him at punitive rates. There was in theory the option of deliberate default to which French and other rulers had had recourse in the past. But once default was declared, or even suspected, the government risked finding itself unable to borrow at all. No historian claims that the venality of financial offices made the French Revolution inevitable. But venality is a textbook example of a parasitical practice which continued to live off its hosts.

Even the vote of the National Assembly on the night of 3 August 1789 did not drive the practice altogether extinct. In 1866, when Napoleon III allowed 628 commodity brokers to be dispossessed and compensated at the average of seven years' sales paid by the other, freely operating, brokers, 'The success of the operation sent a wave of panic through the 9,824 notaries, 3,419 *avoués*, 7,850 process servers, 412 auctioneers, 3,457 registrars, and 60 advocates at the court of cassation, who made up the venal professions' (Doyle 1996: 315). The functions performed by the incumbents of these roles were, admittedly, very different from those of the Farmers-General, whose vested interests had retarded what might otherwise have been the reform of the system of government finance under the *ancien régime*. Nor were they made available for purchase in the same way as those advertised and marketed before the Revolution. The payments to the government were now made as forced loans defined as 'caution money', and a right of presentation of a chosen successor was substituted for the traditional practice of resignation *in favorem*. But the survival of these offices is a striking illustration of the capacity of parasitical practices for continuing reproduction even in a much more unfavourable environment than they had previously enjoyed.

14

There are, however, many sociologists who, while accepting that the future direction of social evolution is not predictable, still see it as having moved in the past, and continuing to move in the present, in a general direction which, despite the occasional reversal or retardation, is plain to see. It was, after all, just such an awareness that inspired much of the agenda of the nineteenth-century sociologists whose influence lingers to this day. Whatever their hopes or fears, or their Eurocentric bias (to which I return in Chapter 5), they all saw themselves as living through an unprecedented series of fundamental changes about whose general trend there could be little scope for disagreement. They could hardly fail to observe in the world around them an evolution out of agricultural towards industrial modes of production, out of theocratic towards secular modes of persuasion, and out of monarchical and oligarchic towards democratic modes of coercion. The pace of change might be different in some parts of the world from others. But it was a change from whose impact no society could much longer escape entirely.

For it, the term 'modernization' came to be increasingly widely used by sociologists writing in the second half of the twentieth century. But that word has no explanatory value in itself. In the ongoing course of social evolution, all societies and their modes of production, persuasion, and coercion are modern at first and ancient in due course. The implication of an underlying teleology, whether intended or not, is difficult to avoid: as many commentators pointed out at the time, the writings of twentieth-century American theorists of 'modernization' for whom their own society was the model which others were destined to follow mirrored the writings of their Marxist opponents for whom the model which others were destined to follow was the Soviet Union. If, on the other hand, no predetermined sequence of any kind is in the author's mind, to characterize an institutional change as a transition out of what is by definition 'pre-modernity' is merely to signal a personal criterion by which the change so characterized is accorded exceptional significance. To claim, for example, that 'By general consent, modernization was first achieved in Great Britain' (N. Davies 1996: 764) is to say little if anything more than that British society evolved in unprecedented ways associated with the so-called 'Industrial Revolution'; and to claim that the economy of the Netherlands was the 'first modern economy' (de Vries and van der Woude 1997: 257) is to say little if anything more than that no other society had as little of its labour force employed in agriculture as early as the Netherlands did.

But it does not follow that the concept of modernization has no place whatever in selectionist sociology. This is because, as the historian C. A. Bayly puts it in writing about what he calls the 'birth of the modern world' between 1870 and 1914, 'an essential part of being modern is thinking you are modern' (2004: 10). Being 'modern' is not a state of society. It is a state of mind, and it has its contribution to make to the explanation of what is going on whenever the right just-so story is one of meme-practice co-evolution in which the phenotypic effects of that state of mind play a part. Institutional innovators are modernizers to the extent that they are motivated by the desire to replace existing practices and roles with others which will be perceived as a 'modernization', whether they are imitating or learning from the modernizers of another society or creating the precedent themselves. (Recall from Section 6 the Brazilian abolitionists.) At the same time, nothing prevents them from carrying both modernizing and archaizing memes in their heads. In the case of the French Revolution, its historians are all aware of the revolutionaries' 'obsessive yet mysterious recourse to antiquity' (Ozouf 1988: 271) whereby the imagined virtues of Republican Rome were invoked side by side with a millenarian vision of a future society purged of the injustice and corruption of the past.

'Ancient' modernity is not, therefore, a contradiction in terms within selectionist theory. The outstanding example is 'ancient' Athens, whose articulate members were not only aware, but proud, of its differences both from other contemporary societies and from what it had itself been in its recent past. It makes no difference that there is no word in Greek which corresponds to the English 'modern'. No reader of Thucydides can doubt that he thinks of himself as a modern historian and the citizen of a modern state which has been fighting a modern war of which he himself was a veteran.[37] Equally, no reader of Euripides' *Suppliants* can doubt that he thinks of himself and his audience as members of an 'equal-voting' (*isopsēphos*) polity in which they take pride not – despite invocation of the legendary Theseus – because it is a revival of a glorious past but because it has made the holders of political office accountable in an unprecedented way to the citizens from among whom they have been chosen by election or lot. The 'modernity' of the Athenian mode of production has long been a topic of scholarly debate: if a 'modern' economy requires factory production, a stock exchange, double-entry book-keeping, and textbooks of economic theory, then the Athenian economy is irredeemably 'ancient'. But the Athenian citizens and metics (and on occasion slaves) who lent, borrowed, traded, taxed, mortgaged, discounted, foreclosed, insured, budgeted, price-fixed, dowered, embezzled, audited, and litigated as they did (Cohen 1992; Loomis 1998) cannot have been unaware that in so doing they were 'modernizing', however they may have put it to themselves, the

---

[37] If, moreover, 'functional differentiation' is the integrating concept of 'all modernization theories irrespective of their different schools of thought and disciplines' (Schelkle 2000: 92), then Thucydides' view that 'less complicated and less organized = early' (Hornblower 1991: 10) makes him a 'modernization theorist' who sees his own society as exemplifying precisely that change.

practices by which the roles constitutive of their society's mode of production was defined.

Even, however, where self-consciously 'modernizing' memes can be clearly identified in the heads of the carriers of mutant or recombinant practices, there is the need to establish how far those memes are the driving force of economic, ideological, or political evolution. When Bayly says of what he calls the 'central' Islamic world and Northern and Eastern Africa that 'the aspiration to create modern states spread with bacillus-like speed in the early nineteenth century' (2004: 280), he is telling a just-so story of cultural selection in which memes constitutive of the representation of the institutions of a 'modern' state were being rapidly transmitted by imitation and learning from the mind of one ruler to another. But it is sometimes difficult to detect how far cultural rather than social selection is just what is going on. A test case is a society not referred to by Bayly: nineteenth-century Afghanistan. Although the soldiers in the army of Amir Sher Ali wore European-style uniforms 'as a symbol of modernity' (Kakar 1979: 95), the practices which gave nineteenth-century Afghan rulers significantly tighter control over the mode of coercion were not an expression of the ruler's self-conscious wish to appear 'modern'. The two most effective innovations were the attachment to the roles of generals rather than provincial governors of control of the means of coercion and the employment of a network of paid informers reporting directly to the amir (for which the model was not Britain or Russia but the neighbouring kingdom of Bukhara). Amir 'Abd al-Rahman Khan further tightened his hold over his insubordinate and quarrelsome subjects by evicting from their roles those mullahs who refused to interpret the Quran in such a way as to bolster his authority. But many rulers at different times and places have put pressure on the controllers of the means of persuasion to further their political aims. What looks like imitation or learning from the example of others in the cause of 'being modern' may turn out to be another just-so story of convergent social evolution, and some means has to be found for discovering which it is.

15

If there is any unilinear trend which social evolution can be shown to have followed across the globe in the millennia since the transition from culture to society, it is 'globalization' itself. But this means no more than that the geographical diffusion of economic, ideological, and political practices from place to place has reached the point that autonomous social evolution has become a thing of the past. For more than ten thousand years, there have been societies evolving outside the reach of any possible invasion by exogenous practices. Only in the middle of the twentieth century CE did two Australian prospectors stumble, to mutual astonishment, on the hitherto unknown societies of the New Guinea Highlands. By now, it has ceased to be possible for there to be cases of convergent evolution of the kind which produced the resemblances between the modes of production, persuasion, and coercion of Hammurabi's Babylonia and those of Anglo-Saxon England, or between those of the Aztecs and those of their Spanish conquerors. Even so, it is possible to envisage a future in which natural and man-made catastrophes combine to isolate the few surviving human societies from one another and to extinguish the techniques which would bring them back into contact. But for the time being both memes and practices can travel anywhere in the world. We have arrived at the end of a long and fascinating story of increasing mutual awareness among the hitherto separate human populations of the globe. Whether, in hindsight, that story can be divided into evolutionary stages or periods which are anything more than extrapolations by elective affinity from presuppositions of the narrator's own is a question to be briefly addressed in the chapter which follows.

CHAPTER 5

Selectionist theory as narrative history

STORIES OF STORIES

I

To insist, in the same breath as proclaiming the merits of a neo-Darwinian approach to comparative sociology, that there is no master narrative of human history is to invite the rejoinder that selectionist theory itself is an attempt to impose a master narrative of its own (Landau 1991). But although selectionist theory does bring with it a multitude of narratives, they are narratives of a kind which leave room for many others compatible with them. Since the agenda of comparative sociology is set by the observed resemblances and differences between human cultures and societies, every explanation of how a culture or society has evolved into being of the kind that it is will be a story about winning and losing memes and practices. But the just-so stories which succeed in so doing do not have authorial 'plots' in the way that 'good' stories, whether factual or fictional, are required to do (Welleman 2003). They have no conclusive endings, no contrived denouements, no privileged vantage-points, no preferential fields of thought and action, no paeans to virtue, and no denunciations of wickedness. They are stories about what has happened to go on in one or another part of the ever-branching evolutionary tree (or ever-flowing braided stream) out of which there continue to emerge new and distinctive cultural and social behaviour-patterns which are neither inexplicable nor pre-ordained.

That does not mean that selectionist stories may not be, in their per-locutionary effects, as exciting or dismaying or encouraging as if they had been deliberately constructed with those effects in view. Although, from a selectionist viewpoint, the French Revolution can be seen to have been in a double sense unnecessary, that does not make any less compel-lingly readable the sequences of dramatic events narrated by Carlyle or Michelet or their many imitators and successors. Nor are stories about the extinction of memes and practices by which seemingly enduring cultures and societies were previously being sustained any less dramatic than stories about the lives of their carriers. The felling of the last palm tree left on Easter Island was an event which, however dispassionately told, can leave few readers wholly unmoved, even though nothing is known about the person who felled it. Selectionist stories can be as effective as any conventional tale of triumphs and disasters, unexpected reversals of fortune, astonishing coincidences, and individual or collective joys and sorrows in generating an emotional response among even those readers who are most firmly committed to the proposition that history-writing is, or should be, more a science than an art. Since, indeed, chance plays as large a part as it does in cultural and social evolution alike, selectionist just-so stories have a capacity to elicit responses of just the kind which both tragic and comic dramatists and novelists actively exploit in the plots which they concoct for that purpose.

But a right just-so story, if such it is, is right whatever reactions it provokes. Since selectionist stories are always stories of winners and losers, it is inevitable that they will be differently told by narrators who side with the one or the other. One temptation to which this can lead is the unblushing complacency nicely caricatured by the cultural historian Ralph Samuel in his remarks about the schoolbook histories of British imperialism (1998: 86): 'Incidents double in the character of parables, pointing up lessons in manners and morals. Intrepid explorers push into the unknown; martyr-missionaries, like Bishop Harrington, brave the wrath of cannibals; besieged soldiers, surrounded by howling dervishes, display tremendous pluck.' Or in the rather different phrasing of an eminent military historian, 'The empires *were* won; and they were won, in the overwhelming majority of cases, by small groups of men exceptional in their energy, intelligence, endurance, and physical courage, even if they had all the power of industrial civilization behind them' (Howard 1984: 34). Inevitably, storytelling like this provokes anti-stories in which the heroes become villains and the villains heroes and counterfactual hypotheses are advanced for the overt purpose of persuading the reader that the winners did not deserve their success and ought not to be admired for achieving it. But the difference made by British imperialism to what would otherwise have been the evolution of the cultures and societies which were for a short time constituent parts of the British Empire is the same whatever different moral judgements different readers may be disposed to pass on the carriers of the memes and practices which made the difference that they did.

The charge of Eurocentrism frequently levelled against the best-known sociologists of the nineteenth and twentieth centuries is difficult to rebut. They did underestimate the extent of autonomous evolution in non-European cultures and societies and the extent to which the evolution of European cultures and societies had been influenced by innovations diffused from the Eastern to the Western parts of the Eurasian landmass. But they were not mistaken in their awareness that there was something that needed to be explained in the inter-societal imbalances of economic, ideological, and political power which they saw in the world around them. It was not as if they saw African colonies being founded on the coasts of North America, or Chinese armies fighting for control of the territory of France, or Islamic mosques replacing the cathedrals and churches of Italy, or the products of Polynesian factories being imported into Britain. The so-called 'Industrial Revolution', however defined by reference to new energy sources, new technology, or new methods of production, had taken place in Britain and not, however nearly it might have done, in China. But then the human diaspora began in Africa, the domestication of plants and animals began in Southwest Asia, and primary state formation began in Mesopotamia. Those are the places where those things happened first to happen and where the just-so stories of how they did have therefore to be set. Nor is it as if Eurocentrics were under the illusion that the hegemony of the West was unchallengeable. It was, after all, Kipling who wrote the poem 'Recessional' and Macaulay who envisaged a New Zealander contemplating the ruins of St Paul's. Tocqueville turned out to be remarkably prescient about a future in which America and Russia would one day divide the world between them. But he did not suggest that at that point history would come to an end.

2

Just as the long quarrel between 'Individualists' and 'Holists' to which I referred in Section 15 of Chapter 1 can (for sociologists, if not for philosophers) be laid to rest within selectionist theory, so can that between the partisans of 'Idiographic' and 'Nomothetic' explanation. The supposed contradiction between 'history' and 'science' has its 'evolutionary solution' (Blute 1997): while every sequence of heritable variation and competitive selection which creates novel biological, cultural, or social forms is historically unique, it would not be a sequence of causes and effects if there were no lawlike regularities in the workings of the world at an underlying level. Often enough, these can be taken for granted, just as they can in the just-so stories of natural science: a geologist who solves the puzzle of a hitherto unexplained plateau by demonstrating that it is the result of sub-aerial denudation down to a sea-level below that of the present day has no need to invoke a physical law, any more than a sociologist needs to invoke a psychological one when explaining an upsurge in social mobility by pointing to the changes in the economy which have led to an increase in the ratio of non-manual to manual occupational roles. But sometimes, it may be by direct appeal to a lawlike regularity that the puzzle is solved: if it turns out that the members of a group or community whose behaviour is exceptionally altruistic are (or believe themselves to be) genetically related then Hamilton's Rule will do very well. Explanations of resemblances between cultures or societies in terms of convergent evolution imply an underlying generalization of the form 'similar environment, similar response', whereas explanations in terms of homologous descent imply that environmental similarity is less important than the details of the local sequence of vertical transmission by cultural or social inheritance. But the relative evolutionary significance of analogy and homology in one or another case is not something which can usefully be debated a priori.

Once, however, a selectionist hypothesis has been shown to fit the relevant evidence as well or better than its competitors, the just-so story accepted as the right one may become a candidate for inclusion among the 'sooner-or-later' stories, which can be as persuasive, but also as problematic, for evolutionary biologists as they are for evolutionary sociologists. Was the human species bound sooner or later to emerge on the planet where it did, or did it do so only because of a wholly extraordinary series of mutations of which any one might never have occurred and human beings never have evolved at all? Is the story of the evolution of species a story of 'a myriad of possible evolutionary pathways, all dogged by the twists and turns of historical circumstances' which will therefore 'end up with wildly different alternative worlds', or is it a story in which 'the constraints we see on evolution suggest that underlying the apparent riot of forms there is an interesting predictability' (Conway Morris 1998: 139)? In cultural and social evolution, although the 'riot of forms' is – to date – less diverse than that of the billion or more biological species which have evolved since life on earth began, it is quite diverse enough to invalidate any would-be lawlike generalizations put forward to cover them all. But not only is the range of possible forms far from unlimited; so is the range of possible sequences along which one succeeds another.

Conway Morris gives as an example the evolution of the whales (1998: 202). From the perspective of the Cambrian, they are no more likely than hundreds of other possibilities, but 'the evolution of some sort of fast, ocean-going animal that sieves sea-water for food is probably very likely and perhaps almost inevitable'. Given sufficient knowledge of the previous history and the ongoing constraints, it becomes increasingly plausible to suppose that sooner or later certain cultural and social traits will appear in one or another culture or society, just as certain biological traits will sooner or later appear in one or another species. The stories of the domestication of plants and animals, or of urbanization, or of state formation, or of industrialization, can, like the story of the whales, be said to be about something which after a certain point was 'waiting to happen' or 'just around the corner' or 'only a matter of time' without any surreptitious reintroduction of illegitimate teleological presuppositions.

This claim – or, if you will, concession – may seem to sit uncomfortably with the insistence that sociology is not and never will be a predictive science, any more than biology will. But outcomes which had once been impossible to imagine, let alone to predict, can come in due course to be so increasingly probable that by the end of the sequence the result does come to be seen by contemporary observers to be inevitable. By the time that mineral resources, new technology, and available human labour had come together in the British environment, a 'factory system' of industrial production was as foreseeable by those who deplored it as by those who welcomed it. But it had not been foreseeable when Adam Smith published *The Wealth of Nations* in 1776, any more than when Alfred Marshall published *Industry and Trade* in 1919, with its story of 'the business point of view' as what he called a 'chief feature of economic evolution', he or anyone else could have foreseen the mode of production which was by then evolving in the Soviet Union.

3

The history of history-writing can itself be told as a selectionist just-so story, as chronicles, annals, and folktales are displaced by narratives based on eyewitness testimony or documentary records from which reported outcomes can convincingly be linked to antecedent causes. But they are not mutually exclusive. Selectionist just-so stories about human behaviour-patterns do not put all the chroniclers, annalists, and folklorists out of business or deny their ability to construct stories capable of being shown to be true. Nor are selectionist sociologists in competition with other sociologists whose purpose is something other than the explanation of how the collective behaviour-patterns of the populations of different cultures and societies have come to be what they are. Sociologists may want only to use reports of the behaviour-patterns of people very different from themselves to convey to their readers what it feels like to be one of 'them'. (I return yet again to the relation between description and explanation later in this chapter.) Others may want only to collect data from which to estimate frequencies, or calculate trends. Others may want only to offer general comment on some aspect of the human condition, or to construct concepts with which to reformulate empirical generalizations about collective human behaviour in more abstract terms. And yet others may want above all to put before their readers observations of behaviour which will cause their readers to share the emotions of approval or disapproval which those observations have evoked in themselves.

There are, however, two kinds of story-telling, in addition to the mythical and the providential, which selectionist theory does categorically disavow. The first is the story-telling of self-styled 'no-nonsense' historians for whom 'the record speaks for itself' and explanation is a matter only of ascertaining the motives of the particular individuals whose decisions influenced the course of subsequent events and the consequences which followed from those decisions. This type of narrative is well illustrated in, for example, the writings of Geoffrey Elton (Skinner 2002: Ch. 2). To it, the selectionist response is that narratives that are limited in this way, well-validated though they may be, ignore the questions which they themselves raise about what makes the decision-makers' decisions effective in altering the course of cultural and social evolution from what it would otherwise have been. The second is story-telling of the kind in which the narrator illustrates a preconceived theme about the course of cultural and social history without reference to the relevant comparisons. To it, the selectionist response is that just as synchronic correlation is no proof of underlying causality, so is diachronic sequence no proof of underlying process. This type of narrative is well illustrated by Norbert Elias's *The Civilizing Process*. Elias tells a well-documented and convincing story of sequential changes in European manners and mores over a chosen period. But he ignores similar changes in non-European cultures, including the courtly subculture of Japan; and as has been pointed out ever since its original publication in Germany in 1939, the assumption implicit in his chosen title was being falsified in the very society in which it was being written during the very years in which he was writing it.

AGES AND STAGES

4

As I lamented in Section 8 of Chapter 4, sociology has as yet no taxonomy of either cultures or societies with anything approaching an adequate Linnaean-cum-Darwinian rationale. But no sociologist will deny that there is a demonstrable sequence of modes of production, persuasion, and coercion of different kinds, just as there are demonstrable institutional resemblances across societies widely separated in both time and place. Symphony orchestras could no more have preceded chanting or singing in cultural evolution, or parliamentary democracy big-men or lineage heads in social evolution, than elephants could have preceded bacteria in biological evolution. Imagine what would happen if an archaeologist discovered a series of marks on the wall of one of the Lascaux caves alongside the depictions of animals and people which turned out to be the notation of a piece of music which could have been written by Mozart! The whole evolutionary paradigm would fall apart.

On the other hand, the appearance of similar institutions at different times and places does face selectionist sociologists with the need to establish which similarities between roles and practices are adaptations whose common form is explained by their common function as opposed to either exaptations which have a reproductive advantage for a different reason from that for which they were originally selected or by-products with no effect at all on the subsequent course of the society's evolution. Which resemblances matter, and which don't? To base a taxonomy on a resemblance which has no evolutionary rationale is to invite the famously disobliging comment made by Edmund Leach (1961: 4) when he likened ill-conceived classifications by unthinking anthropologists to the idea that identifying a class of 'blue butterflies' could contribute to the understanding of the anatomical structure of lepidoptera.

Consider the sociological category 'city-state'. A large number are documented in detail in widely separate parts of the world, from the Near East to Greece, Italy, Germany, Russia, Asia (including Southeast Asia), Mesoamerica, and Africa both north and south of the Sahara. They can all be compared with one another by reference to an ideal-typical list of family resemblances (Griffeth and Thomas 1981; Hansen 2000). But they have in common only that, by definition, their rulers all exercise control over a surrounding territory and/or associated trading network from a single urban centre. What is gained in the understanding of social evolution by putting Sparta (which in any case lacked an urban centre) together with Florence, Amalfi, the German *Reichstädte*, Novgorod, Kano, Tenochitlan, and Monaco? Their family resemblances and differences in modes of production, persuasion, and coercion apply no less to societies which fall outside the definition, including among others nomadic states, oasis states, and the Swiss cantons which swore mutual allegiance in the Rütli meadow in 1293. If, on the other hand, the story being told is about the consequences for a society's evolutionary trajectory of the dominance of one disproportionately influential urban centre, then the dominance of London over England between 1650 and 1750 (Wrigley 1987: Ch. 6) is as relevant a case as Sparta's over Lakonia or Florence's over Tuscany. Or if the story is about the trade-offs negotiated by the rulers of small states in an environment dominated by large ones, then the independent existence of Switzerland is as relevant as that of Singapore.

This does not make it a mistake to speak, in a familiar example, of both an 'Age of the *Polis*' in 'ancient' Greece and an 'Age of the *Statto-Città*' in 'medieval' Italy. The resemblances in their combination of hostility between, and conflict within, a multitude of separate societies seeking to extend their control from a single centre over their surrounding territories include similar inter-systactic relationships which affected their modes of production, persuasion, and coercion alike. In both their modes of production, landed interests competed with mercantile; in both their modes of persuasion, status-groups defined by birth competed with status-groups defined by personal achievement; and in both their modes of coercion, would-be monopolists of the use of force competed with assemblies, committees, and councils. But there are differences as striking as the resemblances. There is no equivalent in Italy to the 'hoplite revolution' in Greece; there is no parallel in the age of the *poleis* to the roles of bishops and clergy in medieval Italy; and although the economic practices and roles of Athens, in particular, were less dissimilar to those of medieval Italy than some historians of Greece have maintained, there are no roles in any Greek *polis* equivalent to those of the banking dynasties like the Bardi and Peruzzi. Nor, in any case, was the 'city-state' universal in either 'ancient' Greece or 'medieval' Italy: the *poleis* co-existed with powerful tribal *ethnē* like Thessaly, just as the *statti-città* coexisted with municipal communes which neither achieved, nor in some cases wished for, independence from the principalities embracing them.

From a selectionist viewpoint, the interesting parallel is not the conjunction of urban centre with rural periphery, but the re-emergence among the Italian city-states of the determination to reduce, so far as possible, the likelihood of an evolution out of oligarchy into tyranny similar to that documented among the *poleis*. The limits imposed by citizen bodies on the tenure of office by a *podestà* or incumbent of some other quasi-consular and therefore potentially monarchical role is at once reminiscent of similar limitations imposed by the citizens of some of the *poleis* on their magistrates (*kosmoi*, *archontes*, or *prytaneis*).[1] In neither case did there evolve institutions which could be labelled 'democratic' as that term is now understood. A Greek *dēmos* was no more all-inclusive, let alone egalitarian, than an Italian *popolo*. The differences were between practices constitutive of more and less restricted forms of an oligarchic mode of coercion. Sometimes a larger and sometimes a smaller proportion of citizens – always male – were entitled to participate in political decision-making, and leading families had sometimes more and sometimes less influence over the selection of political office-holders and the decisions that they made. The peasantry of the Italian *contadi* had no more say in those decisions than the Spartan Helots (or Syracusan *Killyrioi* or Argive *Gymnētes* or Locrian *Woikiatai* or Cretan *Apetairoi*). But this makes it all the easier to see that what was going on was the selection under similar environmental pressures of similar memes and practices. It was not the result of convergent evolution alone. Not only did the Italian constitution-makers learn from and imitate one another, just as the *nomotheteis* of Greece had done, but they were explicitly conscious of the Roman past, in particular, as a precedent.[2] But by the time that, in the early tenth century, the institutions of the Italian state had been weakened beyond the point of recovery, the cities were, to use that way of speaking, 'waiting' to become – sooner rather than later – the centres in which local elites, including resident bishops, would be the carriers of the practices defining political roles. In Greece, it took much longer after the fall of the Mycenaean palaces before the world of scattered villages, depleted populations, small-scale trading, patriarchal retinues, guest-friendships, and local or tribal chieftains and warbands evolved into the world of the *poleis* with their citizen armies and their formal diplomatic relations with one another. But there is no covert teleological implication in pointing out the resemblances which there were between the evolution of the oligarchic

---

[1] The similarities are sometimes so close that, for example, the three 'heads' drawn from a committee of forty drawn from a 'Great Council' of 300 or 400 in thirteenth-century Venice (Lane 1973: 100) match the equivalent three drawn from a committee of fifteen drawn from a council of 600 in Massilia in the sixth century BCE (Strabo 179).

[2] Venice, which might have been expected to be among the first, was in fact 'late in developing an interest in Roman republicanism as a political model' (Brown 1991: 102). But Venice had no role equivalent to the Roman 'tribune of the people'.

practices and roles of the age of the *polis* and, a millennium later, the evolution of those of the age of the Italian *stati-città*.

These 'ages', however, were not stages in either a cycle from monarchy to oligarchy to democracy and back to monarchy again or a linear progression from tribes to states to empires. Nor was there anything about the roles constitutive of the institutions of the city-states which destined them either to abandon an oligarchic for a monarchic mode of coercion or to surrender their sovereignty to some larger territorial entity. Venice did not merely retain its independence but acquired – for a time – an empire, as Rome had done. It is true that twice during the fourteenth century Venice only narrowly escaped *signoria*. It is also true that the failure of the Roman oligarchy to attach the legionaries' loyalty to the *Senatus Populusque Romanus*, whose acronym they carried on their standards, rather than to their individual commanders, led to a protracted period of civil war which was resolved only by an evolution out of oligarchy into monarchy. But in neither case can the outcome be explained by the concentration of power in a single urban centre. Conversely, despite the inability of the Greek *poleis* to unite against Macedon as they had done (with some exceptions) against Persia, the Athenians might have won the Peleponnesian War and might then have assembled a pan-Hellenic army to launch an invasion of Persia, as Isocrates, for one, explicitly recommended. The selectionist just-so story is no more (but also no less) than a story of a similar sequence of meme-practice co-evolution which happened at two separate times and places and happened to involve a number of relatively small urban centres controlling their adjoining territories and fighting regularly but inconclusively with one another.

5

Yet there are some 'ages' which *were* stages of a kind. In the evolution of both technology and art there are some which, like for example the 'Bronze Age' or the 'Age of the Baroque', can uncontentiously be distinguished in terms of what can be seen with hindsight to have been a coherent transitional sequence of variation and selection between what preceded and what followed them. For the purposes of comparative sociology, however, to report them in those terms contributes to the explanation of the ongoing course of cultural and social evolution only to the extent that they specify qualitative population-level changes in shared beliefs or attitudes in the collective mind in the one case, and in roles constitutive of different modes of production, persuasion, or coercion in the other. The boundaries can seldom be marked by a single date, even where the change has come about through a punctuated equilibrium rather than an incremental mutation of memes or practices; and even if they can, whenever an age is claimed to be a stage, the Fallacy of Pre-emptive Periodization needs to be no less carefully guarded against than the Fallacy of Elective Affinity.

The Fallacy of Pre-emptive Periodization is clearly exemplified by the conventional division of human history into 'ancient', 'medieval', and 'modern' which is owed to an otherwise obscure German scholar of the late seventeenth century CE (Burrow 2007: 416). Historians seem as unable to discard the 'middle ages' from their standard vocabulary as they are the 'feudalism' which is regularly associated with them, and many are as happy to apply it to the histories of the Near and Far East as to that of Europe. But in relation to the story of human evolution to date, it is as parochial as it is misleading (Smail 2008). In cultural evolution, the big transitions are first, the emergence of language and symbolism, and second, the emergence of literacy. In social evolution, the big transitions are first, the emergence of the practices and roles constitutive of states, and second, the institutional outcome of the break-out – for as long as it lasts among the populations to which it applies – from the Malthusian constraint of demographic growth on food supply (Clark 2007). Odd though it would sound to call the period between the first and second of these transitions 'medieval', it would have as much of a rationale as calling the period between the fall of the Roman Empire and the so-called European Renaissance 'medieval'. I have already, in Section 14 of Chapter 4, remarked that 'ancient' Athens was, for Thucydides and others of his contemporaries, 'modern' in relation to what preceded it; and although, in previous chapters, I have referred in the conventional fashion to the 'early modern' period of English society, the term is a twentieth-century coinage which has, for comparative sociology, no explanatory value whatever.

The Fallacy of Elective Affinity is clearly exemplified in the concept of the so-called 'Axial Age' in the story of human cultural evolution (Eisenstadt 1982; Bellah 2005). For Karl Jaspers, who coined the phrase, it was in the same pre-Christian centuries that there emerged in China, India, Iran, Israel, and Greece the first self-conscious exercises in critical reflection on the human condition by reference to a transcendental standard arrived at by theoretical speculation. The originality of the doctrines expounded by such remarkable innovators as Zoroaster, Confucius, Buddha, the Hebrew prophets, or the Greek philosophers is not in doubt. But to bring them all together, as Jaspers does, as belonging to a single distinctive 'age' in which, as he put it, 'Man, as we know him today, came into being' does nothing to explain the very different evolutionary trajectories which account for their varying degrees of reproductive success. There is, no doubt, something in common between the environments in which there emerge, then and since, 'new models of reality, either mystically or prophetically or rationally apprehended' which are 'propounded as a criticism of, and an alternative to, the prevailing models' (Momigliano 1975: 9). But there is no just-so story of convergent evolution like that of the evil eye, or of homologous descent like that of the Austronesian languages as they spread out into the Pacific, or of lateral diffusion like that of the techno-memes carried by itinerant craftsmen from one society to another. There are resemblances, but also very large differences, not only in the memes constitutive of their teachings and the social environments into which they introduced them but in their extended phenotypic effects on the behaviour of the members of the different populations. The beliefs of the Greek philosophers are not at all the same as those of the Hebrew prophets with their uniquely disorienting experience of desecration and exile; the *Analects* of Confucius are as different from the Platonic dialogues or the Zoroastrian *Avesta* as they are from the Books of Hosea or Amos or Ezekiel or deutero-Isaiah; the Buddhist attitude to political power and those who wield it is no more that of Confucius than that of either the Greek philosophers or the Hebrew prophets; the *varna* model of the four orders is unique to Vedic India; and so on. And what about the culture of 'ancient' Rome in the 'Axial Age'? As I argued already in Section 12 of Chapter 3, no tension between worldly power and a transcendental standard by which its possession and use was to be criticized was ever conceptualized in Roman culture. Nor, for all the long-lasting influence of Plato's *Republic* (which took the continuance of both slavery and warfare for granted) did there evolve anywhere in Hellenic culture any conception of human rights possessed independently of any given social order. Perhaps the environments of the *poleis* of Greece and the 'warring states' of China were similarly favourable to critical reflection on politics; perhaps the worship of Allah in Islam can be traced back by homologous descent to the worship of Yahweh in Israel; perhaps there was some diffusion of theoretical speculation across societal frontiers in which Achaemenid Persia played a part. But Jaspers' 'Axial Age' is a category derived from neo-Hegelian philosophical anthropology, not neo-Darwinian comparative sociology. It is defined by elective affinities which are the product more of Jaspers' own existential philosophy than of the selective affinities in the world whose distinctive cultures and societies evolved as they did. Well-documented stories can always be narrated in such terms as 'the growth of human self-understanding' or 'the cultural crystallization of conceptual change' or 'the triumph of reason'. But they are not stories which explain why the mutant memes referred to in these terms out-competed their rivals where and when they did. Nor are they stories in which memes constitutive of critical reflection about the human condition drive their mythical competitors to extinction: Zoroaster's most influential cultural legacy was the eschatological myth of the ultimate victory of the good God (Ahura Mazda) over the wicked Satan (Angra Mainyu).

6

Just as, however, you are 'modern' if you think of yourself as modern, so are you living in a distinctive 'age' if that is what, descriptively speaking, it feels like to you. As I remarked in Section 12 of the Prologue, mid-Victorians who saw themselves as living in an 'Age of Improvement' *were* living in one to the extent that, by their personal standards, that was what it was. Likewise, the Christians who saw themselves as living in a *medium aevum* between the First and Second Comings of Christ *were* living in a 'middle age' to the extent that they believed that the Second Coming was an event waiting – sooner rather than later – to occur. The difference is that you can't see yourself as living in what Karl Jaspers will subsequently christen an 'Axial' any more than in a 'pre-Christian', or 'pre-Renaissance', or 'pre-Industrial' age. You can, perhaps, see yourself as living in a 'golden' age if you are convinced that one day in the future your descendants will look back nostalgically on the period of your lifetime as 'golden'. But there remains the perennial disjunction between explanation and description from Section 5 of the Prologue and Section 12 of Chapter 2. Yes, you are privileged over the academic observer in your sense of what your experience feels like for *you*. Introspection, as I said in Section 11 of the Prologue, can tell you quite a lot about yourself, however vehemently the Behaviourists may deny it. But the academic observer is privileged over you in explaining why your experience is what it is. Your own explanation *may* be as good as, or better than, the academic observer's. But if it is, it is because you are yourself looking at it from an academic observer's viewpoint. Your subjective experience is relevant to the explanation of your cultural and social behaviour only where it is because of the terms in which you describe it to yourself that your behaviour is different from what it would otherwise be. You may be reflecting as deeply as you know how about your sense of living in an Age of Improvement, or Barbarism, or the Common Man, or Warring States, or Chivalry, or Imperialism, or in a Romantic Age, or a Dark Age, or an Age of Faith. But it doesn't follow that you know how and why your and your contemporaries' behaviour is being influenced by that feeling, let alone that you have traced the selection of the memes and practices which distinguish one such age from another and identified the environmental pressures which have caused them to be selected instead of their competitors.

TELLING IT LIKE IT FELT LIKE

7

It is not only because human informants can be as unashamedly devious and wilfully untruthful as they often are that sociologists may find that they have misled their readers. It is also because even the most candid and self-aware informants can be as seriously mistaken as they often are about what is going on inside their heads. If, to take a present-day example, you live in a 'democratic' society and take part in its periodic elections to governmental roles, you may think that you know better than anyone else, and be ready to tell the sociologist who is questioning you on your doorstep, that in a recent election you voted for candidate A because of your personal antipathy to candidate B despite your upbringing in a family which supported the party of candidate A. You also know better than anyone else what it feels like to feel the antipathy that you do. But are you sure that you know why you do, and why you do to that degree? In any case, do you know why you and others of the electorate bother to vote at all when the chance that your vote will decide the outcome is so small as to be negligible? Are you aware that you're more likely to vote if at the last election you voted for the winning candidate or didn't turn out to vote but supported the losing candidate (Kanazawa 2000)? A well-informed sociologist is much better placed than you are to explain voter turnout at population level and the extent to which it is a function of expressive motivation, or tactical calculation, or a sense of civic duty, or 'weak altruism' – that is, utility derived from support for a candidate who will help to implement programs that differentially help others with whom you, the voter, feel sympathy (Jankowski 2007).

Some empirically minded readers may want to argue at this point that individual agents' descriptions of their own experiences are wholly irrelevant to the agenda of selectionist sociology. Interesting as it may be to be told what it felt like to be one of 'them', what difference does it make to the correct identification of the selective pressures acting at population level on the phenotypic effects of the genes, memes, and practices which are the protagonists in just-so stories of biological, cultural, and social evolution? There will always be the very different way of answering the 'just what is going on here?' question which generates the stories of immediate personal experience of the kind for which the sociologist Erving Goffman is rightly celebrated – stories about 'impression management', 'breaking frame', and the whole repertory of behavioural devices by which we all, whether consciously or unconsciously, deploy the manoeuvres and subterfuges which are an inescapable part of human interaction at the day-to-day, face-to-face level. But however revealing about other people's inner lives such stories may be, and however entertaining they may be to read, what do they contribute to the explanation of how the cultures and societies within which they are going on have evolved into being what they are?

The answer is that to exclude altogether from the literature of comparative sociology the subjective experiences of the carriers of the bundles of heritably variable and competitively selected information which make cultures and societies into what they are would be to treat those carriers as if they were not, after all, psychologically different from Frans de Waal's chimpanzees. To say that a human culture or society is of a certain kind is to say among other things that representative members of its constituent sub-cultures and systacts are likely to have certain subjective experiences which are likely to influence their behaviour in certain ways. Description of these experiences calls for skills in the choice of words and phrases, and the construction of metaphors and similes, which are obviously different from the skills taught in courses on mathematical modelling or statistical methods. But both depend equally on the evidence: the academic observer is no more entitled to tell you that you feel things that you don't (however little you can explain them) than you are to tell the academic observer that your culture or society has come to be what it is through a sequence of causes and effects that it hasn't (however convinced you are that it has).

8

For all the demonstrable ability of some historians, anthropologists, and sociologists (and many novelists) to describe just what 'their' experiences felt like to 'them', there are too many alternative perspectives from which cultures and societies are viewed by their members, and too many relevant details out of which too many stories could be presented to the reader, for sociological descriptions by different observers to be ranked above or below one another on a single ordinal scale of authenticity and representativeness. But authentic and representative descriptions can still be distinguished from inauthentic and unrepresentative ones. The practical difficulty is that historians cannot interrogate the dead, and it is relatively seldom that the anthropologists on whose testimony comparative sociologists have to rely have conducted extended conversations with the natives designed to test as rigorously as can be done the authenticity of the descriptions to be presented to the readers back home. Some, like for example the Colombian anthropologists Gudeman and Rivera (1990: 4, 8), are at pains to make clear that they conduct their fieldwork as 'a perpetual discussion', and to assure their readers that 'Almost everything we describe was put to the "test" of conversation by the rural folk.' But notice the quotation-marks round the word 'test'. The danger is that such conversation will distort the natives' subjective experience through the very act of exploring them. Far from helping the anthropologists to arrive at a better explanation of why the natives behave as they do, it may simply mislead them. What is needed is for the anthropologists to have conducted extended conversations with knowledgeable native informants who are also thoroughly familiar with the anthropologist's own culture and can therefore arrive at a shared understanding of the difference between authenticating the description and validating the explanation of the distinctive behaviour-patterns which the anthropologists have observed.

An example which illustrates this more clearly than any other I have been able to find is the anthropologist Caroline Humphrey's account (Humphrey 1996) of the lengthy exchanges which she had about Daur Mongolian Shamanism with her informant and friend Urgunge Onon, whose upbringing in a remote Mongolian village was followed by capture by bandits, schooling in Qiqihar, service in the Mongolian freedom movement, graduation from a Japanese university, flight to the Chinese Nationalists, and emigration to the United States at the age of twenty-eight in 1948. Caroline talks of Urgunge as wanting to 'explain' Shamanism, but it is clear from her text that he is concerned neither with the historical origins of Mongolian Shamanism, nor with the reasons for the inheritance and selection of its constitutive memes in competition with its rivals, but with getting Caroline to understand what Daur Shamanism means to *him* so that she can use *her* anthropological expertise to describe it to *us*. The exercise is conducted on the assumption that four presuppositions are shared by Urgunge, Caroline, and Caroline's prospective readers. First, there is a clear distinction between the literal and metaphorical: in Caroline's example, we, she, and Urgunge all know that when an English newspaper carries the headline 'Six Cheat Death in Freak Accident', it would be a mistake to infer that English people think of Death as a person who can be literally cheated. Second, there is a range of basic human responses shared between his, her, and all other cultures: Caroline has no difficulty in recognizing in shamans' songs an intuitive understanding of the psychology of human relationships. Third, belief is not a clear-cut, hard-and-fast matter: Urgunge remarks on the ambiguity with which some Daur beliefs about shamans are held and expresses uncertainty about what his ancestors 'really' believed. Fourth, the attitudes and beliefs of different members of the same culture are affected by their personal traits: Caroline sees, for example, that Urgunge has, as a man, failed to recollect the part that, to her knowledge, women sometimes played in Daur Shamanism. Neither Urgunge nor Caroline expect Caroline's readers to be persuaded by her account to come to share Urgunge's world-view. They only want us to see it as intelligible and coherent and to understand how Shamanism can seem to Urgunge, although not to Caroline or to us, to be 'the best orientation for living in our times'.

The way in which they set about it is by suggesting parallels between 'their' beliefs and attitudes and 'ours', as when Caroline sees shamans' dress as sharing the historical resonances of a priest's vestments as well as objectivizing shamans' power. Her readers, indeed, are likely to find that such parallels occur to them almost automatically. When Urgunge says that he thinks of *tengger* (the sky) as both an ancient sage and a timeless metaphysical entity, that is immediately reminiscent of Christian representations of God as both an all-wise father-figure and an eternally immanent non-corporeal presence,[3] and when he tells Caroline that he thinks of the *Usun-Khan* (water-lord) of a large river as an old man with a long beard, we can remind ourselves of the statues of the old men with long beards that depict the mythical river-gods ornamenting parks and statues in some of our cities. Urgunge's claim that Daur go to shamans for help in illness, and particularly mental illness, which they cannot cure by themselves in the same way that people like Caroline go to their GPs

---

[3] Caroline confesses to having difficulty with Urgunge's insistence that *tenggur* is both a person and a place, like Irmu Khan, the lord of the netherworld (1996: 109). She half agrees with his laughing rejoinder that when students say, 'I went to Cambridge,' they mean both the place and the people, but they then settle by mutual agreement on 'upstairs' for *tengger* and 'downstairs' for Irmu Khan.

is likewise not difficult for Caroline to accept. Shamans, admittedly, have acquired their skills through the experience of an 'inner metamorphosis' which activates 'special means of engaging with unseen forces' rather than the kind of professional training undergone by medical students in our culture. But then we need only remind ourselves of the Ndembu 'doctor adepts' whom I cited as a parallel to 'our' Freudian psychoanalysts in Section 5 of Chapter 3.

It comes as no surprise that Caroline is left uncertain about whether Urgunge is, perhaps, making an anthropological joke at her expense when he tells her that shamans and wild animals (which shamans are excluded from hunting) are 'cross-cousins'. But he leaves her in no doubt that Daur live in a world which is peopled by spirits intermediate between earth and heaven and that shamans, as well as divining illnesses and explaining dreams, invoke and bargain with spirits, conduct rituals of sacrificial payment to spirits, expel or calm spirits when they attack people, exorcize spirits through substitute objects, and retrieve human souls which have been stolen by them. Caroline sees the shamanic construction of causality, in contrast to that of the knowledgeable old men who preside over the Daur hunting-camps and make the nightly meat-offerings necessary to ensure the success of the hunt, as 'founded on a particular, flagrantly non-realistic, premise' (1996: 39). But she accepts that the Daur's 'visions of externality' were 'real, in the sense that they were the understandings of real psychological processes, and it was the shaman's task to catch them and control them, to re-create a unity and balance' (1996: 226–7). Her willingness to see the world, with Urgunge's help, as the Daur see it does not extend to seeing spirits 'slugging it out', as she puts it, 'against other powers in the world' (possible affinities with Zoroastrian and Christian angels and demons notwithstanding). But she feels both that she understands how Daur see the world as well as it is possible to do without actually doing so herself, and that Urgunge is satisfied that she has done so and that he has used his familiarity with her culture as best he can to help her. Her conversations with him give her readers the sense that between them they have succeeded in getting into the collective Daur mind to the point of being able to give the most nearly authentic description possible of what it feels like to see the world as representative members of the Daur Mongol population do.

The exercise so carefully conducted by Caroline and Urgunge is still not without dangers familiar to anyone who has ever conducted extended conversations with native informants about their attitudes and beliefs, including sociologists who have conducted 'depth' interviews, so called, with fellow members of their own culture in which respondents are asked questions of a kind which they have never had occasion to put to themselves. First, the quest for the vivid and illuminating detail may lead the questioner to construct a description which loses in representativeness what it gains in authenticity. Second, the respondent's willingness to help the questioner may lead the questioner to construct what is in effect a redescription manufactured by the respondent's incorporation of presuppositions which are the questioner's rather than the respondent's own. Third, both questioner and respondent may be equally unaware of the degree to which the questioner's questions reflect presuppositions unique to the questioner's own culture. Mary Douglas, in discussing the difference between the French and British schools of ethnography, asks the disturbing rhetorical question 'What would we know of the Nuer if they had been in the French Sudan – and of the Dogon if they had been on the banks of the White Nile? It is hard to imagine, because the Dogon now seem so unmistakably French, so urbane, so articulate, with such philosophical insight' (1975: 124), and Evans-Pritchard has sometimes been suspected of projecting onto the Nuer presuppositions about the nature of subjective religious experience which are in part a reflection of his own. But the difficulties in the way of presenting to the reader an authentic and representative description of a culture – whether extravagantly remote from the reader's or the reader's very own – is not a reason to abandon the attempt, any more than the difficulties of finding evidence which provides a quasi-experimental test of a causal hypothesis about the evolution of a distinctive pattern of collective behaviour are a reason to abandon the attempt to explain it. There is nothing in the neo-Darwinian paradigm which prevents the right just-so stories of how cultures and societies have come to be what they are from including descriptions of the subjective experiences of the men and women who were the carriers in their minds and roles of the memes and practices constitutive of them. Nor are descriptive stories any more arbitrarily conjectural than explanatory ones. They are, rather, discretionary in a way that explanatory stories are not to the extent that the narrator is free to select and emphasize some parts of the evidence in preference to others as best conveying 'their' experience to 'us'. And although description is a speech-act categorically different from explanation, it is perfectly possible that it may on occasion bring out from inside the natives' heads something of what is going on there which helps to explain what has made the memes constitutive of their culture adaptive in their local environment. (Recall from Section 8 of Chapter 1 the historian William H. McNeill's subjective experience of the bonding effects of close-order infantry drill.)

9

Constructive discussion of the relation between the description and the explanation of distinctive behaviour-patterns has been further complicated in the literature of sociology by the notion of 'thick description' which was borrowed by the anthropologist Clifford Geertz from the philosopher Gilbert Ryle. In the example from Ryle with which Geertz opened his influential exposition of the difference between 'thin' and 'thick' description (1973: 7), he contrasted a 'thin' description of what someone is doing ('rapidly contracting his right eyelid') with a 'thick' description ('practising a burlesque of a friend faking a wink in order to deceive an innocent into thinking a conspiracy is in motion'). But this is no more than an elaborately concocted illustration of the observer's need to understand what a person is doing in performing a physical action whose defining intention cannot be inferred from the action itself. Geertz, however, had more than this in mind. The actions whose defining intentions the ethnographer must get right have also to be placed within a context of others which provide what Geertz called the 'background information' necessary to enable the ethnographer to elucidate the 'structures of significance' of focal rituals or traditional customs or dramatic events in the way that a literary critic elucidates the latent assumptions and implicit nuances of a text. Where this is done – and many anthropologists and historians do it as a matter of course without feeling any need for methodological justification – it can be presented, and often is, as an explanatory exercise in the sense that answers are being offered to 'why?' questions. Why are the natives dressed like that? Because these are military uniforms and this is a victory parade. Why are they reciting these words and phrases in unison? Because they are drawn from a holy book and this is a funeral service. And so on. But how has this society come to be of the kind where military parades of this kind are held? How has this culture come to be of the kind where recitations of this kind are thought to be appropriate for commemorating the dead? Why, in other words, are *these* the evolved behaviour-patterns which the ethnographer is reporting and describing to prospective readers? To that question, 'thick descriptions' do not, and do not pretend to, offer answers.

It is because of this confusion of purposes that Geertz can be singled out as he has been by the evolutionary psychologists John Tooby and Leda Cosmides as exemplarily guilty of the ill-conceived invocation of culture as 'the universal glue and explanatory variable that held social science explanations together' (1992: 41). The trouble, in their view, is not so much the different meanings which different authors give to 'culture' as its use as an all-purpose and therefore unfalsifiable explanation of the typical form of 'women want to look younger because youthful appearance is valued in their culture'. As in many such academic disputes, there is a temptation to both sides to exacerbate their disagreement by attributing to each other opinions which they do not in fact hold. But for the purposes of this book, and of this chapter within it, the mistake to be avoided is that of assuming too easily that cultural anthropology as practised by Geertz and evolutionary psychology as practised by Tooby and Cosmides are in irreconcilable contradiction with one another. They are not. Comparative sociology needs both of them.

Geertz's critics are right that he makes too much of 'hunting the exotic' (his own phrase), just as Tooby's and Cosmides' critics are right that they are too ready to assume a uniform ancestral environment and therefore a uniform human mind designed in response to it. But there is no contradiction between an authentic description in Geertz's terms of what is going on inside the natives' heads during a Balinese cockfight and a valid explanation of the status rivalry involved in it as an example of a psychological disposition latent in all human beings which this cultural form is particularly well able to evoke. The authenticity of the description and the validity of the explanation have then to be established in the usual way by pitting them against whatever alternative descriptions and explanations rival observers may put forward – not in a contest between description and explanation, but in a contest between rival descriptions on the one hand and rival explanations on the other. Comparative sociology is quite difficult enough without sociologists who have innocuously different purposes and interests being goaded into dispute over yet another false dichotomy.

Sociology in a post-Darwinian world

TWO DISENCHANTMENTS

I

To any present-day sociologist, the word 'disenchantment' at once brings to mind Weber's '*Entzauberung der Welt*' – the displacement, in a 'demagified' world, of the supernatural, the numinous, and the occult by direct observation, controlled experiment, and logical argument. It was not – or not to the extent that he supposed – an evolution unique to the West. Nor was it either as irreversible or as pervasive as he and many of his contemporaries and successors have been disposed to assume. But in the aftermath of the so-called 'Enlightenment', the collective European mind of the so-called 'Middle Ages' could be viewed with the complacency of hindsight as a culture of mysticism, bigotry, and superstition in which angels and demons fought for possession of human souls, the workings of nature were apprehended through signs, portents, and miracles, and Heaven was, so to speak, as close above our heads as Hell beneath our feet. By the time that T. H. Huxley had debated with Bishop Wilberforce, and Marx had published Volume I of *Capital*, theology had lost the hold it once had over the study of the workings of the world. It had not been comprehensively replaced by 'natural' or 'mechanical' philosophy. But it had been forced to surrender its erstwhile authority in the steadily widening area which *Wissenschaft* now claimed as its own.

There was, however, a different disenchantment still to come. What eighteenth- and nineteenth-century European intellectuals preserved is as notable as what they rejected. It is not just that the beliefs and attitudes inside the heads of bourgeois rationalists conversing in drawing-rooms and coffee-houses were still very different from those inside the heads of traditionally minded nobles, clerics, and an indifferent and uneducated populace. Even the most radical of the secular commentators on the human condition were less disenchanted than they thought themselves to be if they are judged by the standards of their twenty-first-century counterparts. In two respects, in particular, they were not so much disenchanted as optimistically, not to say cheerfully, re-enchanted by the prospect that the discredited dogmas of the priest-ridden past would be replaced by certainties of a new and better-founded kind. The demise of teleology was, if not inconceivable, at any rate not conceived; and none of them anticipated the debates that were to exercise their successors on the topics of chance on the one hand and morality on the other.

Older conceptions of chance in the European intellectual tradition had been a shifting and sometimes contradictory amalgam of the ideas of the capriciousness of the unseen powers by which human lives are influenced on the one hand and the inexorability of the pre-ordained on the other. But the underlying concern was the distressing inability of human beings to foresee, and therefore to guard against, whatever unpleasantness Fate (or 'the Fates'), Providence, Luck, Destiny, God (or *a* god), or Fortune and the 'Wheel of Fortune' (Murray 1978: 98–101) might hold in store. The Homeric hero is at the same time at the mercy of sudden and uncontrollable impulses which are visited on his *thymos* from without and driven relentlessly towards an inescapable death whose manner, time, and place cannot be altered even by a god or goddess who is by way of being on his side. The Christian *preux chevalier*, however strong his faith and sincere his prayers, is prey to supernatural terrors, hideous temptations, and the risk of dying unshriven with his salvation itself at stake. But by the eighteenth century, if not before, the mysteriousness of what lay in the impenetrable future had begun to be not merely demystified but tamed. The distinction between the 'natural' and the 'preternatural' could now be resolved by simply absorbing within the first whatever of the second retained its credibility. Actuarially calculated life-tables, fire-insurance premiums, public lotteries, and political arithmetic (Davenant's 'art of reasoning by figures upon things related to government') made the uncertainties of human life both less frightening and more manageable. Yet it was an intellectual world as far from that of Darwin or Nietzsche as it was from that of Aquinas or Dante – a world in which the laws of nature to which mankind was subject along with the rest of God's creation, although they might not yield predictive knowledge of individual futures any more than of next year's market price for a bushel of wheat, were taken to be uncompromisingly true. As apt an example as any is Joseph Massie's remark of 1760, in the context of the study of commerce, that 'it would be possible, with good statistics, to discover the laws governing the mechanism' (Hoppit 1996: 521).

As with the laws of nature, so with the laws of conduct. Sin, Redemption, and the Day of Judgement were replaced not by nihilism but by 'moral science' – psychology in the service of virtue. The utilitarianism which was to dominate British thought on these topics, and thereby to incur Nietzsche's contempt, was implicit in the 'moral sense' theory of eighteenth-century authors who, as Elie Halévy pointed out (1928: 13), had already inferred from the psychological principle of sympathy a fusion of our personal interests with the happiness of our neighbours. The dilemmas which Mill and Sidgwick were to find so hard to reconcile, and which were to lead Weber to invoke 'old Mill', as he called him (meaning John Stuart, not his father James), in the name of 'polytheism' of values, were not yet enunciated or even perceived. To be sure, there was Hobbes in the background with his *bonum* and *malum* as mere *nomina* signifying appetite or aversion. But then Hobbes was as much an advocate of the duty, as well as the prudence, of political obedience as Adam Smith, despite his much-quoted insistence on the self-interested motives of professionals and tradesmen, was an advocate of the 'moral sentiments' of sympathy, benevolence, and fellow-feeling. Nobody suggested that virtue might not be something desirable in itself or truth not necessarily a good.

2

One of the several ironies in the second disenchantment is that throughout the history of twentieth-century sociology scientific method in general, and statistical techniques in particular, appeared to make human behaviour easier not only to explain but also to control. Their application came to extend beyond demography, criminology, and medicine to the pre-testing of consumer tastes in food and drink by producers and advertisers and the interviewing of samples drawn from now enfranchised populations by opinion pollsters in such a way as to permit not only more accurate forecasting of the outcome of parliamentary and presidential elections but the modification of political programmes in the light of the preferences and prejudices thereby revealed. Condorcet's conviction that 'Only calculation, practised faithfully and mindfully, could create justified certainty, as opposed to the spurious certainty generated by mere reiteration of impressions' (Daston 2007: 128) seemed to be increasingly, not to say triumphantly, justified.

The disenchantments still to come were partly technical. But the appearance of these was accompanied by a growing awareness of problems of a more fundamental kind. It is only to be expected that in the practice of *Wissenschaft* the solution of one problem will lead to the emergence of another. If, for example, the successful use of tests of statistical significance raised hitherto unnoticed puzzles in the notion of randomness itself, that did not deprive the tests of their usefulness. Estimation of the likelihood that an apparently significant correlation might be due purely to chance doesn't lose its point because of a concern about whether disturbingly long strings of the same digits may not be part of a genuinely random sequence which cannot be derived from an algorithm shorter than itself. But what about the uncertainties introduced by the very act of measurement? Or about the unmanageably large effects which can be produced by extremely small disturbances even within strictly deterministic systems? Might it be that twenty-first-century sociologists have to face up to the implications of living in a universe where chance, in the words of C. S. Peirce, 'pours in at every avenue of sense' (Hacking 1990: Ch. 23)? What would Spencer, or Marx, or Weber, or Durkheim have said in response to Jacques Monod's remark that 'chance *alone* is at the source of every innovation, of all creation, in the biosphere' (1972: 110)? In a post-Darwinian world, understanding of the underlying process which has made species, cultures, and societies into what they are comes at the price of surrendering any vestigial hope of predicting what they are going to become.

3

No twenty-first-century sociologist talks any longer about 'moral science' any more than about 'laws of commerce'. The welfare economists and social choice theorists who are the intellectual descendants of Bentham and Mill have abandoned any claim to be able to prove to policy-makers what transcendental ideal of the good society they should have in mind in their attempts to base their decisions on arithmetical calculation and logical inference. To Spencer or Marx or Weber or Durkheim, however, the Wittgensteinian notion that morality cannot be put in propositional form, but merely demonstrated by being lived, would have seemed eccentric if not perverse. They would have been as nonplussed to hear the literary critic Lionel Trilling, in his opening remarks in a lecture series on 'Sincerity and Authenticity', say to a Harvard audience in 1970 that 'Nowadays, *of course* [the italics are mine], we are all of us trained to believe that the moral life is in ceaseless flux' (1972: 1), as to find a prominent neuroscientist saying at the end of the twentieth century, 'There cannot be any social order or moral order that is objectively desirable' (Varela 1999: 64). Any twenty-first-century sociologist who looks back to the time when the four of them were composing the works by which the agenda of twentieth-century sociology was largely set is likely to be struck not merely by their confidence in the progress of social alongside natural science but by their readiness to see themselves as not only researchers but preceptors whose researches entitled them to pronounce on how the members of both their own and other societies should regulate their lives. This is as obviously so, albeit for different reasons, in the case of Durkheim as in that of Marx or Spencer. Marx's injunctions to proletarians and right-minded bourgeois to hasten the impending overthrow of capitalism, like Spencer's injunctions to governments not to intervene in the elimination of the unfit, are too familiar to need comment. Likewise, Durkheim's explicit moral didacticism is as familiar as his hypotheses about the division of labour or suicide rates or the primordial origins of religion. But Weber too, for all his insistence that sociology, although it cannot but be 'value-relevant', must at the same time be 'value-free', leaves his readers in no doubt about the moral standards to which he thinks the people whose behaviour he has analysed should conform. The student audiences who attended his celebrated lectures on the vocations of *Wissenschaft* and *Politik* cannot have left the lecture-hall without recognizing that he regarded intellectual honesty as a moral duty incumbent on university teachers and politicians guided by an ethic of responsibility as more to be admired than those guided by an ethic of absolute ends.

The same holds for the British sociologists of the early twentieth century, including those who came to it by way of statistics no less than those who came to it by way of philosophy. Beatrice Webb, although she saw herself as engaged in creating a 'science of society', had no doubt about the ethical standard by which the institutions of a scientifically ordered society would be an improvement on what they replaced. Indeed, she and her contemporaries were heirs to a tradition which 'from its very foundation was premised on the use of social knowledge in the service of reform' (Goldman 2007: 434). However much they might differ among themselves in their views about the powers and functions of the state, they shared a common commitment to the goal of improving the condition of the people. Loss of Christian faith, whether or not under the influence of either Darwin or Nietzsche, did not undermine their inherited convictions about right and wrong in matters of both personal conduct and public policy. None of them would have been willing to accept the characterization of the moral life as 'in ceaseless flux'.

It is, therefore, another of the ironies of twentieth-century intellectual history that the cultural, and therewith moral, relativism which was to accompany the abandonment of teleological theories of progress derived in part from the same sociological evidence that had once been invoked in support of it. The early advances in knowledge of the ideas and behaviour of peoples from outside the literate civilizations of Europe and Asia had seemed to confirm a just-so story of the evolution of mankind in which phylogeny replicated ontogeny and the 'people without history', as the anthropologist Eric Wolf was to call them (Wolf 1982), would in due course catch up with their betters. By the end of the twentieth century, such presuppositions had been so far discredited that many of the pioneering observers who had first reported on the behaviour of such peoples were being pilloried by their successors as insensitive, patronizing, and wedded alike to colonialist prejudices about supposedly backward cultures and to capitalist prejudices about the virtues of the supposedly rational pursuit of individual self-interest. To Spencer, Marx, Weber, or Durkheim, the idea that their own moral standards should be placed on a par with those whom Frazer had no compunction about calling 'savages' would have seemed unwarranted if not positively offensive. But any comparative sociologists of the twenty-first century who venture to privilege their own parochial standards of behaviour over those of others can expect to be told that the claim is indefensible as well as condescending. In a post-Darwinian world, every code of morality is as much a locally adaptive variant of a shared cultural inheritance as any other. The difference between then and now is neatly captured in the contrast between L. T. Hobhouse's *Morals in Evolution* of 1906, with its story of the progress of humanity in the direction of Hobhouse's own liberal ethical standards, and Richard Joyce's *The Evolution of Morality* of 2006, with its story of the human capacity for making moral judgements as a product of natural selection and the enhancement of the biological fitness of those of our ancestors who made and acted on them.

DOUBTERS AND DIE-HARDS

4

The resistance of twentieth-century sociologists to neo-Darwinian theory is itself an intriguing topic in the sociology of sociology. When John

Maynard Smith, not yet known as the father of evolutionary game theory, addressed a meeting of the Scottish branch of the British Sociological Association on 'Evolution and History' in 1959 (1961: 83–94), he was as aware as anyone in his audience of the misuses of Darwinism in support of racist ideologies and policies directed against sub-populations culturally stigmatized as unfit. The recollection of those misuses is one of the reasons for the die-hards' continuing resistance. But to resist the application of Darwinian concepts and methods to sociology because neo-Darwinian sociology might be put to uses which the resisters would deplore is not an argument against their validity so much as a reflection of a fear that they will lend themselves all the more effectively to such uses if neo-Darwinian theory turns out to be right. The irony here is that the decoding of the human genome raises the prospect that genetic engineering could be imposed by twenty-first-century rulers on their subordinate populations in ways which can no longer be dismissed, as could twentieth-century 'eugenics', on scientific as well as ethical grounds.

Resistance sometimes finds expression in imputations of motive whereby neo-Darwinians are accused by the resisters of wanting to justify the outcomes of the evolutionary process rather than explain them. This is on occasion extended to Darwin himself, who is charged with condoning the evils of capitalism, endorsing the doctrine of *laissez-faire*, and 'siding with the bosses and his fellow investors' against the shop-floor (Desmond and Moore 1991: 421). But even supposing that Darwin's reading of Malthus led him to see the 'struggle for existence' as no less inescapable in the world of political economy than in the world of plant and animal species, that bears neither one way nor the other on the capacity of the theory of natural selection to withstand attempted disconfirmation. As it happens, Wallace and Darwin held widely divergent political views, and 'the theory of natural selection as applied to the animal world is the only thing on which they were in agreement' (Winch 2001: 428). Among Darwin's most influential twentieth-century British successors, J. B. S. Haldane was as far to the Left in politics as R. A. Fisher was to the Right, and Maynard Smith was for many years a member of the Communist Party. Maynard Smith, towards the end of his life, wondered whether his becoming more reductionist as he grew older might have something to do with his progressive disenchantment with Marxism, and acknowledged that there appears to be an association between holistic views about development and left-wing political opinions. But that did not lead him to compromise his endorsement of the view that 'scientific issues should be decided by the evidence, not by ideological bias' (1998: 43). Sociologists, even more than biologists, may hope that their findings will encourage others to share their views about how the world might be changed for what they would personally regard as the better. But the response of many sociologists (myself included) will be to say: if only that were so!

There is a particular irony in the vehemence of the hostility directed by late twentieth-century Marxists against late twentieth-century Darwinians[1] in the light of Marx's letter to Lassalle with which this book begins and Marx's respectful presentation to Darwin of a copy of the second edition of *Das Kapital*. Like the late nineteenth-century Christians outraged by what they saw as the threat posed to their cherished convictions about the part played by God in humanity's past, some late twentieth-century Marxists were outraged by what they saw as the threat posed to their cherished convictions about the part to be played by secular revolutionaries in humanity's future. But they might equally have seen in the underpinning of evolutionary theory and population genetics by molecular biology a vindication of Marx's insistence on the material base on which the whole of human history rests. To an avowedly Marxist historian who recognizes that 'developments in the natural sciences have put an evolutionary history of humanity back on the agenda', it explicitly follows that 'the DNA revolution calls for a specific, historical method for studying the evolution of the human species' and that history is 'the continuance of the biological evolution of *homo sapiens*, but by other means' (Hobsbawm 2007: 185–6). Although no reconciliation is possible between neo-Darwinian selectionist theory and the teleological presuppositions of Marxist theory in its original form, Hobsbawm's characterization of human history as the continuance of biological evolution by other means can quite well stand as an apposite summary of what this book is about.

5

A further influence on late twentieth-century sociologists' resistance to neo-Darwinian theory was the intellectual movement known as 'post-modernism'. To empirical sociologists concerned only about the accuracy of their data, the consistency of their definitions, and the reliability of their techniques, the doubts voiced in the name of post-modernism are of scarcely more interest than Zeno's paradox to a ballistics expert. But behind the post-modernists stands Nietzsche, whose part in undermining

---

[1] For some vehement examples, see Pinker (2002: Ch. 7), and for some temperate comments, see Laland and Brown (2002: Ch. 3).

complacent certainties about 'man's place in nature' has, as I remarked in the Prologue, been hardly less influential than Darwin's own. Their unconscious alliance has meant that the post-Darwinian world is one in which the once-confident search for proven, authoritative, encyclopaedic knowledge has had not only to give way to causal indeterminism and moral relativism but to confront the disconcerting suggestion that what passes for discovery about the workings of the world is merely a function of different researchers' perspectives whereby they impose on the evidence they present the conclusions which they claim to have extracted from it. But although Nietzschean diatribes against the pretentions of self-deceiving priests, professors, and pundits cannot be dismissed out of hand by simply pointing to 'the facts', Nietzsche did not deny that there are truths, with a small t, of *Wissenschaft*, whatever doubts are appropriate about Truth with a large one. He did, after all, continue to characterize himself as a *wissenschaftlicher Mensch* who hates the Christian God because the Christian God hates mankind for being *wissenschaftlich* (*The Antichrist*, §48); and when, in *The Will to Power* (§462), he says that instead of 'sociology' we need a 'theory of power structures' (*Lehre von der Herrschaftsgebilden*), my own response is that it is precisely such a theory to which Chapter 4 of this book offers a contribution.

Post-Darwinian sociologists, ready as they must be to be (in Nietzsche's favourite metaphor) 'unmasked', can safely ignore the more extravagant forms of doubt voiced by those of his interpreters for whom there are no truths about human behaviour (or anything else) which are other than a reflection of the observer's personal and social circumstances. They can agree that many claims to have arrived at such truths are fraudulent because the narrator's perspective excludes inconvenient evidence or arguments which might tell against a conclusion to which the narrator is committed in advance. But this is a test to which the post-modernists have to subject themselves as well. If they go so far as to respond by saying that that test is merely another spurious appeal to an illusory criterion of objective truth, they lay themselves open to the knock-down counter-argument which is at least as old as Plato's *Euthydemus*: if the very idea of making a mistake has no meaning, what is it that you are trying to teach us? Or if they plead that the difference between themselves and those whose claims they have deconstructed is that they, unlike their victims, are speaking only in irony, they lay themselves open to the knock-down argument that it is impossible to engage ironically in the enterprise of justifying a post-modernist (or any other) assertion about the world for the simple reason that to say that it is justified entails a claim that it is true.

Explanations of beliefs and attitudes by reference to bias, self-interest, or unexamined presuppositions inherited from parents, mentors, or peer-group members are not only compatible with, but familiar within, selectionist theory. Selectionist sociologists are as dismissive as any post-modernist of answers to the question 'Why did the so-and-so believe such-and-such?' or 'Why did they behave as they did?' of the form of 'Because they were right to do so'. The right just-so story will have to identify the selective pressures which enhanced the relative reproductive fitness of the memes carried in their heads and the practices carried in their roles, and these may well turn out to be the same as those identified by post-modernists in the name of the sociology of knowledge. Post-modernists and selectionists part company altogether when, but only when, the post-modernists' exercise in explaining beliefs – or explaining them away – turns out to depend on 'the remarkable assumption', as the philosopher Bernard Williams rightly calls it, 'that the sociology of knowledge is in a better position to deliver truth about science than science is to deliver truth about the world' (2002: 3).

6

It may be the lack of agreement among selectionists about what exactly is being selected which has encouraged some of the doubters to persist in their doubts. But enough has (I hope) been said in this book to show that neither the disanalogies between genes and memes or practices nor the complexities of multi-level selection are reasons to deny that first cultural and then social selection are continuous with, and analogous but not redu-cible to, natural selection. Admittedly, mere assertion of what some readers may regard as by now hardly more than a truism does not by itself generate the just-so stories which have to be formulated and tested before any claim to have explained how a reported cultural or social change in the state of a specified population over a specified period came about. But that is not a reason for denying that the truism is true. A rhetorical device sometimes deployed by the die-hards is the claim that selectionist explanations are merely 'old wine in new bottles' (Benton 2001: 216). But the accusation of restating in other terms what is already familiar sits oddly with the attempt to show that selectionist theory is fundamentally flawed (and selectionist explanations therefore inherently misconceived). Doubters are always enti-tled to raise their doubts. But they are not entitled to have it both ways.

The die-hards need to be listened to not because selectionist theory has been, or is likely to be, overturned by their objections to it but because selectionists have sometimes made larger claims for it than it can sustain. By now, the quantity and quality of findings about human behaviour from within the neo-Darwinian paradigm is such that they are making their way onto syllabuses that will be taught by the die-hards' successors to students who will wonder, like present-day geologists reading about the nineteenth-century arguments between 'Neptunists' and 'Vulcanists', what the fuss was about. Admittedly, not all these findings will. But that, far from undermining the paradigm, is inherent in the evolutionary nature of science itself.[2] The perennial risk is that the advocates of any novel paradigm will overstate their case to the point that they provoke a reaction which goes too far in its turn. Not only are there questions about the evolution of collective behaviour-patterns which selectionists have answered wrongly, but there are questions which they will never be able to answer at all. No amount of additional evidence of any conceivable kind will yield a definitive account of the difference made by the First World War to Germany's evolution into a society of the kind that it became under what its rulers called "National Socialism", or the difference made to the evolution of the economic, ideological, and political institutions of the Soviet Union by the death of Lenin. Neo-Darwinian sociology, however far it extends our understanding of the mechanisms at work in cultural and social selection, will never be able to tell us more than a limited part of what we would like to know. But it will generate some much better-validated just-so stories than we presently have about what has made the cultures and societies in the archaeological, ethnographic, and historical record into what they have been and are.

CONCLUSION

7

I said in the Prologue that the purpose of this book is not so much to defend selectionist theory against its critics as to suggest how the traditional agenda of comparative sociology might usefully be reconstructed in its terms. I have, in the end, done little more than sketch the outline of such a reconstruction and put forward some examples from a range of

---

[2] On which it may be worth quoting from Kuhn's own concluding chapter (1962: 171): 'The analogy that relates the evolution of organisms to the evolution of scientific ideas can easily be pushed too far. But with respect to the issues of this closing section it is very nearly perfect. The process described in Section III as the resolution of revolutions is the selection by conflict within the scientific community of the fittest way to practice future science.'

different times and places to show how the understanding of just what is going on in distinctive cultural and social behaviour-patterns can be advanced by it. But the selectionist agenda for comparative sociology can be summarized, with one proviso, in a simple diagram:

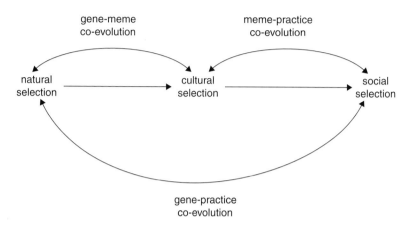

The proviso is that the straight arrows fail to make it clear that while they depict a historical sequence at the same time as an analytical distinction, social selection has been at work for only a very small fraction of the time since natural selection was first supplemented by cultural selection. In the course of these few millennia, however, the rates of mutation and extinction of both memes and practices have accelerated exponentially. The same evolutionary forces which have caused hitherto separate cultures and societies to come to resemble each other under pressures from an increasingly global environment have at the same time generated a multitude of new and unprecedented cultural and social forms which have reached their own locally optimal fitness peaks. The only certainty is that the future course of cultural and social, as of biological, evolution will continue to be as unforeseeable as ever. In a hundred years' time, the cultures and societies of the twenty-second century of the Christian era will be different from anything envisaged by any sociologist of today, and so will twenty-second-century sociology itself.

References

Abels, R. P. 1988. *Lordship and Military Obligation*. London
Aeschylus. *Seven Against Thebes*
Ammianus Marcellinus. *History*
Anderson, B. 1983. *Imagined Communities*. London
Andress, D. 2004. *The French Revolution and the People*. London
Appian. *Bellum Civile*
Aristophanes. *Knights*
Aristotle. *Nicomachean Ethics*
    Politics
Arno, A. 2003. 'Aesthetics, intuition, and reference in Fijian ritual communication: Modularity in and out of language', *American Anthropologist* 105: 807–19
Aronson, E. and Miles, J. 1959. 'The effect of severity of initiation on liking for a group', *Journal of Abnormal and Social Psychology* 59: 177–81
Avital, E. and Jablonka, E. 2000. *Animal Traditions: Behavioural Inheritance in Evolution*. Cambridge
Ayalon, D. 1975. 'Preliminary remarks on the *Mamlūk* military institution in Islam', in V. J. Parry and M. E. Yapp (eds.), *War, Technology, and Society in the Middle East*. Oxford
Ball, J. A. 1984. 'Memes as replicators', *Ethology and Sociobiology* 5: 145–61
Banaji, J. 2007. *Agrarian Change in Late Antiquity: Gold, Labour, and Aristocratic Dominance*. Oxford
Banks, J. A. 1981. *Victorian Values: Secularism and the Size of Families*. London
Bar-Yosef, O. 1998. 'The Natufian culture in the Levant, threshold to the origins of agriculture', *Evolutionary Anthropology* 6: 159–77
    2001. 'From sedentary foragers to village hierarchies: The emergence of social institutions', *Proceedings of the British Academy* 110: 1–38
Baranowski, A. 1998. 'A psychological comparison of ritual and musical meaning', *Method and Theory in the Study of Religion* 10: 1–38
Barthélemy, D. 1997. *La Mutation de l'an mil a-t-elle eu lieu? Servage et chevalerie dans la France des Xe et XIe siècles*. Paris
Bascom, W. R. 1948. 'Ponapae prestige economy', *Southwestern Journal of Anthropology* 4: 211–21

Bassett, S. R. 1989. 'In search of the origins of Anglo-Saxon kingdoms', in S. R. Bassett (ed.), *The Origins of Anglo-Saxon Kingdoms*. Leicester

Bateson, P. and Martin, P. 1999. *Design for a Life: How Behaviour Develops*. London

Bayly, C. A. 2004. *The Birth of the Modern World 1780–1914*. Oxford

Beard, M., North, J., and Price, S. 1998. *Religions of Rome*. Cambridge

Becker, G. S. 1996. *Accounting for Tastes*. Cambridge, Mass.

Bede. *Ecclesiastical History*

Bellah, R. N. 2005. 'What is axial about the axial age?', *Archives Européennes de Sociologie* 46: 69–89

Benton, T. 2001. 'Social causes and natural relations', in H. Rose and R. Rose (eds.), *Alas Poor Darwin: Arguments against Evolutionary Psychology*. London

Bergucki, P. 1999. *The Origins of Human Society*. Oxford

Berlin, I. 1998. *Many Thousands Gone: The First Two Centuries of Slavery in North America*. Cambridge, Mass.

Bianchi, S. 1987. *Révolution culturelle de l'an II: Elites et peuples, 1789–1799*. Paris

Binmore, K. 2001. 'How and why did fairness norms evolve?', *Proceedings of the British Academy* 110: 149–70

Black-Michaud, J. 1975. *Cohesive Force: Feud in the Mediterranean and the Middle East*. Oxford

Blair, J. 2005. *The Church in Anglo-Saxon Society*. Oxford

Blanning, T. C. W. 2002. *The Culture of Power and the Power of Culture: Old Regime Europe, 1660–1789*. Oxford

Bloch, M. 1961. *Feudal Society*. London

Blute, M. 1997. 'History versus science: the evolutionary solution', *Canadian Journal of Sociology* 22: 345–64

Borgerhoff Mulder, M. 2000. 'Optimizing offspring: the quantity–quality trade-off in agropastoral Kipsigis', *Evolution and Human Behavior* 21: 391–410

Borofsky, R. 1987. *Making History: Pukapukan and Anthropological Constructions of Knowledge*. Cambridge

Bostridge, I. 1997. *Witchcraft and its Transformaions c.1650–c.1750*. Oxford

Bowlby, J. 1969. *Attachment and Loss. I: Attachment*. London
    1973. *Attachment and Loss. II: Separation*. London

Bowser, F. P. 1974. *The African Slave in Colonial Peru, 1524–1650*. Stanford, Calif.

Boyd, R., Gintis, H., Bowles, S., and Richerson, P. J. 2003. 'The evolution of altruistic punishment', *Proceedings of the National Academy of Sciences* 100: 3,531–5

Boyer, P. 2001. *Religion Explained: The Human Instincts that Fashion Gods, Spirits and Ancestors*. London

Braudel, F. 1966. *La Méditerranée et le monde méditerranéen à l'époque de Philippe II*. Paris

Brewer, J. 1982. 'Commercialization and politics', in N. McKendrick, J. Brewer, and J. H. Plumb (eds.), *The Birth of a Consumer Society: The Commericalization of Eighteenth-century England*. London
    1997. *The Pleasures of the Imagination: English Culture in the Eighteenth Century*. London

Brodie, R. 1996. *Virus of the Mind: The New Science of the Meme*. Seattle

Brosnan, S. F. and de Waal, E. B. M. 2003. 'Monkeys reject unequal pay', *Nature* 425: 297–9

Schiff, H. C., and de Waal, E. B. M. 2005. 'Tolerance of inequity may increase with social awareness in chimpanzees', *Proceedings of the Royal Society of London Series B* 272: 253–8

Brown, A. 1991. 'City and citizen: Changing perceptions in the fifteenth and sixteenth centuries', in A. Molho, K. Raaflaub, and J. Emlen (eds.), *City-States in Classical Antiquity and Medieval Italy*. Stuttgart

Brown, E. A. R. 1974. 'The tyranny of a construct: Feudalism and historians of medieval Europe', *American Historical Review* 79: 1,063–88

Brown, P. 1971. *The World of Late Antiquity: From Marcus Aurelius to Muhammad*. London

1981. *The Cult of the Saints: Its Rise and Function in Latin Christianity*. Chicago

1995. *Authority and the Sacred: Aspects of the Christianization of the Roman World*. Cambridge

Bruce, S. 1998. *Conservative Protestant Politics*. Oxford

Buckland, W. W. 1908. *The Roman Law of Slavery: The Condition of the Slave in Roman Law from Augustus to Justinian*. Cambridge

Bull, L., Holland, O., and Blackmore, S. 2001. 'On meme-gene co-evolution', *Artificial Life* 6: 227–35

Burke, M. A. and Young, P. 2001. 'Competition and custom in economic contracts: A case study of Illinois agriculture', *American Economic Review* 19: 559–73

Burkert, W. 1996. *Creation of the Sacred: Tracks of Biology in Early Religions*. Cambridge, Mass.

Burroughs, P. 1999. 'Imperial institutions and the government of empire', in *The Oxford History of the British Empire. III: The Nineteenth Century*. Oxford

Burrow, J. 2007. *A History of Histories: Epics, Chronicles, Romances and Inquiries from Herodotus and Thucydides to the Twentieth Century*. London

Byock, J. L. 1982. *Feud in the Icelandic Saga*. Berkeley, Calif.

Byrne, B. 2007. 'England – whose England? Narratives of nostalgia, emptiness, and evasion in imaginations of national identity', *Sociological Review* 53: 509–30

Byrne, R. W. and Whiten, A. 1988. *Machiavellian Intelligence: Social Expertise and the Evolution of Intellect in Monkeys, Apes, and Humans*. Oxford

Cain, P. J. and Hopkins, A. G. 1993. *British Imperialism: Innovation and Expansion 1688–1914*. London

Camerer, C. 2003. *Behavioral Game Theory: Experiments in Strategic Interaction*. Princeton, N.J.

Campbell, A. 1999. 'Staying alive: Evolution, culture, and women's intrasexual aggression', *Behavioral and Brain Sciences* 22: 203–52

Campbell, C. 1996. 'Half-belief and the paradox of ritual instrumental activism: A theory of modern superstition', *British Journal of Sociology* 47: 151–66

Campbell, D. T. 1960. 'Blind variation and selective retention in creative thought as in other knowledge processes', *Psychological Review* 67: 380–400

   1974. 'Evolutionary epistemology', in P. A. Schilpp (ed.), *The Philosophy of Karl Popper*. La Salle, Ill.

   1975. 'On the conflicts between biological and social evolution and between psychology and moral tradition', *American Psychologist* 30: 1,103–26

Campbell, J. 2000. 'Some agents and agencies of the Late Anglo-Saxon State', in David A. E. Pelteret, (ed.), *Anglo-Saxon History: Basic Readings*. London

Carey, S. 1985. *Conceptual Change in Childhood*. Cambridge, Mass.

Carmona, J. 2006. 'Sharecropping and livestock specialization in France, 1830–1930', *Continuity and Change* 21: 235–59

Catullus. *Carmina*

Centola, D. and Macy, M. 2007. 'Complex contagions and the weakness of long ties', *American Journal of Sociology* 113: 702–34

Cheney, D. L. and Seyfarth, R. M. 1990. *How Monkeys See the World: Inside the Mind of Another Species*. Chicago

Christ, M. R. 2006. *The Bad Citizen in Classical Athens*. Cambridge

Church, C. H. 1981. *Revolution and Red Tape: The French Ministerial Bureaucracy 1770–1850*. Oxford

Cicero. *Republic*
   Philippics

Cipolla, C. M. 1972. 'The diffusion of innovations in Early Modern Europe', *Comparative Studies in Society and History* 14: 46–52

Clarence-Smith, W. G. 2006. *Islam and the Abolition of Slavery*. Oxford

Clark, G. 2007. *A Farewell to Alms: A Brief Economic History of the World*. Princeton, N.J.

Clark, S. 1997. *Thinking with Demons: The Idea of Witchcraft in Early Modern Europe*. Oxford

Claude, D. 1980. 'Freedmen in the Visigothic Kingdom', in E. James (ed.), *Visigothic Spain: New Approaches*. Oxford

Clauss, M. 2000. *The Roman Cult of Mithras: The God and his Mysteries*. Edinburgh

Cloak, Jr, F. T. 1975. 'Is a cultural ethology possible?', *Human Ecology* 3: 161–82

Cobban, A. 1964. *The Social Interpretatin of the French Revolution*. Cambridge

Cohen, E. E. 1992. *Athenian Economy and Society: A Banking Perspective*. Princeton, N.J.

Cohn, N. 1993. *Cosmos, Chaos and the World to Come: The Ancient Roots of Apocalyptic Faith*. New Haven, Conn.

Coleman, J. S. 1990. *Foundations of Social Theory*. Cambridge, Mass.

Coleman, S. 2004. 'The charismatic gift', *Journal of the Royal Anthropological Institute* n.s. 10: 421–42

Colley, L. 1992. *Britons: Forging the Nation 1707–1837*. London

Connor, W. R. 2004. 'Early Greek land warfare as symbolic expression', *Past &
Present* 119: 3–29

Conway Morris, S. 1998. *The Crucible of Creation: The Burgess Shale and the Rise
of Animals*. Oxford

Cosmides, L. and Tooby, J. 1992. 'Cognitive adaptations for social exchange',
in J. H. Barkow, L. Cosmides, and J. Tooby (eds.), *The Adapted
Mind: Evolutionary Psychology and the Generation of Culture*. Oxford

Crick, F. 1988. *What Mad Pursuit: A Personal View of Scientific Discovery*.
London

Countryman, L. W. 1980. *The Rich Christian in the Church of the Early Empire*.
New York

Darnton, R. 1979. *The Business of Enlightenment: A Publicity History of the
'Encyclopédie' 1775–1800*. Cambridge, Mass.
  1996. *The Forbidden Best-Sellers of Pre-Revolutionary France*. London

Darwin, C. 1882. *The Descent of Man, and Selection in Relation to Sex*. 2nd,
revised edition. London

Daston, L. 2007. 'Condorcet and the meaning of enlightenment', *Proceedings of
the British Academy* 151: 113–34

Daube, D. 1952. 'Slave-catching', *Judicial Review* 64: 12–28

Davies, N. 1996. *Europe: A History*. London

Davies, W. 1987. *Small Worlds: The Village Community in Early Medieval Brittany*.
London
  1996. 'On servile status in the early Middle Ages', in M. L. Bush (ed.), *Serfdom
and Slavery: Studies in Legal Bondage*. London

Davis, D. B. 1984. *Slavery and Human Progress*. Oxford

Dawson, D. 1996. *The Origins of Western Warfare: Militarism and Morality in the
Ancient World*. Boulder, Col.

De Vos, G. and Wagatsuma, H. 1966. *Japan's Invisible Race: Caste in Culture and
Personality*. Berkeley, Calif.

De Vries, J. and van der Woude, A. M. 1997. *The First Modern Economy: Success,
Failure, and Perseverance of the Dutch Economy, 1500–1815*. Cambridge

De Waal, F. 1996. *Good Natured: The Origins of Right and Wrong in Humans and
Other Animals*. Cambridge, Mass.
  2005. *Our Inner Ape: The Best and Worst of Human Nature*. London

Dennett, D. 1995. *Darwin's Dangerous Idea: Evolution and the Meanings of Life*.
London

Descola, P. 1996. *The Spears of Twilight: Life and Death in the Amazon Jungle*.
London
  2005. *Par-delà nature et culture*. Paris

Desmond, A. and Moore, J. 1991. *Darwin*. London

Diamond, J. 1997. *Guns, Germs and Steel: The Fates of Human Societies*. London
  2005. *Collapse: How Societies Choose or Fail to Survive*. London

Dickie, M. W. 2001. *Magic and Magicians in the Greco-Roman World*. London

Dio Cassius. *Roman History*

Diodorus Siculus. *History*

Diogenes Laertius. *Lives of the Philosophers*

Dobres, M. A. and Hoffman, C. R. 1994. 'Social agency and the dynamics of prehistoric technology', *Journal of Archaeological Method and Theory* 1: 211–58

Donoghue, J. D. 1957. 'An Eta community in Japan: The social persistence of outcaste groups', *American Anthropologist* 59: 1,000–17

Douglas, M. 1966. *Purity and Danger: An Analysis of Concepts of Pollution and Taboo*. London

    1975. *Implicit Meaning: Essays in Anthropology*. London

Douglass, F. 1855. *My Bondage and My Freedom*. New York

Dover, K. J. 1974. *Greek Popular Morality in the Time of Plato and Aristotle*. Oxford

Doyle, J. A. 1887. *The English in America*. II: *The Puritan Colonies*. London

Doyle, W. 1980. *Origins of the French Revolution*. Oxford

    1996. *Venality: The Sale of Offices in Eighteenth-century France*. Oxford

Drescher, S. 1988. 'Brazilian abolition in historical perspective', *Hispanic American Historical Review* 68: 249–60

Du Boulay, J. 1974. *Portrait of a Greek Mountain Village*. Oxford

Dunbar, R. 2004. *The Human Story: A New History of Mankind's Evolution*. London

    Clark, S. and Hurst, N. L. 1995. 'Conflict and cooperation among the Vikings: Contingent behavioural decisions', *Ethology and Sociobiology* 16: 233–46

Durham, W. H. 1991. *Coevolution: Genes, Culture, and Human Diversity*. Stanford, Calif.

Edgerton, R. B. 1992. *Sick Societies: Challenging the Myth of Primitive Harmony*. New York

Eisenstadt, S. N. 1982. 'The axial age: The emergence of transcendental visions and the rise of clerics', *Archives Européennes de Sociologie* 23: 294–314

Elliott, J. H. 2006. *Empires of the Atlantic World: Britain and Spain in America 1492–1830*. New Haven, Conn.

Endicott, K. 1988. 'Property, power, and conflict among the Batek of Malaysia', in T. Ingold, D. Riches, and J. Woodburn (eds.), *Hunters and Gatherers*. 2: *Property, Power, and Ideology*. Oxford

Epstein, S. R. 1999. 'The rise and decline of Italian City States', *Working Paper 51/99*. London School of Economics

Ermisch, J. 2005. 'The puzzling rise in childbearing outside marriage', in A. F. Heath, J. Ermisch, and D. Gallie (eds.), *Understanding Social Change*. Oxford

Eusebius. *Ecclesiastical History*

Evans-Pritchard, E. E. 1937. *Witchcraft, Oracles, and Magic among the Azande*. Oxford

    1940. *The Nuer: A Description of the Modes of Livelihood and Political Institutions of a Nilotic People*. Oxford

    1956. *Nuer Religion*. Oxford

1962. *Essays in Social Anthropology*. London

1965. *Theories of Primitive Religion*. Oxford

Faith, R. 1997. *The English Peasantry and the Growth of Lordship*. London

Faraone, C. A. 1993. 'Molten wax, spilt wine and mutilated animals: Sympathetic magic in Near Eastern and Early Greek oath ceremonies', *Journal of Hellenic Studies* 13: 60–80

Feeny, D. 1993. 'The demise of corvée and slavery in Thailand, 1782–1913', in M. A. Klein (ed.), *Breaking of the Chains*. Madison, Wis.

Fehr, E. and Gachter, S. 2002. 'Altruistic punishment in humans', *Nature* 415: 137–40

Feil, D. K. 1987. *The Evolution of Highland Papua New Guinea Societies*. Cambridge

Fentress, J. and Wickham, C. 1992. *Social Memory*. Oxford

Ferrill, A. 1985. *The Origins of War: From the Stone Age to Alexander the Great*. London

Fessler, D. M. T. and Navarette, C. D. 2003. 'Meat is good to taboo: Dietary proscriptions as a product of interaction of psychological mechanisms and social processes', *Journal of Cognition and Culture* 3: 1–40

Finley, M. I. 1959. 'Was Greek civilization based on slave labour?', *Historia* 8: 145–64

1965. 'Technological innovation and economic progress in the ancient world', *Economic History Review* 18: 29–45.

Fletcher, R. 1997. *The Conversion of Europe: From Paganism to Christianity 371–1386 AD*. London

Flint, V. I. J. 1991. *The Rise of Magic in Early Medieval Europe*. Princeton, N.J.

Fogel, R. W. 1989. *Without Consent or Contract: The Rise and Fall of American Slavery*. New York

Foley, R. 1996. 'The adaptive legacy of human evolution: A search for the environment of evolutionary adaptedness', *Evolutionary Anthropology* 4: 194–203

Foote, R. G. and Wilson, D. M. 1970. *The Viking Achievement*. London

Fouracre, P. 2005. 'Marmoutier and its serfs in the eleventh century', *Transactions of the Royal Historical Society* 15: 29–49

Fredegar. *Chronicle*

Friedman, J. 1975. 'Tribes, states, and transformations', in M. Bloch (ed.), *Marxist Analyses and Social Anthropology*. London

1982. 'Catastrophe and continuity in social evolution', in C. Renfrew, M. J. Rowland, and B. Segraves (eds.), *Theory and Explanation in Archaeology*. London

Froese, P. 2001. 'Hungry for religion: A supply-side interpretation of the Hungarian religious revival', *Journal for the Scientific Study of Religion* 40: 257–68

Gager, J. G. 1992. *Curse Tablets and Binding Spells from the Ancient World*. Princeton, N.J.

Galenson, D. W. 1981. *White Servitude in Colonial America: An Economic Analysis*. Cambridge

Garlan, Y. 1974. *Recherches de poliorcétique grecque*. Paris

Geertz, C. 1973. *The Interpretation of Cultures*. New York

Gellner, E. 1989. 'Culture, constraint and community: Semantic and coercive compensations for the genetic under-determination of *Homo sapiens sapiens*', in P. Mellars and C. Stringer (eds.), *The Human Revolution*. Edinburgh

Gentile, E. 1996. *The Sacralization of Politics in Fascist Italy*. Cambridge, Mass.

Gernet, L. 1982. *A History of Chinese Civilization*. Cambridge

Gigerenzer, G. and Goldstein, D. G. 1996. 'Reasoning the fast and frugal way: Models of bounded rationality', *Psychological Review* 103: 650–69

Gil-White, F. J. 2001. 'Are ethnic groups biological "species" to the human brain? Essentialism in our cognition of some social categories', *Current Anthropology* 42: 515–54

Gillingham, J. 1995. 'Thegns and knights in eleventh-century England: Who was then the gentleman?', *Transactions of the Royal Historical Society* 6th series 5: 129–53

Gilsenan, M. 2000. *Recognizing Islam: Religion and Society in the Modern Middle East*. London

Gintis, H. 2000. 'Strong reciprocators and human sociality', *Journal of Theoretical Biology* 206: 169–79

Godechot, J. 1965. *La Prise de la Bastille, 14 Juillet 1789*. Paris

Goetz, H. W. 1993. 'Serfdom and the beginnings of a "seigneurial system" in the Carolingian period', *Early Medieval Europe* 2: 29–51

Goldman, L. 2007. 'Foundations of British sociology 1880–1930: Contexts and biographies', *Sociological Review* 55: 431–40

Goody, J. 1971. *Technology, Tradition, and the State in Africa*. London

Gordon, H. S. 1954. 'The economic theory of a common-property resource: The fishery', *Journal of Political Economy* 62: 124–42

Gorski, P. S. 2000. 'Historicizing the secularization debate: Church, state, and society in late medieval and early modern Europe', *American Sociological Review* 65: 138–67

Gould, R. V. 2000. 'Revenge as sanction and solidarity display: An analysis of vendettas in nineteenth-century Corsica', *American Sociological Review* 65: 685–704

Green, P. 1963. 'The world of William Golding', *Essays by Divers Hands* n.s. 32: 37–57

Greif, A. 2006. *Institutions and the Path to the Modern Economy: Lessons from Medieval Trade*. Cambridge

Gresle, F. 1989. 'La Révolution française: Notes et commentaires sur des ouvrages récents', *Revue Française de Sociologie* 30: 639–49

Griffeth, R. and Thomas, C. F. (eds.) 1981. *The City-State in Five Cultures*. Santa Barbara, Calif.

Gudeman, S. and Rivera, A. 1990. *Conversations in Colombia: The Domestic Economy in Life and Text*. Cambridge

Hacking, I. 1990. *The Taming of Chance*. Cambridge

Hahn, S. 1990. 'Class and state in postemancipation societies: Southern planters in comparative perspective', *American Historical Review* 95: 75–98

Haidt, J. 2001. 'The emotional dog and its rational tail: A social intuititionist approach to moral judgement', *Psychological Review* 108: 814–34

Halévy, E. 1928. *The Growth of Philosophic Radicalism*. London

Halstead, P. and O'Shea, J. 1989. *Bad Year Economics*. Cambridge

Hamilton, W. D. 1996 [1975]. 'Innate social aptitudes of man: An approach from evolutionary genetics', in *Narrow Roads of Gene Land: The Collected Papers of W.D. Hamilton*. I: *Evolution of Social Behaviour*. Oxford

Hands, A. R. 1968. *Charities and Social Aid in Greece and Rome*. London

Hansen, M. H. (ed.) 2000. *A Comparative Study of Thirty City-State Cultures: An Investigation Conducted by the Copenhagen Polis Centre*. Copenhagen

Harris, J. 1981. 'The red cap of liberty: A study of dress worn by French Revolutionary partisans 1789–94', *Eighteenth-Century Studies* 14: 283–312

Harris, J. R. 1998. *The Nurture Assumption: Why Children Turn Out the Way They Do*. New York

Harrison, C. F. 1999. *The Bourgeois Citizen in Nineteenth-Century France*. Oxford

Harvey, P. D. A. 1993. 'Rectitudines singularum personarum and Gerefa', *English Historical Review* 426: 1–22

Hayden, B. 1998. 'Practical and prestige technologies: The evolution of material systems', *Journal of Archaeological Method and Theory* 5: 1–55

Heath, C., Bell, C. and Sternburg, E. 2001. 'Emotional selection in memes', *Journal of Personal and Social Psychology* 2: 563–9

Hébert, F. 1995. 'Une dramaturgie en Révolution: La Fête révolutionnaire à Rouen (1789–An III)', in M. Vovelle (ed.), *1789–1799: Nouveaux chantiers d'histoire révolutionnaire: Les institutions et les hommes*. Paris

Heckhamen, J. and Schultz, R. 1999. 'The primacy of primary control is a human universal: Reply to Gould's (1999) critique of the life-span theory of control', *Psychological Review* 106: 605–9

Hedström, P., Sandell, R., and Stern, C. 2000. 'Mesolevel networks and the diffusion of social movements: The case of the Swedish Social Democratic Party', *American Journal of Sociology* 106: 145–72

Hemmings, F. W. J. 1987. *Culture and Society in France 1789–1848*. Leicester

Henrich, J. and McElreath, R. 2003. 'The evolution of cultural evolution', *Evolutionary Anthropology* 12: 123–35

Boyd, R., Bowles, S., Camerer, C., and Gintis, H. (eds.). 2004. *Foundations of Human Sociality: Economic Experiments and Ethnographic Evidence from Fifteen Small-scale Societies*. Oxford

Herman, B., Thöni, C., and Gachter, S. 2008. 'Antisocial punishment across societies', *Science* 319: 1,362–7

Herodotus. *Histories*

Herzfeld, M. 1986. 'Closure as cure: Tropes in the exploration of bodily and social disorder', *Current Anthropology* 27: 107–20

Hewlett, B. S. and Cavalli-Sforza, L. L. 1986. 'Cultural transmission among Aka Pygmies', *American Anthropologist* 88: 922–34

Hilton, B. 1988. *The Age of Atonement: The Influence of Evangelicalism on Social and Economic Thought, 1795–1865*. Oxford

Himmelfarb, G. 1984. *The Idea of Poverty: England in the Early Industrial Age*. London

Hobsbawm, E. 2007. 'Marxist historiography today', in C. Wickham (ed.), *Marxist History-writing for the Twenty-first Century*. Oxford

Hoffman, M. L. 1981. 'Is altruism part of human nature?', *Journal of Personality and Social Psychology* 40: 121–37

Holden, C. J. and Mace, R. 1997. 'Phylogenetic analysis of the evolution of lactose digestion in adults', *Human Biology* 69: 605–28

Homer. *Odyssey*

Hoppit, J. 1996. 'Political arithmetic in eighteenth-century England', *Economic History Review* 49: 516–40

Hornblower, S. 1991. *A Commentary on Thucydides*. I: Books I–III. Oxford

Howard, M. 1984. 'The military factor in European expansion', in H. Bull and A. Watson (eds.), *The Expansion of International Society*. Oxford

Hufton, O. 2001. 'Altruism and reciprocity: The early Jesuits and their female patrons', *Renaissance Studies* 15: 328–53

Humphrey, C. 1996. *Shamans and Elders: Experience, Knowledge, and Power among the Dauer Mongols*. Cambridge

   2005. 'Ideology in infrastructure: Architecture and Soviet imagination', *Journal of the Royal Anthropological Institute* 11: 39–58

Humphreys, S. C. 1978. *Anthropology and the Greeks*. London

Hunt, L. 1984. *Politics, Culture, and Class in the French Revolution*. Berkeley, Calif.

Hunt, T. L. 2007. 'Rethinking Easter Island's ecological catastrophe', *Journal of Archaeological Science* 34: 485–502

Huxley A. F. 1983. 'How far will Darwin take us?', in D. S. Bendall (ed.), *Evolution from Molecules to Man*. Cambridge

Iannacone, L. R. 1995. 'Household production, human capital, and the economics of religion', in M. Tommasi and K. Ierulli (eds.), *The New Economics of Human Behaviour*. Cambridge

Iliffe, J. 1983. *The Emergence of African Capitalism*. London

   2005. *Honour in African History*. Cambridge

Innes, M. 2000. *State and Society in the Early Middle Ages: The Middle Rhine Valley 400–1000*. Cambridge

Irons, W. 1999. 'Adaptively relevant environment versus the environment of evolutionary adaptedness', *Evolutionary Anthropology* 6: 194–204

Jablonka, E. and Lamb, M. J. 1995. *Epigenetic Inheritance and Evolution: The Larmarckian Dimension*. Oxford

Jankowski, R. 2007. 'Altruism and the decision to vote: Explaining and testing high voter turnout', *Rationality and Society* 19: 5–34

John, E. 1977. 'War and society in the tenth century: The Maldon campaign', *Transactions of the Royal Historical Society* 5th series: 173–95

Jolowicz, H. J. and Nicholas, R. 1972. *A Historical Introduction to Roman Law*. Cambridge

Jones, A. H. M. 1964. *The Later Roman Empire 284–602: A Social, Economic, and Administrative Survey*. Oxford

Kakar, H. K. 1979. *Government and Society in Afghanistan: The Reign of Amir 'Abd al-Rahman Khan*. Austin, Tex.

Kanazawa, S. 2000. 'A new solution to the collective action problem: The paradox of voter turnout', *American Sociological Review* 65: 433–42

Kang, G. E. 1979. 'Exogamy and peace relations of social units: A cross-cultural test', *Ethnology* 18: 85–99

Kaplan, S. 1979. 'Réflexions sur la police du monde de travail, 1700–1815', *Revue Historique* 261: 17–77

Katz, E. and Lazarsfeld, P. F. 1955. *Personal Influence: The Part Played by People in the Flow of Mass Communications*. Glencoe, Ill.

Keeley, L. 1996. *War Before Civilization*. Oxford

Kelly, R. C. 1985. *The Nuer Conquest: The Structure and Expansion of an Expansionist System*. Ann Arbor

Kelly, R. L. 1993. *The Foraging Spectrum: Diversity in Hunter-Gatherer Lifeways*. Washington, D.C.

Kieckhefer, R. 1989. *Magic in the Middle Ages*. Cambridge

Kiernan, B. 1996. *The Pol Pot Regime: Race, Power, and Genocide in Cambodia under the Khmer Rouge, 1975–79*. New Haven, Conn.

Kirk, G. S. 1980. *Myth: Its Meaning and Function in Ancient and Other Cultures*. Cambridge

Klein, H. S. 1982. *Bolivia: The Evolution of a Multi-Ethnic Society*. Oxford
  1986. *African Slavery in Latin America and the Caribbean*. Oxford

Knauft, B. 1991. 'Violence and sociality in human evolution', *Current Anthropology* 32: 223–45

Kopytoff, I. and Miers, S. 1977. 'Introduction', in S. Miers and I. Kopytoff (eds.), *Slavery in Africa: Historical and Anthropological Perspectives*. Madison, Wis.

Kroll, E. 1997. 'Dogs, Darwinism, and English sensibilities', in R. W. Mitchell, N. S. Thompson, and H. Lyn Miles (eds.), *Anthropomorphism, Anecdotes, and Animals*. Albany, N.Y.

Kuhn, D. 1991. *The Skills of Argument*. Cambridge

Kuhn, T. S. 1962. *The Structure of Scientific Revolutions*. Chicago

Kuran, T. 1995. *Private Truths, Public Lies*. Cambridge, Mass.

Kurzban, R. and Leary, M. R. 2001. 'Evolutionary origins of stigmatization: The function of social exclusion', *Psychological Bulletin* 127: 187–208

Lactantius. *Divine Institutes*

Lake, M. 1998. 'Digging for memes: The role of material objects in cultural evolution', in C. Renfrew and C. Scarre (eds.), *Cognition and Material Culture: The Archaeology of Symbolic Storage*. Cambridge

Laland, K. N., Odling-Smee, J., and Feldman, M. W. 2000. 'Niche construction, biological evolution and cultural change', *Behavioural and Brain Sciences* 23: 131–75
  and Brown, G. R. 2002. *Sense and Nonsense: Evolutionary Perspectives on Human Behaviour*. Oxford

Lamont, P. 2004. 'Spiritualism and a mid-Victorian crisis of evidence', *Historical Journal* 47: 897–920

Landau, M. 1991. *Narratives of Evolution*. New Haven, Conn.

Landes, D. S. 1998. *The Wealth and Poverty of Nations: Why Some Are So Rich and Some So Poor*. New York

Lane, C. 1981. *The Rites of Rulers: Ritual in Industrial Society – The Soviet Case*. Cambridge

Lane, F. C. 1973. *Venice: A Maritime Republic*. Baltimore

Lankaster, W. 1981. *The Rwala Bedouin Today*. Cambridge

Lawson, M. K. 1993. *Cnut: The Danes in England in the Early Eleventh Century*. London

Le Goff, J. 1984. *The Birth of Purgatory*. London

Leach, E. R. 1961. *Rethinking Anthropology*. London

    1982. *Culture and Communication: The Logic by which Symbols Are Connected: An Introduction to the Use of Structuralist Analysis in Social Anthropology*. Cambridge

Lee, B. B. 1979. *The !Kung San: Men, Women, and Work in a Foraging Society*. Cambridge

Lefebvre, G. 1939. *Quatre-Vingt-Neuf*. Paris

    1954. *Études sur la Revolution Française*. Paris

Lennard, R. 1959. *Rural England 1086–1135*. Oxford

Lévi-Strauss, C. 1963. *Structural Anthropology*. New York

Levy, D. A. and Nail, P. R. 1993. 'Contagion: A theoretical and empirical review and reconceptualization', *Genetic, Social, and General Psychology Monographs* 119: 235–84

Lewis, G. 1980. *Day of Shining Red: An Essay on Understanding Ritual*. Cambridge

Libby, D. C. and Paria, C. A. 2000. 'Manumission practices in a late eighteenth-century Brazilian slave parish: Sâo José d'El Rey in 1795', *Slavery and Abolition* 21: 96–127

Liebermann, F. (ed.) 1903. *Die Gesetze der Angelsachsen*. Halle

Liebeschutz, J. H. W. G. 1979. *Continuity and Change in Roman Religion*. Oxford

Limberis, V. 1991. 'The eyes infected by evil: Basil of Caesarea's homily, On Envy', *Harvard Theological Review* 84: 163–84

Livy. *History of Rome*

Lloyd, G. E. R. 2007. *Cognitive Variations: Reflections on the Unity and Diversity of the Human Mind*. Oxford

Loomis, W. T. 1998. *Wages, Welfare Costs, and Inflation in Classical Athens*. Ann Arbor

Loyn, H. R. 1955. 'Gesiths and thegns in Anglo-Saxon England from the seventh to the tenth century', *English Historical Review* 277: 529–49

    1962. *Anglo-Saxon England and the Norman Conquest*. London

Lucian. *The Passing of Peregrinus*

Lynch, A. 1996. *Thought Contagion: How Belief Spreads Through Society.* New York

MacCulloch, D. 2003. *Reformation: Europe's House Divided 1490–1700.* London

MacDonald, K. B. 1993. *A People That Shall Dwell Apart: Judaism as a Group Evolutionary Strategy.* Westport, Conn.

Mace, R., Holden, C. J., and Shennan, S. (eds.) 2005. *The Evolution of Cultural Diversity: A Phylogenetic Approach.* London

Macleod, W. C. 1925. 'Debtor and chattel slavery in aboriginal North America', *American Anthopologist* 27: 370–80

MacMullen, R. 1984. *Christianizing the Roman Empire (A.D. 100–400).* New Haven, Conn.

Macy, M. W. 1991. 'Learning to cooperate: Structure and tacit collusion in social exchange', *American Journal of Sociology* 97: 808–43

Maguire, H. 1994. 'From the evil eye to the eye of justice: The saints, art, and justice in Byzantium', in A. E. Laiou and D. Simon (eds.), *Law and Society in Byzantium: Ninth-Twelfth Centuries.* Washington, D.C.

Malaussena, K. 2004. 'The birth of modern commemoration in France: The tree and the text', *French History* 18: 154–72

Malinowski, B. 1935. *Coral Gardens and their Magic: A Study of the Methods of Tilling the Soil and of Agricultural Rites in the Trobriand Islands.* London

Mallon, R. and Stich, S. P. 2000. 'The odd couple: The compatibility of social construction and evolutionary psychology', *Philosophy of Science* 67: 133–54

Mannheim, K. 1936. *Ideology and Utopia.* London

Marcus Aurelius. *Meditations*

Marshall, G. 1981. *Presbyteries and Profits: Calvinism and the Development of Capitalism in Scotland 1560–1707.* Oxford

Maschner, H. D. G. and Patton, J. Q. 1996. 'Kin selection and the origins of hereditary social inequality: A case study from the Northern Northwest Coast' in H. D. G. Maschner (ed.), *Darwinian Archaeologies.* New York

Massey, D. S. 2002. 'A brief history of human society: The origin and role of emotions in social life', *American Sociological Review* 67: 1–29

Matthias, P. 1979. *The Transformation of England: Essays in the Social and Economic History of England in the Eighteenth Century.* London

Maynard Smith, J. 1961. 'Evolution and history', in M. Banton (ed.), *Darwinism and the Study of Society.* London

1982. *Evolution and the Theory of Games.* Cambridge

1998. *Shaping Life: Genes, Embryos, and Evolution.* London

Maza, S. 2003. *The Myth of the French Bourgeoisie: An Essay on the Social Imaginary 1750–1850.* Cambridge, Mass.

McGrew, W. 2004. *The Cultured Chimpanzee: Reflections on Cultural Primatology.* Cambridge

McKechnie, P. 1989. *Outsiders in Greek Cities in the Fourth Century B.C.* London

McNeill, W. H. 1982. *The Pursuit of Power: Technology, Armed Force, and Society since A.D. 1000.* Oxford

Meeks, W. A. 1993. *The Origins of Christian Morality.* New Haven, Conn.

Miller, G. F. 1998. 'How mate choice shaped human nature: A review of sexual selection and human evolution', in C. Cranford and D. L. Krebs (eds.), *Handbook of Evolutionary Psychology: Ideas, Issues, Applications.* Mahwah, N.J.

Millett, P. 1989. 'Patronage and its avoidance in classical Athens', in A. Wallace-Hadrill (ed.), *Patronage in Ancient Society.* London

Mithen, S. 2004. 'From Ohalo to Çatalhöyük: The development of religiosity during the early prehistory of Western Asia, 20,000 to 7000 BCE', in H. Whitehouse and L. H. Martin (eds.), *Theorizing Religions Past: Archaeology, History, and Cognition.* Walnut Creek, Calif.

Momigliano, A. 1975. *Alien Wisdom: The Limits of Hellenization.* Cambridge

Monod, J. 1972. *Chance and Necessity: An Essay on the Natural Philosophy of Modern Biology.* London

Moore, J. S. 1998. 'Domesday slavery', *Anglo-Norman Studies* 11: 190–220

Morgan, P. D. 1988. *Slave Counterpoint: Black Culture in the Eighteenth-Century Chesapeake and Lowcountry.* Chapel Hill, N.C.

Murra, J. V. 1980. *The Economic Organization of the Inka State.* Greenwich, Conn.

Murray, A. 1978. *Reason and Society in the Middle Ages.* Oxford

Murray, O. 1991. 'War and the Symposium', in W. J. Slater (ed.), *Dining in a Classical Context.* Ann Arbor, Mich.

Nietzsche, F. *The Antichrist*
  The Will to Power
  Genealogy of Morals

Nisbett, R. E. 2003. *The Geography of Thought: How Asians and Westerners Think Differently … and Why.* New York
  and Cohen, D. 1996. *Culture of Honor: The Psychology of Violence in the American South.* Boulder, Col.

Nock, A. D. 1933. *Conversion: The Old and the New in Religion from Alexander the Great to Augustine of Hippo.* Oxford

Oates, J. 1979. *Babylon.* London

Ogden, D. 2001. *Greek and Roman Necromancy.* Princeton, N.J.

Orians, G. H. and Heerwagen, J. H. 1992. 'Evolved responses to landscapes', in J. H. Barkow, L. Cosmides, and J. Tooby (eds.), *Evolutionary Psychology and the Generation of Culture.* Oxford

Ostrom, E. 1990. *Governing the Commons: The Evolution of Institutions for Collective Action.* Cambridge
  Walker, J., and Gardner, R. 1992. 'Covenants with and without the sword: Self-governance is possible', *American Political Science Review* 86: 404–17

Otterbein, K. 2000. 'Five feuds: An anlysis of homicides in Eastern Kentucky in the late nineteenth century', *American Anthropologist* 102: 231–43

Ovid. *Fasti*

Owen, A. 2004. *The Place of Enchantment: British Occultism and the Rise of the Modern*. Chicago

Ozouf, M. 1988. *Festivals and the French Revolution*. Cambridge, Mass.

Palmer, C. A. 1976. *Slaves of the White God: Blacks in Mexico, 1570–1650*. Cambridge, Mass.

Parker, J. 2004. 'Witchcraft, anti-witchcraft and trans-regional innovation in early colonial Ghana', *Journal of African History* 45: 393–420

Parkin, D. 1985. (ed.), *The Anthropology of Evil*. Oxford

Parry, J. and Bloch, M. 1989. 'Introduction: Money and the morality of exchange', in J. Parry and M. Bloch (eds.), *Money and the Morality of Exchange*. Cambridge

Patterson, O. 1982. *Slavery and Social Death*. Cambridge, Mass.

Paul the Deacon. *History of the Lombards*

Pausanias. *Description of Greece*

Pessar, P. R. 2004. *From Fanatics to Folk: Brazilian Millenarism and Popular Culture*. Durham, N.C.

Pinker, S. 1994. *The Language Instinct*. New York
  2002. *The Blank Slate: The Modern Denial of Human Nature*. London

Plato. *Laws*
  Menexenus

Pliny. *Natural History*

Plumb, J. H. 1967. *The Growth of Political Stability in England 1675–1725*. London

Pomeranz, K. 2000. *The Great Divergence: China, Europe, and the Making of the Modern World Economy*. Princeton, N.J.

Raha, M. K. 1978. 'Stratification and religion in a Himalayan society', in J. S. Fisher (ed.), *Himalayan Anthropology: The Indo-Tibetan Interface*. The Hague

Rappaport, R. A. 1999. *Ritual and Religion in the Making of Humanity*. Cambridge

Rathbone, D. W. 1983. 'The slave mode of production in Italy', *Journal of Roman Studies* 73: 160–8

Rawson, B. 1989. 'Spurii and the Roman view of illegitimacy', *Antichthon* 23: 10–41

Readman, P. 2005. 'The place of the past in English culture, c. 1890–1914', *Past & Present* 186: 147–99

Richards, A. 1935. 'A modern movement of witch finders', *Africa* 8: 448–60

Richerson, P. J. and Boyd, R. 1999. 'Complex societies: The evolutionary origins of a crude superorganism', *Human Nature* 10: 253–89
  2005. *Not by Genes Alone: How Culture Transformed Human Evolution*. Chicago

Ridley, M. 1996. *The Origins of Virtue*. London

Ritner, R. K. 1995. 'The religious, social, and legal parameters of traditional Egyptian magic', in M. Meyers and P. Mirecki (eds.), *Ancient Magic and Ritual Power*. Leiden

Roberts, J. H. 1988. *Darwinism and the Divine in America: Protestant Intellectuals and Organic Evolution 1859–1900*. Madison, Wis.

Robertson, A. F. 1980. 'On sharecropping', *Man* 15: 411–29

Robertson, A. J. (ed.) 1939. *Anglo-Saxon Charters*. Cambridge

Roffe, D. 1990. 'Domesday Book and Northern Society: A reassessment', *English Historical Review* 105: 310–36

Runciman, W. G. 1972. 'Describing', *Mind* 81: 372–88

    1983. *A Treatise on Social Theory*. I: *The Methodology of Social Theory*. Cambridge

    1990. 'Doomed to extinction: The *polis* as an evolutionary dead-end', in O. Murray and S. Price (eds.), *The Greek City: From Homer to Alexander*. Oxford

    1991. 'Are there any irrational beliefs?', *Archives Européennes de Sociologie* 32: 215–28

    2001a. 'Was Max Weber a selectionist in spite of himself?', *Journal of Classical Sociology* 1: 13–32

    2001b. 'From Nature to Culture, from Culture to Society', *Proceedings of the British Academy* 110: 235–54

Sahlins, M. 1974. *Stone Age Economics*. London

    1983. 'Other times, other cultures: The anthropology of history', *American Anthropologist* 85: 517–44

Samuel, R. 1998. *Island Stories: Unravelling Britain: Theatres of Memory* II. London

Sawyer, R. 1986. *Slavery in the Twentieth Century*. London

Schapera, I. 1956. *Government and Politics in Tribal Societies*. London

Schelkle, W. 2000. 'Summary: Modernization', in W. Schelkle, W.-H. Krauth, M. Kohli, and G. Elwert (eds.), *Paradigms of Social Change: Modernization, Development, Transformation, Evolution*. Frankfurt

Schoeck, H. 1969. *Envy: A Theory of Social Behaviour*. London

Schwartz, S. B. 1985. *Sugar Plantations in the Formation of Brazilian Society: Bahia, 1550–1835*. Cambridge

Scott, C. 1988. 'Property, practice, and aboriginal rights among Quebec Cree hunters', in T. Ingold, D. Riches, and J. Woodburn (eds.), *Hunters and Gatherers 2: Property, Power, and Ideology*. Oxford

Scott, S. F. 1978. *The Response of the Royal Army to the French Revolution: The Rise and Development of the Line Army 1787–93*. Oxford

Searle, J. R. 1995. *The Construction of Social Reality*. London

Seneca. *Epistles*

Sewell, W. H. 1981. 'La confraternité des proletaires: Conscience de classe sous la monarchie de juillet', *Annales* 36: 650–71

Shapin, S. 1994. *A Social History of Truth: Civility and Science in Seventeenth-Century England*. Chicago

Shennan, S. 2002. *Genes, Memes, and Human History*. London

Silk, J. B., Brosnan, S. F., Vonk, J., Henrich J., Povinelli, D. J., Richardson, A. S., Lambeth, S. P., Mascaro, J., and Schapiro, S. J. 2005. 'Chimpanzees are indifferent to the welfare of unrelated group members', *Nature* 437: 1,357–9

Simon, H. A. 1990. 'Invariants of human behavior', *Annual Review of Psychology* 41: 1–19

Skinner, Q. 2002. *Visions of Politics*. I: *Regarding Method*. Cambridge

Skyrms, B. 1996. *Evolution of the Social Contract*. Cambridge

Smail, D. L. 2008. *On Deep History and the Brain*. Berkeley, Calif.

Smith, A. D. 2003. *Chosen Peoples*. Oxford

Smout, T. C. 1969. *A History of the Scottish People 1560–1830*. London

Snell, K. D. M. 2003. 'The culture of local xenophobia', *Social History* 28: 1–30

Snodgrass, A. 1980. *Archaic Greece: The Age of Experiment*. London

Sober, E. and Wilson, D. S. 1998. *Unto Others: The Evolution and Psychology of Unselfish Behavior*. Cambridge, Mass.

Solow, R. M. 1997. 'How did economics get that way and what way did it get?', *Daedalus* 126: 39–58

Soltis, J., Boyd, R., and Richerson, P. J. 1995. 'Can group-functional behaviors evolve by cultural group selection? An empirical test', *Current Anthropology* 36: 437–94

Somerset, A. 2003. *The Affair of the Poisons: Murder, Infanticide, and Satanism at the Court of Louis XIV*. London

Sosis, R. 2003. 'Why aren't we all Hutterites? Costly signaling theory and religious behavior', *Human Nature* 14: 91–127

  and Alcorta, C. 2003. 'Signaling, solidarity, and the sacred: The evolution of religious behavior', *Evolutionary Anthropology* 12: 264–74

Speer, A. 1970. *Inside the Third Reich*. London

Spooner, B. 1976. 'Anthropology and the Evil Eye', in C. Maloney (ed.), *The Evil Eye*. New York

Stankiewicz, R. 2000. 'The concept of design space', in J. Ziman (ed.), *Technological Innovation and the Evolutionary Process*. Cambridge

Stark, R. 1996. *The Rise of Christianity: How the Obscure, Marginal Jesus Movement Became the Dominant Religious Force in the Western World in a Few Centuries*. Princeton, N.J.

Stedman Jones, G. 2004. *An End to Poverty? A Historical Debate*. London

Strabo. *Geography*

Suetonius. *Grammarians*

Sugden, R. 2002. 'Beyond sympathy and empathy: Adam Smith's concept of fellow-feeling', *Economics and Philosophy* 18: 63–67

Sugiyama, L. S., Tooby, J., and Cosmides, L. 2002. 'Cross-cultural evidence of cognitive adaptations for social exchange among the Shiwiar of Ecuadorian Amazonia', *Proceedings of the National Academy of Sciences* 99: 11,536–11,542

Sulloway, F. J. 1996. *Born to Rebel: Birth Order, Family Dynamics, and Creative Lives*. New York

Tacitus. *Agricola*

  Annals

Tainter, J. A. 1988. *The Collapse of Complex Societies*. Cambridge

Talbot, C. 2001. *Precolonial India in Practice: Society, Religion, and Identity in Medieval Andhara*. Oxford

Tanner, T. 2000. *The American Mystery*. Cambridge

Thomas, K. 1971. *Religion and the Decline of Magic: Studies in Popular Beliefs in Sixteenth and Seventeenth Century England*. London

Thucydides. *History*

Tilley, C. 1999. *Metaphor and Material Culture*. Oxford

Tonkinson, R. 1988. '"Ideology and domination" in Aboriginal Australia: A Western Desert test case', in T. Ingold, D. Riches, and J. Woodburn (eds.), *Hunters and Gatherers*. 2: *Property, Power, and Ideology*. Oxford

Tooby, J. and Cosmides, L. 1992. 'The psychological foundations of culture', in J. H. Barkow, L. Cosmides, and J. Tooby (eds.), *The Adapted Mind: Evolutionary Psychology and the Generation of Culture*. Oxford

1996. 'Friendship and the banker's paradox: Other pathways to the evolution of adaptations for altruism', *Proceedings of the British Academy* 88: 119–143

Toulmin, S. and Baier, K. 1952. 'On describing', *Mind* 61: 13–38

Trilling, L. 1972. *Sincerity and Authenticity*. London

Tuchman, B. 1962. *August 1914*. London

Turley, D. 1991. *The Culture of English Antislavery, 1780–1860*. London

Turner, M. 1982. *Slaves and Missionaries: The Disintegration of Jamaican Slave Society, 1787–1834*. Urbana, Ill.

Turner, V. W. 1968. *The Drums of Affliction: A Study of Religious Processes among the Ndembu of Zambia*. Oxford

Van den Berghe, P. L. 1997. 'Rehabilitating stereotypes', *Ethnic and Racial Studies* 20: 1–16

Vanberg, V. J. 2002. 'Rational choice versus program-based behaviour: Alternative theoretical approaches and their relevance for the study of institutions', *Rationality and Society* 14: 7–54

Varela, F. J. 1999. *Ethnical Know-How: Action, Wisdom, and Cognition*. Stanford, Calif.

Varro. *De Re Rustica*

Veyne, P. 1981. 'Clientèle et corruption au service de l'état: La vénalité des offices sous le bas-empire romain', *Annales* 36: 339–60

Viveiros de Castro, E. 1998. 'Cosmological deixis and Amerindian perspectivism', *Journal of the Royal Anthropological Institute* 4: 469–88

Weber, M. 1922. *Gesammelte Aufsätze zur Religionssoziologie*. Tübingen

Webster, T. B. L. 1953. *Studies in Later Greek Comedy*. Manchester

Welleman, J. D. 2003. 'Narrative explanation', *Philosophical Review* 112: 1–25

Whitehouse, H. 2004. *Modes of Religiosity: A Cognitive Theory of Religious Transmission*. Oxford

Whitelock, D. 1979. (ed.), *English Historical Documents* I. Cambridge

Whiten, A., and Byrne, R. W. (eds.) 1997. *Machiavellian Intelligence*. II: *Extensions and Evaluations*. Cambridge

Horner, V., and Marshall-Pescini, A. 2003. 'Cultural panthropology', *Evolutionary Anthropology* 12: 92–105

Whiting, R. C. 1983. *The View from Cowley: The Impact of Industrialization upon Oxford 1918–1939*. Oxford

Wickham, C. 1994. *Land and Power: Studies in Italian and European Social History, 400–1200.* London

2005. *Framing the Middle Ages: Europe and the Mediterranean 400–800.* Oxford

Wierzbicka, A. 1992. *Semantics, Culture, and Cognition: Universal Human Concepts in Culture-Specific Configurations.* Oxford

Wiley, A. S. 2007. 'Transforming milk in a global economy', *American Anthropologist* 109: 666–77

Williams, B. 2002. *Truth and Truthfulness: An Essay in Genealogy.* Princeton, N.J.

Williams, G. C. 1966. *Adaptation and Natural Selection: A Critique of Some Current Evolutionary Thought.* Princeton, N.J.

Wilson, E. O. 1978. *On Human Nature.* Cambridge, Mass.

Winch, D. 2001. 'Darwin fallen among political economists', *Proceedings of the American Philosophical Society* 145: 415–37

Winch, P. 1958. *The Idea of a Social Science.* London

Wittgenstein, L. 1953. *Philosophical Investigations.* Oxford

Wolpert, S. 1977. *A New History of India.* Oxford

Wolf, E. R. 1982. *Europe and the People without History.* Berkeley, Calif.

Woolf, G. 1990. 'Food, poverty, and patronage: The significance of the epigraphy of the Roman alimentary schemes in early imperial Italy', *Papers of the British School in Rome* 58: 197–228

Wrangham, R. and Peterson, D. 1996. *Demonic Males: Apes and the Origins of Human Violence.* London

Wrigley, E. A. 1987. *People, Cities and Wealth: The Transformation of Traditional Society.* Oxford

2003. 'The Quest for the Industrial Revolution', *Proceedings of the British Academy* 121: 147–70

Wyatt-Brown, B. 1982. *Southern Honor: Ethics and Behavior in the Old South.* Oxford

Yair, G. 2007. 'Existential uncertainty and the will to conform: The expressive basis of Coleman's rational choice paradigm', *Sociology* 41: 681–98

Zafirovski, M. 1999. 'What is really rational choice? Beyond the utilitarian conception of rationality', *Current Sociology* 47: 47–113

Zeldin, T. 1973. *France 1848–1945.* I: *Ambition, Love and Politics.* Oxford

Index